AMERICA BRUSHES UP

AMERICA BRUSHES UP

The Use and Marketing of Toothpaste and Toothbrushes in the Twentieth Century

Kerry Segrave

McFarland & Company, Inc., Publishers
Jefferson, North Carolina, and London

LIBRARY OF CONGRESS CATALOGUING-IN-PUBLICATION DATA

Segrave, Kerry, 1944–
   America brushes up : the use and marketing of toothpaste and
toothbrushes in the twentieth century / Kerry Segrave.
      p.   cm.
   Includes bibliographical references and index.

   ISBN 978-0-7864-4754-1
   softcover : 50# alkaline paper

   1. Mouth — Care and hygiene — United States — History.
2. Toothpastes — United States — History.   3. Toothbrushes —
United States — History.   4. Advertising — Toothpaste — United
States.   5. Advertising — Dental instruments and apparatus —
United States.   I. Title.
RK61.S44   2010
617.6'010688 — dc22   2009047870

British Library cataloguing data are available

Cover photograph ©2010 Shutterstock

Manufactured in the United States of America

*McFarland & Company, Inc., Publishers
   Box 611, Jefferson, North Carolina 28640
   www.mcfarlandpub.com*

Contents

Preface 1

Introduction 3

1. From Ancient Times to 1899 5
2. Toothbrushes, 1900–1945 15
3. Toothpaste, 1900–1945 34
4. Toothpaste, Advertising and Marketing, 1900–1945 48
5. Toothpaste, Advertising Challenged, 1900–1945 63
6. Toothpaste, 1946–1960 80
7. Toothpaste, Advertising and Marketing, 1946–1960 101
8. Toothpaste, Advertising Challenged, 1946–1960 109
9. Toothbrushes, 1946–2008 117
10. Electric Toothbrushes, 1940s–2008 134
11. Crest Toothpaste, 1960–2008 145
12. Toothpaste, New Wonders, 1960–2008 157
13. Toothpaste, General, 1960–2008 172
14. Toothpaste, Advertising and Marketing, 1960–2008 184
15. Conclusion 202

Chapter Notes 207
Bibliography 217
Index 225

Preface

This book looks at the use of toothpaste and toothbrushes in America over the period 1900 to 2008, mainly the 20th century. This period was chosen because it was then that the modern dental care industry was really born and took shape.

The work examines the use of these products, their advertising and marketing to the public, and how the products were treated in the newspapers and mass circulation general interest magazines.

The purpose of the book is to look at the rise and spread of the dental care industry, specifically the toothpaste (including the powders that were the dominant form of the product in its earliest years) and the toothbrush aspects of the personal tooth care industry in America.

By the end of the 19th century there was much tooth decay in the land, relative to earlier times, due largely to the growing general availability of industrially processed foods in the Western world. When that was combined with the rise of modern advertising methods and the rapid growth of that industry, it made the 20th century an ideal time for the marketing and selling of toothpaste and toothbrushes.

Research for the book was conducted in Vancouver, British Columbia, at the University of British Columbia, Simon Fraser University, and the Vancouver Public Library. Sources used were hard copy indexes such as *Readers' Guide to Periodical Literature* and various online databases such as historical newspapers.

Introduction

This book examines the history of dentifrices (toothpaste and tooth-powder) and toothbrushes in 20th century America. Back around 1900 most people in the U.S. did not use commercially prepared dentifrices but were content to use homemade preparations. It was left to the power of the advertising industry to convert Americans into faithful users of toothpaste. Beginning with a quack preparation called Sozodont (introduced in 1859, 37 percent alcohol) the toothpaste industry has embraced and utilized false claims in its efforts to sell more paste. Whitening pastes were big in the 1920s and then again much later. Plaque attacker toothpastes were big in the 1920s (under another name) and again years later.

For some 70 years now dentists and their organization, the American Dental Association, have engaged in on and off battles with toothpaste makers over what they have seen as a variety of outrageously false ad claims. The U.S. government has also done battle with the paste manufacturers from time to time but without too much success. Arguably, the toothpaste ad claims of today vary little in their falsity from those of the 1980s, the 1960s, the 1920s, and so on.

Over the decades a constant stream of wonder ingredients have been announced as having been added to toothpastes, allowing them to perform miracles. Equally miraculous changes happened to the shape of a toothbrush head, or to the angle of its handle. Behind such activity lay the idea that something new and different had to happen in an industry every now and then, and if technology did not oblige, advertising would. A notable failure has been the attempt to equip every American with an electric toothbrush, despite half a century of effort. Yet that has not deterred efforts by makers who continue to promote new power models. Against all that stands the one great success — fluoride toothpaste. In over 100 years of the modern toothpaste industry, it represents just about the only positive accomplishment of that industry.

1

From Ancient Times to 1899

A few grains of gunpowder on a chewed skewer will remove every spot and blemish and give your teeth an inconceivable whiteness. — Anonymous, 18th century

Sozodont is "the most convenient, efficacious and beneficial article for the Teeth the world has ever seen." — Sozodont ad, 1864

Oral hygiene went back as far as the record can be traced, although it wasn't until the 1800s that the forerunners of modern toothpaste and toothbrushes came into being. According to historian David McLean, writing in the 1930s, wherever there had been a trace of civilization, white and even teeth had been valued, and there had always been some practice of mouth hygiene. Around 300 B.C. Theophrastus wrote that in ancient Greece it was a virtue to shave frequently and to have white teeth. Dentifrices were used by the Romans, who believed white teeth were the first requisite of gentility. Hippocrates, a Greek, later derived a dentifrice made of the burnt head of a hare and three burnt mice. Roman writers gave numerous other formulas for dentifrices, some containing myrrh, an astringent for the gums.[1]

Implements that were in all probability toothpicks, McLean continued, had been unearthed in prehistoric ruins. During the period of the great Roman emperors, toothpicks were in general use and were found in the bedrooms of upper-class women. As late as 1835 Dr. Samuel Fitch in his book *Dental Surgery* argued, "The toothpick should have a place in every gentleman's pocket and every lady's toilet; and should be always used after every meal." Books of etiquette declared the napkin should be gracefully raised to shield others at the table from having to view the toothpick in action. The world's simplest toothbrush was the bare finger, of course. The Talmud spoke of a chip or splinter of wood, the end of which was frayed by chewing, for use as a toothbrush. A similar device was said to have been used by some tribes of American Indians and by natives of South Africa, where the fibrous wood of the palm tree was still used into the 20th century to make excellent brushes. Brahmin priests rubbed their teeth every morning with a twig of the fir tree. Moslem Hindus did the same, using a fresh fir twig every day; reportedly they felt considerable horror at the thought of using brushes made of the hair of animals and of using a brush more than once. McLean believed the modern toothbrush must have made its appearance during the latter part of the 17th century as the wooden stick was still in use in 1650, while in 1728 Pierre Fouchard condemned brushes made of horsehair as being too stiff.[2]

Ancient Indo-Europeans of around 1700 B.C. made a religious rite of the brushing of the teeth, according to Dr. George V. Bobrinskoy, assistant professor of Sanskrit at the University of Chicago. Those early Indians had no toothpastes and used a twig taken from a living tree, with a species of fig tree being recommended. It was said to be imperative the bark remain on the twig; the brush could be used only once. Bobrinskoy also translated a passage from Buddhist literature that read, "There are five evils, O Monks, resulting from the omission of the chewing of the tooth stick. Which five? It is detrimental to the eyesight; the mouth becomes evil smelling; the taste conducting nerves of the tongue are not cleansed; bile, phlegm and food cover the tongue over; and one's mead does not please one."[3]

Reporter Martha Hommel remarked that in the *Han Wo Chuan* (China), a record of the Tang dynasty (A.D. 618 to 907), was found the mention of tooth powder. She also related that among the personal belongings of Roman Emperor Charles V (1500–1558) were a basin in the shape of a tortoise, used by Charles in washing his teeth, and a salt-box of Moorish workmanship, an indication that at the time teeth were also cleaned with salt in Europe. Among his other belongings were 18 files to file his teeth and a number of gold toothpicks. According to Hommel, use of the modern-type toothbrush in Europe was mentioned in a 1749 text but was not then common. A 1754 European text recommended the application of toothpowder with the root of the marshmallow for cleaning teeth. Hindus in India and Japan used salt as a toothpowder, applied with a willow stick whose end was frayed with incisions by a knife.[4]

One of the earliest ads for toothpaste, this one appeared in the *New York Times* in 1860.

Dentist Lon Morrey commented that since earliest times alchemists, beauticians, and healers had prescribed various concoctions to whiten the teeth, strengthen the gums, sweeten the breath and prevent dental decay. Early Roman apothecaries offered burnt, powdered staghorn as a dental aid. They also prescribed cow's anklebones mixed with myrrh, swine's hoofs and powdered eggshells. Octavia, sister of Emperor Augustus, used a dentifrice of barley, vinegar, honey, rock salt, and nard oil baked to charcoal and pulverized.[5]

Journalist Morton Pader was another who remarked that the value of practicing oral hygiene procedures was recognized in the ancient Hebrew, Greek, Roman, and other civilizations. Products employed for the purpose ranged from chew sticks to dentifrices of sorts containing, in some cases, highly abrasive minerals. Pader thought it was unlikely that any sophistication in dentifrice formulation could have developed under the circumstances prevailing up until about 1840. Prior to that, explained Pader, oral health was the province of practitioners who had received their training as apprentices with their effort devoted mainly to such dental practices as removal of teeth, restoration of single cavities, and so on. About 1840, oral health began to take on the aspects of a profession, with the establishment of a dental school, a dental society and a dental journal. From those beginnings came more and more research, with some of that directed to dentifrices, specifically to their role in the maintenance of oral hygiene and to their evaluation with respect to efficiency and safety, added Pader.[6]

Patrick Ryan reported the ancient Greeks favored white teeth and were accustomed to cleaning them carefully. That the Romans were similarly inclined was confirmed by Catullus in the 1st century B.C. He noted that some of his contemporaries were even prepared to adopt the Spanish custom of cleaning their teeth with stale urine in the belief that it whitened them and

This 1864 ad extolled the virtues of a dentifrice that supposedly removed bad breath from the mouth, as well as pimples and freckles from the skin.

fixed them firmly in the sockets. Over time dentifrices had included cuttlefish bones, powdered pearls, ashes of nettles, salt, tobacco, honey, vinegar, cinnamon, alum, soap, pyrethrum, sulphuric acid, and a resin called dragon's blood. A leading 18th century beauty expert, said Ryan, advised, "A few grains of gunpowder on a chewed skewer will remove every spot and blemish and give your teeth an inconceivable whiteness." A recipe published in 1874 by Dr. Pierre Cazenave recommended a tooth polish comprised of half a gill each of brandy and alcohol, plus 18 grains of oil of mint, well mixed.[7]

Writing in *Family Health,* Ren Glasser mentioned Hippocrates and his dentifrice formula and that other Greeks, after whiter teeth, tried pumice, emery, granulated alabaster, coral powder, trumpet shells mixed with salt, and iron rust. Long before the advent of the toothbrush, added Glasser, teeth were sometimes cleaned with a fiber pencil — the precursor of the toothpick. Picks belonging to the wealthy were made of ivory or gold and were even worn as jewelry on a chain or attached to a belt. For the non-rich, it was more likely their toothpicks came from the mastix tree (Pistacia Lentucus). Chewing pills and toothpowders made from the sap of that particular tree were also common during the Middle Ages. Ancient Arabs carved their dental fiber pencils from a wood rich in sodium bicarbonate, something Glasser described as being a most effective dentifrice, even up to the time in which he was writing —1978.[8]

Another journalist, Deborah Blumenthal, reported the ancient Egyptians used a dentifrice made of equal parts incense, green lead (a toxic metal), and verdigris, a green crust that formed on metal such as copper or brass when exposed to the air or to sea water. The Chinese used the ground bones of fish in their early dentifrices. In the Middle Ages, added Blumenthal, the danger of using highly abrasive agents on tooth enamel was finally recognized by the Arabs, who expressed concern over the fine sand and pumice found in oral hygiene preparations. Meanwhile in Europe at that time, strong acids were being used on the teeth to remove stains, and similar corrosive agents continued to be used in updated formulations until the early part of the 20th century.[9]

Consumer Reports remarked that physicians in ancient Egypt made the first toothpaste, a highly abrasive and pungent mixture of pumice powder and wine vinegar. And in 1500 B.C. a well-known papyrus detailed ancient Egyptian recipes to strengthen teeth — with lead, honey, incense, and powdered flint. According to this magazine, the first toothbrush appeared in China, around A.D. 1000; it had an ivory handle and bristles from a horse's mane.[10]

An article in the *Literary Digest* in 1926 declared the first toothbrush used by ancients was the chew stick, a twig about the size of a carpenter's pencil,

Sozodont was likely the first dentifrice to achieve wide fame in the U.S. This 1865 copy pointed out the many blessings to be had from the red liquid that was in reality a quack patent medicine containing 37 percent alcohol.

with one end beaten to a soft, fibrous condition. Not only did the implement clean the teeth, but it also gave the gums a gentle massage. It was used with the same up and down motion dentists recommended in the 20th century. Used once, the stick was then thrown away and a new one made for the next occasion. A 17th century item used to keep the teeth clean was a strip of linen cloth. Around that time also, several kinds of toothpowder reportedly came into use. One of the simplest of those was a burnt cork concoction that was rubbed on the teeth. When the black charred cork was applied to the teeth it actually whitened them.[11]

Back in 1896 a piece in *Scientific American* stated that in some old books published during 1600 directions were given for preparing certain roots that were used to clean the teeth; Lucerne and licorice roots were specified. Those roots were to be boiled and cut into pieces six inches long with the ends of each being split with a penknife into the form of a little brush, after which the pieces were slowly dried to prevent splitting. To put one of these tools into use, one end was moistened with water, dipped into toothpowder, and rubbed against the teeth until they looked white. Brushes similar to those were said to still be used in 1896 in some parts of Turkey. However, it was admitted that many Turks used ordinary European toothbrushes then, although most looked on the pig as unclean and thus would not defile their mouths with a hog-bristle brush — then the most common type manufactured. Thus, reported *Scientific American*, "The shopkeepers, therefore, swear by their hearts and the souls of their fathers and mothers that the hair of which their brushes are made grew on the back of the camel, cow, or the horse."[12]

According to reporter Anthony Ramirez, Aristotle advised Alexander the

Great to rub a rag against his teeth while George Washington's dentist gave the same advice, suggesting the addition of some chalk to the rag. With the invention of the toothbrush in about 1770 by William Addis, said Ramirez, dental creams and powders became popular. But dentifrices were sold in porcelain jars into which entire families would dip their damp toothbrushes. Anxieties over such an unhygienic practise were not eased until 1892 when Dr. Washington Wentworth Sheffield, a dentist in New London, Connecticut, invented the toothpaste tube. That collapsible metal tube allowed individual, and hygienic, portions of the paste for each member of the family.[13]

Writing in *Barron's* magazine in 1965, Goody Solomon stated the Romans perfumed the mouth with saffron, rose water, fennel, and myrrh mixed with gum Arabic. And while commercial dental creams were manufactured in America in colonial times, most people made up their own at home until about 1900. Another reporter, Esther McCabe argued that it was not until about 1806 that the bristle brush came into general use.[14]

Journalist Don Wharton said that toothpastes were sold in America before the Civil War, with some being imported items and some being items made up by dentists for their own patients. The paste came in small jars and

His Greeting.

"Hooray for Blaine and Logan!"
Cried Miller, stumbling home.
Where a frowning lady—(Mrs. M.)
Waited for him to come.

"Seems to me you smell of liquors,"
She said, with some contempt,
"Not tall—not tall," said Miller,
His plumed hat quite unkempt.

"You'd better buy for the wigwam," she said,
"Some SOZODONT. Beneath
It's odor, liquor's lost. Then, ere you leave,
Make each man brush his teeth!"

A FINE THING FOR THE TEETH.
Fragrant SOZODONT is a composition of the purest and choicest ingredients of the Oriental vegetable kingdom. Every ingredient is well known to have a beneficial effect on the teeth or gums. Its embalming or antiseptic property and aromatic fragrance make it a toilet luxury. SOZODONT removes all disagreeable odors from the breath caused by catarrh, bad teeth, &c. It is entirely free from the injurious and acrid properties of tooth pastes and powders which destroy the enamel. One bottle will last six months.

Strangely, this 1884 ad stated Sozodont (mostly alcohol) should be used when one had been drinking since it purportedly got rid of the smell of liquor.

to use it one had to rub the brush across the surface of the paste. Many people recoiled from such unsanitary dipping. Collapsible tubes had been invented for artists' paints by an American, John Rand, in 1841, wrote Wharton. In the 1880s a son of Dr. Washington Sheffield, the dentist at New London, Connecticut, came home from a trip abroad with the report that Europeans were selling food in tubes. So the Sheffields tried putting toothpaste in imported tubes in 1892. Sales went up so quickly the pair bought a machine to make their own tubes and established their own plant.[15]

During the 1850s in America the big miracle product was a charcoal dentifrice, described by one dental journal as "sharp as diamond dust." In 1859 the same journal commented on a theme that would remain familiar to dentists over time: "What the problem seems to demand in this age of steam is something to whiten the teeth at once, no matter how long they may have been neglected." Around the same time a writer in the *American Journal of Dental Science* was recommending a dentifrice composed of powder of dried bone, 80 parts; precipitated chalk, 20 parts; bicarbonate, five parts; and powdered orris root, two parts. In 1867 a recommended preparation was 10 grams of phenic or carbolic acid (perfumed) for use either as toilet water or as a dentifrice; or used with phenate of soda and a comb as a cure for pityriasis.[16]

Then, in 1859, a New York wholesale druggist, William Henry Hall, started to promote a red liquid dentifrice called Sozodont — a name coined from Greek words meaning "save" and "teeth." It was 37 percent alcohol and became the first dentifrice to be featured in a national advertising campaign. An 1864 ad enthused that Sozodont was "the most convenient, efficacious and beneficial article for the Teeth the world has ever seen." Hall was a pioneer user of advertising strategies that included testimonials, jingles, scare copy and leg art. One ad featured endorsements from 15 leading New York clergymen. Other ads quoted Bismarck; some went so far as to imply the product was used in the White House. The use of legs to sell goods could be found in an old Sozodont ad that featured a scene in a sultan's harem. More sex appeal-style ad copy, directed at women, was prominent in an 1870s ad that declared, "MEN GO WILD about splendid teeth." By 1893 Sozodont was said to be so well known as to be a household word. So popular was the product that even Mark Twain kidded it. In *A Connecticut Yankee in King Arthur's Court* he described a heraldic symbol in which a gauntleted hand clutched a toothbrush, with the motto, "Try NOYOUDONT!" When Hall died in 1894 Sozodont profits had grown to $10 million. But pastes and powders had begun to challenge the dominant position of the red liquid and it quickly fell out of favour. Wharton argued that its ads, however, had at least taught and encouraged people to brush their teeth. The popularity of Sozodont came at

An 1888 ad for Rubifoam, as graphics began to appear more and more in ad copy.

the peak of the craze for patent medicines that came in the late 1800s. Most of those preparations were nothing more than quack medicines.[17]

Another early American pioneer in the field of dentifrices was Dr. Israel Whitney Lyon. He studied dentistry in New York and went west in the 1850s to the California gold fields where he had a colourful life, as he put it, "stuffing gold into the miners' teeth and taking it out of their pockets." In 1866 he returned to New York and when the American Dental Association (ADA) condemned liquid dentifrices and recommended a formula for a powder, Lyon went to work with that formula and produced his own variation; Dr. I. W. Lyon's Tooth Tablets. Those tablets were powder compressed into a thin cake, and scored like a chocolate bar into sections that could be broken off and placed on a toothbrush. In 1874 he brought out Dr. I. W. Lyon's Tooth Powder in green hand-blown glass bottles. Lyon's first trademark was a lion holding a toothbrush; five months later he changed to the head of a beautiful woman, a logo still in use halfway through the 20th century. Then one day he got an inspiration — why not put the product in a can? The can, with Dr. Lyon's telescopic measuring tube was introduced in 1891. In four years his pow-

A more elaborate ad in 1896 for Sozodont. This ad, as well as all the other early ones, were prime examples of the false claims made by dentifrice makers. Those claims started at the beginning of the modern era in dentifrices and continue to the present.

der sales jumped to $63,000 annually while the tablet sales dropped to $2,000. Ten years later powder sales stood at $402,000 per year. Starting off with the backing of some first-class dentists, Lyon used their names to sell his products, although his advertising was described as honest. At a time when there was no law to keep manufacturers from making false claims, Lyon told a magazine reporter, "It is useless to say that any dentifrice will whiten the teeth or change their color one particle — anything which professes to do it is an acid." After Lyon died in 1907 his two sons ran the business for two decades before selling out. Lyon's remained the top selling toothpowder well into the 20th century.[18]

And so, after a long and spotty history, toothpastes and toothbrushes moved into the modern era in the late 1800s. All the items recognizable to people in the 21st century were in place by then: the bristle brush (using real animal hair at the time, not synthetic bristles) and the toothpaste in collapsible metal tubes (although powders were by far the best selling dentifrices then). When advertising lent its full weight to this new field, as it did in the early 20th century, the modern era of oral hygiene had truly begun.

2

Toothbrushes, 1900–1945

If I had my way I'd make it a penal offense for any mother to put a toothbrush in the mouth of a child. — U.S. Representative Cyrus Sulloway, 1912.

But let us start right by abandoning the filthy tooth-brush once and for all. — Dr. Bernard Feldman, 1915.

And it is obvious that with proper food man would have no more need for a toothbrush than a dog or cat does. — *Consumers' Research Bulletin*, 1943.

Annie Lane was an English journalist who in 1905 lamented the state of teeth — neglected and decaying in her view — in her homeland, compared to the good teeth found in prehistoric man and in 1905 America where the people were said to look after their teeth and to visit the dentist. Lane argued that if it was up to her she would require all English school boards to furnish their pupils with toothbrushes and toothpowder, "and I would open the morning session with a general brushing of teeth." She said that a member of a social work agency had recently demanded of the mayor of a city that toothbrushes be provided free for the "pauper children." However, he not only refused but he denounced the proposal as "pampered luxury and extravagance." As far as Lane was concerned, toothbrushes made for health, health made for intelligence, "and it is the intelligent man the world wants and pays for, which proves the incalculable importance of tooth-brushes in the progress of the world." Lane added that in the political economy of nations the toothbrush was of much more importance than the sword, and toothpowder was infinitely more important than gunpowder: "As England never considers the millions she annually spends in gunpowder, why does she not pause in her martial career and spend a few thousand pounds in toothpowder?"[1]

While some favored the idea of providing toothbrushes for children, others opposed the idea, sometimes vehemently. At a 1912 hearing in Washington before the District of Columbia Committee on a bill to regulate dentistry, U.S. representative Cyrus Sulloway (New Hampshire) declared, "If I had my way I'd make it a penal offense for any mother to put a toothbrush in the mouth of a child." Sulloway vigorously denounced the use of the tooth-brush and lauded the good old days of tobacco chewing and dipped snuff— that is, for oral hygiene purposes.[2]

At the other end of the issue, 50 children were given a lecture in 1912 at a New York City playground located at 91st Street and Fifth Avenue. It was a lecture delivered by Theora Carter, president of the Society of Good Cheer, on the necessity and advantages of keeping the teeth clean. At the end of her talk each child received a toothbrush. During her talk Carter told of two lit-tle girls on her block, one cleaned her teeth regularly while the other did not care for her teeth: "When the first little girl smiles she shows a row of nice white teeth. The other can only show blackened, decayed ones." She con-cluded, "So, you see that if you want to be good looking you must clean your teeth." One of Carter's missions in life was to teach parents and children that one way to good health was through the care of the teeth. She also gave a demonstration of the proper way to brush (up-and-down), as a part of her lecture, by selecting one of the children as a volunteer.[3]

A long rant against the toothbrush appeared in a May 1915 issue of the *Literary Digest* in which the anonymous writer began by saying if there ever was an implement generally acknowledged as indispensable to civilization it was the toothbrush. "It has been to most of us almost a religious symbol of that personal cleanliness which the old saw places next to godliness," said the piece. "And now, forsooth, we are told that it is not conformable to modern hygiene and sanitation! Its sins are both of omission and commission." Dr. Bernard Feldman, a dentist, argued the public had become accustomed to looking upon the toothbrush as necessary and that teachers and dentists were all recommending its diligent use. That teaching of schoolchildren and of adults on how to use the brush properly was what Feldman considered to be "the menace of the toothbrush," because it had been proved to him that the brush "is defeating the very purposes of our oral-hygiene movement and that we are actually infecting the mouth instead of cleaning it by the use of the filthy, germ-ridden thing." Research had shown the implement to be germ-laden, he added, and the truth was that the brush was a dangerous instru-ment that was practically impossible to sterilize. Even if the impossible were attained and the brush was rendered sterile it, and its paste or powder, did not reach the places on the teeth where it was most important for the bris-tles to reach since a majority of tooth decay started in those places. "An efficient cleaning is probably never obtained by the brush," declared Feldman. "What is more probable is that many of the germs that are present on the bristles are deposited in these places." For this dentist it meant that no one who could look squarely at facts could continue to either use the toothbrush or advise its use for his clientele. Until a commission of dentists should solve the problem by coming up with a technique that was both sanitary and efficient, Feldman suggested people return to the old Japanese method of using the clean forefinger to massage and clean the gums and outer surfaces of the teeth. "It seems to be Nature's own instrument that just fits the bill," he concluded, "but let us start right by abandoning the filthy tooth-brush once and for all."[4]

A few months later the same magazine presented the other side of the story when it wrote that other dentists denied the brush was a disseminator of infection and that it did not clean the teeth. Those dentists assured their patients that the brush was easily sterilized and capable of efficiently cleaning the teeth. Dr. W. H. Barth felt no dentists would dispute the idea that the mouth in which a toothbrush had been used was cleaner and freer of decay than was a mouth in which it had not been used: "The tooth-brush is handier, and it can be made as clean and aseptic as the forefinger." Dr. Benedict Furniss agreed with Barth but thought the brush should be dipped in a solution of five percent Lysol to sterilize it. Dr. Jules J. Sarazin also favored the toothbrush but argued it should be immersed in an iodine solution and then rinsed after each usage. One controversy that did divide the dental profession was how to brush — some thought the brushing should be crosswise, while others favored the rotary method. Still, a majority of dentists felt the brush was a valuable agent in oral hygiene.[5]

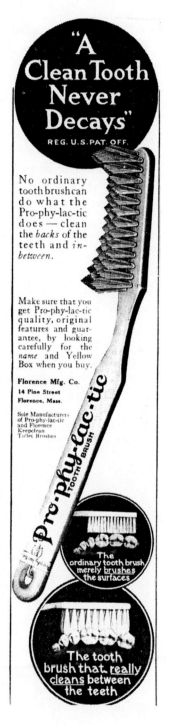

No ordinary tooth brush can do what the Pro-phy-lac-tic does — clean the *backs* of the teeth and *in-between*.

Make sure that you get Pro-phy-lac-tic quality, original features and guarantee, by looking carefully for the *name* and Yellow Box when you buy.

Florence Mfg. Co.
14 Pine Street
Florence, Mass.

Sole Manufacturers of Pro-phy-lac-tic and Florence Keepclean Toilet Brushes

The awkwardly named Pro phy-lac-tic was one of the leading brushes for years. This 1917 ad touted the advantage of its unusual shape.

Dr. Hugh W. MacMillan, writing in *The Dental Summary* in 1916, declared it was then generally conceded that an unsterile brush could be a greater hindrance than a benefit to the health of the mouth, but it was used because there was nothing else. Since it was the best agent people could employ for the stimulation of the gums and for cleaning the teeth, the problem was to find a method to sterilize it quickly and easily without destroying the brush by boiling it or by using strong antiseptics. After use, the brush was to be held under water and rinsed. Salt was then sprinkled on the brush with the salt being dissolved on the wet brush and penetrating through to the center of the tufts of the bristles. Then the brush was hung in its usual place. When it was needed again, the water would have evaporated, leaving a deposit of salt crystals in and around every bristle; said to be an environment in which germs could not live. Then the person was advised to use the brush as it was, after applying the preferred toothpowder.[6]

By the time of World War I, at the latest, American governments at various levels were involved in promoting the use of the toothbrush. Oral Hygiene Week was held in May 1917, conducted by the Educational Bureau of the New York City Health Department, to teach children the value of the proper care of the teeth and mouth. To bring the campaign to a close toothbrush drills were arranged in the different boroughs at which "thousands of children will demonstrate their ability to clean their teeth properly." In Manhattan the drill was held in Central Park wherein judges observed and the winners received badges of merit donated by the First and Second District Dental Societies.[7]

Nor was governmental instruction always limited to children. In accordance with instructions from New York City police commissioner Richard Enright that an active and sustained effort be made to prevent and cure physical disorders of policemen, a booklet titled *Healthy Teeth — Healthy Body* was given to every member of the New York City Police Department in 1922. According to the booklet, "There is no greater asset to a policeman than a good, sound, clean set of teeth" and that over 75 percent of the U.S. population suffered from defective teeth. Among the don'ts listed in the booklet were: "Don't have a family toothbrush" and "Don't stack a lot of toothbrushes together in a glass."[8]

Writing in the advertising trade journal *Printers' Ink* in 1924, W. Thacher recalled the first toothbrush he remembered was a simple tool, fashioned of bone, with bristles inserted in small holes and held in place by glue. And then someone discovered that by treating cotton or other cellulose material, a hard, durable but slightly elastic material could be formed. That became known as celluloid and was found to be excellently adapted to the making of toothbrushes. Around 1900, continued Thacher, all toothbrushes were very much alike and a family kept all of them in a single container, which led to confusion with people using the wrong one. And so an enterprising maker of the brush with the new celluloid handle had the foresight to poke a hole in the end of the handle. Also, he supplied a metal hook to be fastened to the wall from which the brush could be hung, and to make double sure there was no family confusion, put a number on each brush — from one to 10. Bristles in the old brush were set in a solid mass, presenting a closed phalanx of even depth. Following that came an improvement in which the bristles were separated into individual tufts. Even with that improvement, the brush still had one very serious defect. Its bristles would come loose and lodge in the gums or throat of the user. Then a manufacturer conceived of the idea of setting the bristles in rubber so that they were so firmly cemented into the handle they were unlikely to come loose. At the same time that improvement made it possible to cleanse the brush in "germicidally" hot water. And finally the brush, heretofore displayed loose in trays on drugstore counters, was enclosed in an individual container, reaching the purchaser in a clean condition. "And lo!— the modern tooth-brush, a perfect instrument, a sign of sanitation, a mark of modern merchandising methods, a tangible testimonial to the power of advertising," enthused Thacher. Of the half dozen or so improvements in the toothbrush that he mentioned he stated, "Not one of them was made as the result of an outcry or protest on the part of the user. In each case the improvement had to be sold. The want had to be created. Through advertising. Of course. How else could it be done?"[9]

Until the early 1920s toothbrushes sold in America were mainly imported from Japan, had wood or bone handles and were bristled with hogs' hair. Crudely made, they came to the druggist in bulk and unwrapped — and they accumulated dust and germs just in ordinary handling. Employed as a merchandising manager for a wholesale drug sundry house in the early 1920s, J. T. Woodside estimated that only one person in every four in America owned a toothbrush. He determined to produce a standard sanitary brush of good quality and to advertise it widely. The new brush he developed with convex bristles was submitted to the dental profession and to Dr. George N. West, then president of the International Dental Association and dean of the Kansas City Dental College. West approved the new design and agreed to give it the prestige of his name. Thus the Western Company (Weco) was formed. Dr. West's Toothbrush was the first to be sold in sterile, sealed glassine envelopes and helped to banish the unwrapped toothbrush from most drug counters.[10]

The Albright Tooth Brush was launched in 1924, made by the Rubberset Company of Newark, New Jersey, maker of the Rubberset Shaving Brush, among other items. Begun in 1847 as the Celluloid Harness Trimming Company, the firm was initially not involved at all with brushes. Around 1877 its first president and founder, Andrew Albright, was approached by a man with a new idea for making brushes so that the bristles would stay in. They were embedded in soft rubber instead of being held in place by means of shellac, glue or resin. Albright saw the virtue in the idea and took over the manufacture of brushes with bristles set in rubber, changing the soft rubber into hard vulcanized rubber. At the time the company launched its toothbrush it also manufactured paintbrushes, nail brushes, the Rubberset Shaving Brush, and other kinds of brushes.[11]

The Albright Tooth Brush was inserted first in a special sealed sanitary envelope and then placed in a decorated carton. One of the big problems of branded toothbrush exploitation, said reporter August Belden, had always been the matter of counter display. Large quantities of brushes were imported annually with over 34 million arriving in America in 1923, at an average cost of only a few cents each, to retailers. Those imports were sorted by the dealer and placed according to their different retail prices in various baskets or trays. Since the profit from them was greater than the profit from an American-made branded brush, the dealer was inclined to feature the imports. U.S. manufacturers tried to overcome that problem by furnishing dealers with counter cabinets for the display of the domestic product but the cabinets ended up being resting places for all manner of other goods and their effectiveness was lost. Rubberset was said to have overcome that difficulty by designing a package to contain one dozen Albright brushes for the dealer to place on his counter. Each dozen Albright implements were shipped to dealers in one of those display packages. It arrived folded and inserted in a cardboard container and all the dealer had to do was to take it out, unfold it and it was ready to go. When the 12 were sold the dealer just threw the display case away — it was said to be not adaptable to holding other merchandise. Those display packages were said to be "good silent salesmen" for the Albright Tooth Brush, which retailed at 35 cents. Also, the display package reportedly opened a new outlet nationwide for the selling of toothbrushes — the cigar store — to go along with the drugstore.[12]

When advertising for the new Albright Tooth Brush began in February 1924, the copy explained how Andrew Albright Jr., president of the firm, developed the new implement with the aid of 4,118 dentists and that it was the "perfect tooth brush." While the regular price was 35 cents if, during the first week of the campaign you took your old brush and the newspaper coupon to your druggist, you would receive two brushes for the price of one. Reportedly that nationwide campaign succeeded because it caused dealers to make sure they all had some of those items in stock. And, because the coupon was worthless unless accompanied by an old brush, it prevented people from accumulating large numbers of coupons to get a large number of items, "thus overcoming this evil of the coupon plan which gives something away." So, before the first ad appeared, some 2.5 million of these brushes had been sold in just three weeks, to dealers. Rubberset then had 17 branch offices and employed about 45 salesmen but it was not nearly enough. In the campaign's first week 500 extra salesmen went to work on the road, and 300 in the second week. Retailers were called on three times if they did not buy on the first or second visit and each time a different man paid the visit. Every druggist retailer in America was covered personally except those in small towns and villages (and they were hit with letters, copies of the ad, and return postcards to place orders). Window display material was also furnished and part of the campaign was a window display contest with prizes totaling $1,500 in cash. For each photo of a window display a dealer sent to it, Rubberset paid $1.50.[13]

The controversy over whether or not the toothbrush was hygienic continued until the late 1920s, several years after the items began to appear at retail outlets in their own individual packaging. Oliver T. Osborne, a professor at Yale University, argued in 1925, that the toothbrush became contaminated with infection from all diseases of the mouth and throat and the diseases that could "most surely contaminate" the brush were diphtheria, tonsillitis, and pyorrhea of the gums. Because children were so prone to so many diseases he advised that very young children should not use a toothbrush, not even a soft one, and that other methods of cleaning the teeth had to be used. Osborne did not specify those methods, nor did he specify an age for the children. In short, Osborne believed, and argued, that the toothbrush was a menace to health, at least at times.[14]

John Oppie McCall, professor at the College of Dentistry of New York University said, in 1927, that only 15 percent of the total U.S. population used a toothbrush and most that did use one did so in such an automatic fashion that they got little benefit from it. "Eighty per cent of those who use a tooth brush use it like one uses a nail file or a scrubbing brush," explained McCall. "That is, out of force of habit or of social necessity rather than because of a biological reason." McCall added there was an old feeling that a toothbrush produced diseases of the mouth and gums instead of preventing them with a result of that misunderstanding being that people used very soft brushes and carefully avoided striking the gums: "These precautions, of course, did not bring any benefits." If his figures were to be believed only 3 percent of Americans used a toothbrush correctly.[15]

Writing in the American Medical Association's main periodical directed

A 1936 ad for a gimmick toothbrush. Only the head needed replacement when the brush wore out, not the entire implement.

at lay readers, *Hygeia*, in 1928, William Gardner declared that properly used, toothbrushes markedly cut down decay and prevented gum disease, although he admitted care of the toothbrush had never been adequately stressed. Boiling a new brush to sterilize it was wrong, he explained, because boiling destroyed the flexibility of bristles; heat distorted the handle of the brush if it was made of celluloid; and the cement used to cover the wires holding the bristles disintegrated from the heat. Because every brush of good quality was exposed to formaldehyde fumes before it left the factory, Gardner advised that a brush should be rinsed thoroughly after use by holding it under a cold water tap with as much water shaken from it as possible before it was hung up to dry (if placed in a glass, bristles up). In order for the bristles to regain their original shape and stiffness a brush should dry for at least 24 hours. Thus, a person who brushed his teeth twice a day should always have at least two brushes in use. They lasted, he said, about four months. A brush once used became infected by bacteria from the mouth, but they needed moisture, darkness, food and a temperature about 97 degrees F to survive. A dry toothbrush prevented those conditions, said Gardner, and lab tests had shown that 99 percent of bacteria on a brush were eliminated when the above named conditions were denied.[16]

When *Hygeia* offered advice in 1929 on how to select a toothbrush to purchase it ignored the usual brush characteristics such as hard, soft, or medium bristles, concave or convex, straight handle or curved, and so on. A prospective customer entered a drugstore and approached the toothbrush case — a compartment full of a miscellaneous assortment of toothbrushes — went the piece, and in a state of contemplation that customer rubbed his thumb over the bristles. "No toothbrush can be considered fit to enter the sacred precincts of the buccal cavity after it has lain uncovered indefinitely on a counter," explained the article. "Added to the dust and dirt it acquires from the atmosphere, it has on its bristles the sweat and grime of untold numbers of testing thumbs. It may look clean, but it isn't and it should at least enter on its duties in virgin purity." Strongest advice given was to buy one that came in its own container or transparent box, even if it did cost a "trifle more." Concluding advice was to "choose the toothbrush carefully, buy a new one often, keep two on duty at once, and, above all, avoid the brush with the thumb-tested past."[17]

Through the 1920s and into the late 1930s brushes were almost always made of hog bristles, the finest grades of which were said to come from the cold, bleak regions of Russia, Siberia, and China, where wild hogs roamed the wilderness. The thinner the hog, the longer and stiffer were the bristles. As received by the brush manufacturer, those bristles came in bunches varying in diameter from two to 12 inches long with an average length of five inches. There were five different grades with the length, stiffness and color determining the value of the bristles. Longer bristles were better and rated a higher grade. Years earlier the usual type of toothbrush handle was made of beef bone, which was unsatisfactory in many respects, such being prone to breakage. By the late 1920s some 500 different types of toothbrushes were made: big and little, long and short, hard and soft, straight handled and curved, bleached and unbleached.[18]

When the hog bristles, which also were received from India, Poland and Romania, were first received they were far from clean and were turned into bleached or unbleached varieties. The Japanese were said to do their bleaching by way of a chemical process known only to them with no further sterilization until they were made into a toothbrush, accomplished through the heat of the manufacturing process itself. Around 1900 the French had a process of bleaching and sterilization in which the bristles were exposed to sunlight for six months — turned frequently during that time period. Bristles were held in place in toothbrushes by drawn wire or linen thread.[19]

An ad in 1930 for the ungainly named Pro-phy-lac-tic toothbrush declared there were three dental curves in the human mouth — a U shape, a V shape and a U (squared on the bottom) — and three different shapes in the company's product line. And a person could determine his own dental curve through a simple 30-second bite test. All he had to do was go to his neighborhood druggist, take a free folder, and "Bite into the sanitary dental wax." Thus, "scientifically," the person determined his own dental curve. The bite test, explained the ad, "is the new way approved by dentists; 42,819 of them have written us for it."[20]

The patented Prophylactic toothbrush was sold to the Florence Company by a New York dentist, a Dr. Rhein, around 1891 and registered as a name with its hyphenated form in 1905. From 1924 to 1933 the yearly average of sales was in excess of 7.5 million brushes with an annual expenditure in the period on advertising of around $500,000. Pro-phy-lac-tic Tooth Powder also went back to Dr. Rhein who made and sold it by himself or in corporate form until his death in 1922. The container was always a gray or cream-colored can with a purple top. After Rhein's death the tooth powder business went through a series of changes until 1933 when Park & Tilford (New York) obtained the rights to the product.[21]

One ad campaign that garnered a certain amount of attention was launched in 1933 in various cities scattered across the U.S., by the Western Company, manufacturer of Dr. West's Toothbrush. It was a plan that involved a trade-in component and that had been used in a single town several years earlier but then had been abandoned. Under the campaign a trade-in value of 11 cents was allowed on the 50-cent retail cost of a Dr. West brush. Weco advertised, "Go into your bathroom. Inspect your toothbrush. If you find it is old, soggy and useless, as most old toothbrushes are, take it to your druggist and use it for part payment on a new one." Sold in a glass tube with a cellophane cap, a note inside the tube warned the buyer not to keep the product in the tube, as that would prevent proper ventilation. Dealers paid 30 cents for brushes they sold for 50 cents (a 40 percent mark-up). If they participated in the trade-in plan the manufacturer gave them a four-cent allowance, which meant dealers paid 26 cents for a brush to retail at 39 cents (a 33 percent mark-up).[22]

Dr. West's trade-in plan was meant to jolt people out of a buying procrastination that had been perhaps exacerbated by the economic hard times of the Depression. "We are trying out this idea in the belief that it may help toward solving postponed purchasing, which has always been the curse of the toothbrush industry," explained Kenneth Laird, Western vice president in charge of advertising. When a tube of toothpaste is used it's empty and finished, he added, and a new purchase was an automatic necessity. In the case of the toothbrush, however, "there is often a tendency to nurse along an old-timer well past its state of full effectiveness." Still, the campaign was mainly a gimmick since it was not mandatory to bring in an old brush to the druggist. Signing a pledge at the retailer's to trash the old one at home was enough. That alternative was offered, said Laird, because in investigating the trade-in scheme it was discovered that some people were ashamed at the idea of the dealer or anybody else seeing just how sorry was the state of their old toothbrush.[23]

In order to find out how much time the average person spent in cleaning their teeth, the Western Company conducted surveys in 1934 in various parts of the country. Results showed that most people, instead of spending the three to four minutes said to be commonly supposed to be devoted to the task, turned out to perform the teeth cleaning task in about 30 seconds, with even a time as long as 60 seconds being rarely found. Those findings caused Western to launch a new product, Dr. West's Double-Quick Toothpaste.[24]

The Pro-phy-lac-tic Brush Company of Florence, Massachusetts (the firm was then a division of the Lambert Company), launched an ad campaign in 1934 that featured an ideal marriage contest. Each entry blank (available only from dealers) carried pictures of 12 girls and three male movie stars. Described on the form were the personal characteristics of the girls. Contestants selected one of the stars and one of the girls and wrote a letter explaining why that couple would make an ideal marriage. Each letter had to be

Desperate times in the Depression called for drastic measures. In 1933 Dr. West offered customers 11 cents as a trade-in for their old brush toward the purchase of a new Dr. West.

accompanied by one Pro-phy-lac-tic carton or the customary "reasonably accurate copy." Entrants competed for 20 McMurdo Silver radios, which each carried a retail list price of $375.[25]

David McLean, in *Hygeia* in 1935, stated there were nearly 500 toothbrush patents on file in the U.S. Patent Office. He recommended brushes be sterilized occasionally in some "competent germicide" and then rinsed for several minutes under running water. McLean felt they should be allowed to dry in fresh air and sunshine. In his view toothbrushing required not less than three minutes for each jaw and should be done three times a day. "The ordinary use of dental floss between the teeth is taboo," he added. "In the long run it does more harm to the gums than it does good to the teeth." He did not explain why he disliked dental floss.[26]

Natural bristles for toothbrushes started to fade away in the late 1930s, with a major impetus toward synthetic bristles being the war between China and Japan in 1937. China was a major supplier to the world of bristles but Chinese farmers were then too occupied with more serious things than to shave their pigs, sort, and export the bristles with the result being a bristle shortage in many parts of the world in 1938. Nationalistic Japan had tried to produce synthetic bristles long before the war with China started but that conflict sharply speeded up efforts. Early in 1938 the Osaka Industrial Research Laboratory announced it had produced bristles from viscose threads treated in solutions of uric acid at a cost said to be one-fifth that of natural bristles. Japanese exporters made a surprising discovery with toothbrushes made with these artificial bristles. Formerly they had a hard time selling brushes in India and the Near East because the 300 million Muslims there were not supposed to take anything in the mouth that came from pigs. As soon as the new bristles were offered, orders began to multiply. Prior to the advent of synthetic bristles the Muslims reportedly had brushed their teeth with makeshift brushes of vegetable fiber that often made the gums bleed.[27]

A couple of weeks later an announcement was made that American researchers had also come out with synthetic bristles, after a slam at the Japanese ones as being prone to wilt too rapidly upon contact with water and saliva. Ads were scheduled in America for October 1938 to proclaim a new toothbrush: "No bristle shedding ... 100% waterproof ... greater cleansing and long life." It was Dr. West's Miracle-Tuft brush. Behind those boasts was the U.S. development of synthetic bristles, made in the laboratories of E.I. du Pont de Nemours & Company. Research work in America had been spurred by the same shortage from the China war as had caused Japan to speed up research. It was in the summer of 1937 that Du Pont told the Weco firm that it had at last developed and thoroughly tested a synthetic bristle. Exton was the name of the new Du Pont bristle. Wearing machine tests seemed to have proven that toothbrushes made by Exton would outlast natural bristle brushes by a factor of at least two to one. Those new bristles were said not to soften in water or saliva and would not break off in the mouth of the user. Dr. West's Miracle-Tuft Toothbrush was to be packed in the well-known glass tube and to retail for 50 cents; the same price as for the brush it was replacing, Dr. West's Waterproof Toothbrush. According to A. C. Nielsen Company, Dr. West's dollar sales in 1937 were 70 percent ahead of its nearest competitors. The main rivals, Pro-phy-lac-tic and Tek brushes, had no ready response. Exton was to be sold exclusively for use in Dr. West's new brush, for since 1927 Du Pont had operated a factory exclusively for the manufacture of Dr. West's brushes. Tek's only response was to announce a repeat program of its campaign from the previous fall, wherein customers could buy two brushes for 51 cents, a one-cent sale.[28]

West's new synthetic brush had little noticeable difference in appearance with the old natural-bristle tool, both selling at 50 cents. Also, the new item was packed in the same sealed glass tube that was one of the major selling points for the old item. Thus, to clear the old model, the company decided to try and increase its sales by putting the old brush in a different and new package — a blue carton instead of a glass tube — at a lower price of 35 cents. Weco hoped to draw in some people who had in the past been discouraged "by the relatively high 50-cent price." While the carton brushes were claimed to be sterilized they were not what Weco called "surgically sterile," as were the implements in the glass tubes. Retailers were urged to offer both the old and new brushes side by side on their counters. According to Weco, tests of that plan revealed that brushes in cartons sold only 4.6 percent below normal, indicating the big business increases it experienced were obtained mainly at the expense of other brands selling at similar prices. Weco said, oddly, that every survey it conducted of toothbrush users showed that two to three times as many people said they used a Dr. West's as actually did, based on the firm's sales figures. In 1937, for example, when asked that question, 22.5 million people said they used Dr. West's brushes but, according to Weco's sales figures 11 million people bought the brushes. From that data, Weco decided the difference in the numbers —11.5 million people — represented those who apparently were not users but wished they had been able to afford that 50-cent brush. That is, 11.5 million people declared themselves users of Dr. West's brushes even though they did not own a West's product. They did that because they wished they used one.[29]

When Weco Products got the exclusive rights to use Du Pont's new fiber Exton (closely related to the firm's much more widely publicized synthetic silk, nylon) company executives were very worried abut the fact that the synthetic bristles would far outwear any natural hog or boar bristles. Although they assumed that sales to new customers of its Miracle-Tuft brushes would help to compensate for any loss in replacement sales, a reduction in the total volume of all toothbrush sales looked to the industry like a logical outcome of the arrival of synthetic bristles. Yet a year after the launch of synthetic brushes sales totals had actually increased by 2 percent to 4 percent. Sales of Weco's Miracle-Tuft synthetic brush and the natural bristle Waterproof brand had both continued to increase. Several years earlier a survey indicated that, on average, toothbrushes were replaced every 4.88 months. Isolated examples for Dr. West's Miracle-Tuft brand indicated replacements were made after around six months. Because Weco bought natural bristles at least a year before usage (to ensure adequate aging) it had a stockpile and that was the reason it had to develop a strategy to sell its Waterproof brand against the synthetic Miracle-Tuft. The purpose of putting the natural brush in a paper carton priced at 35 cents had been simply to liquidate the item. Instead, it showed such sales vitality — with little advertising promotion behind it the item sold around 70 percent as many units as Miracle-Tuft, and almost 50 percent of Miracle-Tuft's dollar volume — that all ideas of eliminating the Waterproof brand were abandoned.[30]

But by the summer of 1940 *Business Week* was reporting that unit sales of toothbrushes were off 3 percent that year with dollar sales off 13 percent. Leading the industry was Weco Products, whose Dr. West's brushes commanded 34.6 percent of the total volume and accounted for 37.7 percent of all toothbrush advertising. Next came Listerine's Pro-phy-lac-tic, sales 15.6 percent, advertising, 20.1 percent; Johnson & Johnson's Tek, sales 14.1 percent, advertising, 35.3 percent; Bristol-Myers' Double Duty, sales 2.1 percent, advertising, 6.6 percent. All others — meaning non-advertised brands — accounted for 33.6 percent of total sales. While a very few of the latter were high-price lines, most were low-price items sold on drugstore bargain counters, in departments stores, and in five-and-ten-cent stores. Weco was then selling its Exton Miracle-Tuft at 47 cents retail minimum with its hog-bristle Waterproof brand at 25 cents. Despite the competition in the field toothpaste heavyweight company Pepsodent was preparing to enter the brush field.[31]

While Weco still held exclusive rights for the Du Pont synthetic bristles it launched, in mid–1940, a new synthetic model, Dr. West's 25, which retailed for 25 cents and was backed by a large ad campaign that hyped it in a way not to interfere with the Sales of Miracle-Tuft. Dr. West's 25 was advertised as being made with nylon, not Exton, although the only difference between the two (other than price) was the weight of the handle and the caliper of the bristles. That model arrived on the scene a few months before any other manufacturer could come out with a nylon product — due to Weco's exclusive rights to the Du Pont patent. The new model was in direct competition with Weco's hog-bristle Waterproof brand (and at the same price) and was expected to displace it because the synthetic bristles wore longer and did not soften up when wet. Also, the model was seen as gaining an advantage over the still-to-come Pepsodent brush, expected to be aimed at the same medium-priced sector of the market as Dr. West's 25.[32]

When Weco's exclusive franchise on the use of nylon bristles expired in November 1940, Pro-phy-lac-tic promptly announced a nylon toothbrush to retail at 23 cents. To promote the idea of using different brushes for morning and evening use the company offered consumers two of these brushes (in different colors) in one carton for 43 cents. It was a promotion made despite the fact that a nylon brush used twice a day did not get soggy the way a hog-bristle brush did when used twice a day (the idea that a brush should be left to stand 24 hours to dry before being reused was sensible for natural brushes but unnecessary for synthetic ones). Toothbrushes in the U.S. market were said to fall into two major groups: those retailed in drugstores, and those sold in five and dime stores. Of the drugstore items, 54.6 percent fell in the 50-cent bracket, which Dr. West's Miracle-Tuft continued to dominate. Below the half-dollar bracket came the two-bit category, which actually carried an average retail price of 19 cents. Around this time the word Exton was dropped with the synthetic brushes being all described as having nylon bristles, after it was acknowledged that Exton and nylon were the same thing.[33]

Near the end of December 1940, Pepsodent announced its new toothbrush was ready to go — the "50-Tuft." Pepsodent was described by business reporter Andrew Howe as one of the "greatest names" in the field of oral hygiene. It heralded its toothbrush as the "only tooth brush in the world with fifty tufts of Du Pont's synthetic bristles in a small head — twice as many tufts as any other tooth brush" and its introductory ad program stressed the 50-tuft story. Those tufts were ordinary Du Pont nylon bristles but Pepsodent gave them the trademarked name of fibrex, "for advertising convenience." However, admitted Howe, they were the same bristles as Dr. West's products used, and all were the same as Exton. Each of the two Weco synthetic brushes contained 25 tufts and it was at that point that Pepsodent was aiming its ad copy. Various other brush makers used various names for the nylon bristles "but they are all the same, except that they are supplied in several diameters, varying by only one-thousandth of an inch," said Howe. Pepsodent's $1 million ad campaign for 50-Tuft was headed by spots on the Bob Hope radio show beginning in January 1941, along with full page color ads in national weekly magazines and newspaper supplements at the same time.[34]

One of the first evaluations of toothbrushes for general consumers took place in June 1941, in the pages of *Consumers' Research Bulletin*. That article declared there was no question that synthetic bristles were superior to natural ones in that they wore longer, wore better, did not bunch or spread out from use, and were less likely to come loose as individual bristles. All six recommended items contained synthetic bristles; four Dr. West models, two each of Miracle-Tuft and Dr. West's 25, Pepsodent 50-Tuft, and Tek. Three of them retailed at 47 cents, two at 23 cents, and one at 25 cents for an average of 35.7 cents. Five models of natural-bristle brushes (Montgomery Ward, and Pycope, for example) were all given recommended ratings,

Another ad about the end of the old hogs' hair natural bristles, 1943.

WHY CUT 'EM OFF ?...

Pro-phy-lac-tic won't buy 'em!

For years hog bristle made the best tooth brushes... then along came round-end *PROLON*

Next time you buy a tooth brush, keep this in mind: Years of laboratory research have produced amazing new synthetic bristles . . . better, longer-lasting than natural bristle.

And among the new synthetic tooth brush bristles being marketed under various trade names, far and away the best are those made by duPont.

PROLON — no finer bristle made

"Prolon" is our name for the very finest grade of this synthetic bristle that duPont makes. So, when you read or hear competitive tooth brush claims, ask yourself this: *How can the same du Pont bristle, in another brush under another name, last longer or clean better than under the name "Prolon" in a Pro-phy-lac-tic Tooth Brush?* You know

the answer...it can't!

Pro-phy-lac-tic's big *plus* is that Prolon is the only synthetic bristle that is rounded at the ends.

Yes, under a special patented process, exclusive with Pro-phy-lac-tic, we smooth and round the end of each and every Prolon bristle in the Bonded Pro-phy-lac-tic Tooth Brush. See for yourself how much gentler these round ends are on tender gums!

Only PROLON has "round ends"

Remember, no other tooth brush has this important feature. So, next time you buy a tooth brush get the best you can buy for your money . . . get the Bonded Pro-phy-lac-tic Tooth Brush —the only tooth brush, by the way, with a written six-month guarantee.

... and don't miss this new line of hair brushes in gleaming Jewelite!

Pro-phy-lac-tic's latest triumph! Dresser sets and toilet brushes in crystal-clear plastic. Choice of four gleaming, jewel colors. Transparent Jewelite backs Moisture-resistant, snow-white Prolon bristles. $1.50 to $10.00 — at most beauty goods counters Illustrated: Roll Wave, a unique "curved-to-the-head" brush ... with comb. $4.50

but below the nylon products. Prices in this group ranged from 19 cents to 50 cents with an average of 35 cents. In the third and last group were 16 models that were all not recommended. Most of them were natural bristle brushes but a few synthetic brands were included, not the least of which were a few variations of Dr. West's 25 (there were half-a-dozen sub-models under that general brand name), Pro-phy-lac-tic and a Tek. Those 16 rejected items ranged in price from nine cents to 45 cents and averaged 23 cents. Most were rejected for reasons of shape with that defined as bristles too long, tufts too closely set, tufts uneven in height, and so on. One of the unusual brands in that last category was the Tefra Refillable (from the Tefra Company, Indianapolis), which sold for 25 cents complete and refills (the head of the brush alone) at 15 cents.[35]

A couple of years later, in 1943, *Consumers' Research Bulletin* discussed toothbrushes in a more general way. It pointed out that brushing was a cosmetic measure rather than one for health and hygiene "and it is obvious that with proper food man would have no more need for a toothbrush than a dog or a cat does." Said J. Sim Wallace, a distinguished English dental expert, "No amount of antiseptics and toothbrushing ever atones for continuous dietetic error" and "artificial aids to oral hygiene" would not prevent pyorrhea or dental decay. According to a consensus of dental opinion, the following seemed to represent the specifications for an ideal type of brush: the head should be about one inch to 1.25 inches long and about $\frac{5}{16}$ of an inch wide; there may be either two or three rows of bristles in tufts about $\frac{3}{32}$ inches apart in the rows in order that the bristles may easily clean the spaces between the teeth. In a two-row brush the space between rows should be about $\frac{1}{8}$ of an inch and in a three-row brush, about $\frac{1}{16}$ inches; tufts of bristles should be compact, tightly packed, and be trimmed to a rough, blunt cone shape; tufts should be of a uniform height slightly less than $\frac{1}{2}$ an inch, with no tufts standing up above the others. In the view of this account a mild dentifrice could be used once a day when brushing the teeth but on the other brushing in the day no dentifrice should be used (brush only) since the important thing was the brush, not what was on it. Also recommended was that a toothbrush be allowed to dry for 24 hours (hung in sunlight as often as practicable) before reuse and that the brush be sterilized from time to time by placing it in a chloramine solution for about 10 minutes.[36]

In 1944 American civilians spent around $30 million on toothbrushes and by 1945 three major companies, E. R. Squibb & Sons (Squibb brushes), Weco Products (Dr. West) and Johnson & Johnson (Tek) spent a total of about $1.5 million on advertising in magazines and on radio programs. In its 1945 ratings *Consumers' Research Bulletin* recommended five brands (price range from 20 cents to 47 cents, average of 29.6 cents); eight brands were given an intermediate rating (20 cents to $1.46); and five models were not recommended (10 cents to 50 cents, 29.8 cents). One model given an intermediate ranking was the Indexo (35 cents), a rubber toothbrush suitable for slipping over the index finger for use, made by the Indexo Finger Toothbrush Company of New York City.[37]

3

Toothpaste, 1900–1945

Toothpaste is "an agent which may aid the tooth brush in cleaning the surfaces of the teeth. Beyond this the toothpaste has no further function."— American Dental Association, 1932.

It is the brush and not the paste or the powder one puts on it which is of chief importance.—Consumer Reports, 1936.

Dr. Lyon's Tooth Powder was introduced in America in 1866 and went on to become a household word throughout the U.S. with the business reaching a sales peak in 1922. From that year on, sales decreased steadily about 10 percent each year. It was felt that the product suffered from competing against the increasingly dominant paste segment of the dentifrice industry, with the result that the firm added a toothpaste to the line, selling both powder and paste. That was the situation in the latter part of 1927 when R. L. Watkins & Company, owner of Watkins Mulsified Cocoanut Oil Shampoo, Glostora, and liquid Avron, bought the Lyon business for $800,000. The new owners decided to put their faith in the powder, which had once been so successful. Lyon's brand of toothpaste was no longer pushed; it was allowed to gently fade into oblivion. Peak sales of the paste were about $150,000 yearly and when Watkins acquired the concern in 1927 sales of the paste product totalled $57,000 annually. For 1932 sales ran around $6,000. H. A. Weissman, vice president of sales and marketing, explained the paste would not be revived as a companion product because "we can never go back to promotion for the toothpaste and hold faith with our consuming public or the dental profession. We have been sincere in our belief that a tooth powder is the most effective and economical cleansing agent." More vigorous ad campaigns were launched to promote the powder, using slogans such as, "Do as your dentist does — use powder" and "Outlasts tooth paste 2 to 1." Sales were said to have increased 50 percent each year from 1928 through 1932. A 1929 sampling campaign that was started among dentists in Pennsylvania was expanded to a nationwide strategy in 1932. Once each month dentists received a sample of the powder and were told they could have as many more samples as they wanted — the idea was that they would be given out to patients. Whereas the old Lyon ownership had spent $200,000 in 1927 for advertising, the new owners spent about $600,000 in 1932, with $150,000 of that total being for the cost of samples.[1]

Another popular brand in America in the first half of the 20th century was Kolynos toothpaste; it originated abroad. Doctor N. S. Jenkins was born in Boston. After becoming a dentist, he practiced in Bangor, Maine, for a while and then went to Dresden, Germany, where he practiced for years. In the late 1800s, shortly after Professor W. D. Miller concluded mouth bacteria was the local cause of tooth decay, Jenkins began a study to develop an agent that would not only cleanse teeth but also destroy oral bacteria. Collaborating with Miller, Jenkins continued his experiments and clinical observations for 17 years, until 1908. Then he returned to the U.S. to have his findings tested in the chemical laboratory of one of America's leading universities. Reportedly, those studies substantiated Jenkins's conclusions and thus, he introduced Kolynos. Jenkins, though, preferred to remain a scientist and decided against entering commercial business. However, in order to let the public have the benefit of "this new scientific dentifrice," he did permit his son, L. A. Jenkins, to undertake the manufacture of the product. A plant was established at New Haven, Connecticut.[2]

By the mid–1930s the Kolynos company was a unit of the American Home Products Corporation. It was one of the most successful exporters in the U.S. and it had been a successful exporter long before it became part of American Home Products. Kolynos was sold in 88 countries in 1937 and manufactured in whole or in part in more than 20 of them. In most nations it was retailed in drugstores although it was also sold in bazaars in Oriental countries and elsewhere in perfumery shops and also in grocery stores. Kolynos also advertised in most countries in which it was sold, usually in newspapers and magazines. It advertised in a total of 32 languages, 11 in India alone. The name of Kolynos was a combination of two Greek words, meaning "beautifier" and "disease preventer." During the 1930s and 1940s in America millions of people bought Kolynos Dental Cream to make their teeth "gleam like pearls" in only three days. It focused a great deal in its ads on the whiter teeth theme with one of its ad headlines proclaiming, "In 3 days whitens teeth 3 shades." Such ads got the brand as much as 20 percent of the market during its heyday.[3]

Around the end of the 1950s the fall of Kolynos began when, as one industry observer reported, people came to care more about cavities than about looks. One toothpaste executive remarked, in 1968, "Kolynos lost out because it had no fluoride story to tell. Now, ironically, there's a swing back to a white-teeth appeal, but too late to save the brand. You could launch a new brand for less than it would cost to revive Kolynos." At that time, 1968, Kolynos was still owned by the Whitehall Laboratories Division of American Home Products. When asked what it thought about the Kolynos situation company advertising manager Richard G. Rettig responded curtly that Kolynos "doesn't sell much anymore and we don't want to talk about it."[4]

Colgate got into the dentifrice business in 1895 when it began to sell its new Ribbon Dental Cream for 50 cents a jar, at a time when the Sears Roebuck catalog advertised a high-back dining chair for just three cents more. The company substituted collapsible tubes for the jars, then reconfigured the tube opening so the paste would not spurt out and slide off the brush.[5]

When Dr. Richard J. Forhan died at his New York City home late in 1965 he was just short of his 100th birthday and reputed to be one of America's richest dentists. In 1913 Forhan, who had developed an astringent for gum troubles, made it an ingredient of a dentifrice he began making in Brooklyn, and that he called "Forhan's for the Gums." Early ads for the product declared, "Four out of Five Have Pyorrhea," which, allegedly, Forhan's could cure. About $2.5 million worth of the product was sold annually by 1929 when Forhan sold out to the Zonite Products Corporation (in 1956 it became the Chemway Corporation). Shortly after buying Forhan's, Zonite was enjoined by the Federal Trade Commission (FTC) from making any claims about pyorrhea, and all advertising ceased. Sales slumped until 1936 when ads were resumed with the milder claim that the product might help in treating gingivitis, a gum inflammation of varying degrees of severity. Sales boomed again, especially during World War II when it was promoted heavily on the radio. After 1945, though, ads stopped. Forhan's was still sold in small quantities in the U.S. in the mid–1960s, at a time it was said to be the second largest selling toothpaste in Mexico. Also, it was then sold in many South American nations, in Canada, and in Europe.[6]

Introduced in 1915, Ipana gained momentum in the 1930s when its manufacturer, Bristol-Myers, sponsored such popular radio programs as Fred Allen's *Town Hall* show, featuring the Ipana Troubadours, who appeared in red and yellow costumes that matched Ipana's tube and box colors. That comedy program made heavy use of Ipana's "smile of beauty" slogan. During those years and through the 1940s, Ipana was alternately number two and three in market share behind Colgate, with a close competitor being Kolynos.[7]

Like Ipana, Pepsodent toothpaste was introduced around 1915. Albert Lasker, chief of the Lord & Thomas ad agency, felt that a market existed for an inexpensive toothpaste. He was receptive, therefore, when a neighbour, banker Louis Eckstein, introduced him to Douglas Smith, a patent medicine entrepreneur whose Liquozone, a magic cure-all, benefited from ad copy writ-

Why the Brush never touches the Can

"Please hurry with that Dr. Lyon's"

D R. LYON was by no means content with producing the purest, finest and most efficient dentifrice. He deemed it out of equal importance to provide the utmost hygiene and elegance in its manner of use.

To this refinement of method as well as quality, the long established place of distinction, apart from merely commercial tooth preparations, is due.

For it is equally the fame of

Dr. Lyon's
PERFECT
Tooth Powder

(Prepared for nearly half a century by a doctor of dental surgery)

that it is unrivaled for the *life-time* preservation of the teeth, and that any number of persons can use it from the same can, each serene against all thought of common contact.*

The patent measuring tube which forms the neck of the can delivers just the right quantity of powder to the brush by a tap of the finger. The brush and the can never touch.

Yet another vital advantage of Dr. Lyon's being in *powder form:* It brings no saccharine, glycerine, gelatine, glucose or honey to form sticky masses between the teeth to cause decay. It encourages thorough brushing, keeping the gums healthy and hard. Tartar and discoloration disappear. A natural fragrance of breath is maintained.

Use Dr. Lyon's Perfect Tooth Powder night and morning—ABOVE ALL AT NIGHT. Train your children early to its constant use.

What Dr. Lyon's does not do should be entrusted only to your dentist to do.

So long has this feature enjoyed high appreciation that Robert Louis Stevenson, in his famous romance "The Ebb Tide," mentions Dr. Lyon's and the fact that any number of persons can use it with perfect propriety and neatness.

Sold Everywhere

A 1912 ad for Dr. Lyon's Tooth Powder. Note the ad explained the brush never touched the can (it was poured out on to the brush). That was important because of hygienic criticism of the time as family members all rubbed their brushes across the surface of some cans of dentifrices.

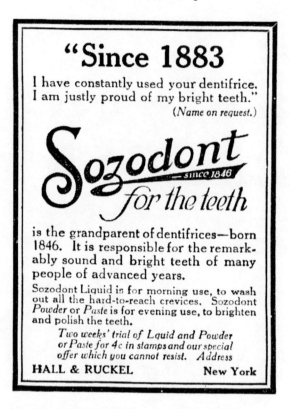

By 1915 Sozodont had expanded to have liquid, powder, and paste dentifrices, but its time was just about over.

ten by Claude Hopkins. Smith, ready to move on to other ventures, had bought a toothpaste formula from a dentist who claimed the formula would remove "mucin plaques" from the teeth. Smith formed the Pepsodent Company with Lord & Thomas taking the advertising account in November 1916, with Lasker acquiring stock in Pepsodent for his fee from the cash-short firm. Hopkins, who worked at Lord & Thomas, bought a $13,000 share in the toothpaste company that went on to pay him $200,000 in dividends before he eventually sold the stock for $500,000. He built the brand with a combination of coupon and free-trial offer advertising. Lasker got rid of the word "plaque" because he felt nobody would know its meaning, although he and Hopkins positioned Pepsodent as the toothpaste that removed "film" from teeth. Later, Lasker added sodium alkyl sulphate, a harmless detergent, and ordered his copywriters to invent a word with three vowels and two consonants to describe the new ingredient. Selected was the word "irium," as Pepsodent underwent its first reformulation. So great was his faith in advertising that Lasker used no sales force for Pepsodent. His formula for product pricing was "one-third to manufacturing; one-third to advertising; one-third to profit."[8]

Most of the toothpaste that would come to dominate the dentifrice industry came into being in the early 1900s, at a time when the market was dominated by tooth powders and when many people, perhaps most, made it themselves at home. Writing in *Scientific American* in 1900, W. A. Dawson advised that a perfect tooth powder that would thoroughly clean the teeth needed only a few ingredients and was easily made. For the base "there is nothing better than precipitated chalk" because it had all the detergent and polishing properties necessary for the thorough cleaning of the teeth and yet was soft enough to not do any damage to the teeth. That was something that could not be said for pumice, cuttlebone, charcoal, and so on, argued Dawson, abradants that were used in tooth powders. Abrading tooth powders, he added, probably had as much to answer for as 20th century ways of living in speeding up the arrival of the "prophesized toothless race." Next in value, he felt, came soap with powdered white castile soap usually being an ingredient of tooth powders. But it tasted bad and so needed a sweetener and a flavoring. Sugar or saccharin was advised for the sweetener and almost anything for the flavouring. One of the more popular commercially available tooth-powders could be made up at home using the following recipe: precipitated chalk, one pound; white castile soap, one ounce; Florentine orris, two ounces; sugar (or saccharin two grains), one ounce; oil of wintergreen, one-quarter ounce. As a home preparation the cost was around 15 cents a pound, one cent per ounce. That same formula, commercially prepared, retailed in two ounce bottles for 25 cents and "most proprietary powders retail at that price," said Dawson. The fancy bottles generally used cost from four to 10 cents each and the powder itself at no more than two cents for the two ounces, leaving the remainder for profit.[9]

As late as 1932 homemade dentifrices were still being promoted over the commercially prepared powders or pastes, with the efficacy of the commercial products being still unclear. In answer to a reader's query on the effectiveness of popular brands of toothpaste and toothpowders, the editor of *Hygeia*, the American Medical Association's official magazine for lay readers, said even the relative cleansing properties of the dentifrices on the market were unknown. Most of those pastes, he said, had as their principal abrasive either calcium carbonate or tricalcium phosphate, to which was sometimes added salt, sodium perborate and a long list of other substances. Toothpastes were said to be the same as tooth powders, but they had been made into paste form by the addition of glycerin and excipients such as tragacanth. "The use of a dentifrice is limited to whatever cleansing properties it may have," said the editor. The Oklahoma State Board of Health, through its dental division, advocated a homemade dentifrice consisting of equal parts of salt, soda and borax, to which a dash of flavoring could be added. *Hygeia*'s editor gave the following recipe for a home-made dentifrice: salt, two ounces; magnesia, calcined light, one-third ounce; oil of wintergreen, 45 drops; oil of peppermint, 10 drops.[10]

With commercial dentifrices becoming more and more prevalent in society the American Dental Association (ADA) established its Council on Dental Therapeutics in 1932 to examine the composition and claims of articles of dental usefulness. Those articles included dentifrices and mouthwashes. It marked the beginning of an often-stormy relationship between the dental profession and the toothpaste industry. Manufacturers who agreed to comply with the provisions of the council for the acceptance of dentifrices submitted the composition of their products to the council and agreed to limit their advertising to the following council definition of a dentifrice as "an agent that may aid the tooth brush in cleaning the surfaces of the teeth. Beyond this the toothpaste has no further function."[11]

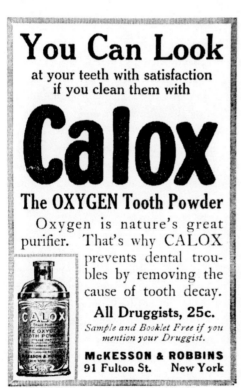

One new type of toothpaste to emerge in the 1930s was the salt-based product. Charles H. Dickson was the vice president of the Worcester Salt Company — its main product, Worcester Iodized Salt, was widely available in grocery stores — and said in 1932 that his firm had for years been contemplating the possibility of marketing a salt toothpaste, one reason being that it had long been a popular ingredient in homemade preparations. In their booklets

Calox claimed, in 1915, that it was, somehow, an oxygen tooth powder. It was another false claim that was eventually stopped.

and literature on Worcester Salt, wherein they recommended many other uses for the product, the company had for some time suggested its use as a dentifrice and mouthwash. "What we really have done, therefore, in our new product, is to interpret this use in terms of the taste, convenience and persuasion which the American people demand," explained Dickson.[12]

Even after they determined to manufacture Worcester Salt Tooth Paste it was two years before the product was ready for market; it retailed at 35 cents a tube. Dickson said it was logical to sell it in grocery stores since it sold its salt there already, "but for a toothpaste the natural outlet is the drug store. The housewife, we reasoned, is not accustomed to asking for tooth paste in a grocery store, nor is she mentally concentrated on that product while there." Thus, the firm concentrated on getting the product into drugstores, where it had no presence. When they launched the new paste they sent an announcement letter, and a full-size tube as a sample to drug stores along with a card to mail back to them with comments. Some 7 percent returned the cards with 99 percent of those said to have approved of the product with their comments. For its first advertising campaign Worcester Salt Tooth Paste adopted for its main slogan, "Your mouth will sing its praises."[13]

A trademark dispute erupted in the industry in 1935 when Pepsodent tried to stop another company from marketing a new toothpaste called Pearledent, claiming its name was too similar to its own and thus violated trademark laws. However, the U.S. Patent Office ruled against Pepsodent, saying people could distinguish between similarly named brands. The Patent Office added that because there were at least 45 dental preparations on the market, it could be said that such a large number was almost conclusive proof that the public was able to distinguish such small differences in notations.[14]

Phillips Dental Magnesia (made by the Chas. H. Phillips Chemical Company, a subsidiary of Sterling Products) entered the paste field in the very early 1930s with a milk of magnesia product. Despite all the competition it had $547,000 of paste sales in 1933 while the Watkins company had sales that year of $1,493,000 of Dr. Lyon's Tooth Powder. Such figures were rarely revealed but had become public when Watkins attempted unsuccessfully to take over Sterling. In the two years from 1933 to 1935 the public reportedly renewed its interest in powder products to such an extent as to worry some of the paste makers. Several paste makers — Pepsodent, Listerine, and Forhan's, for example — had gone so far as to bring out a tooth powder within the last year of that period and, also, Sterling launched a Phillips toothpowder product.[15]

One of the earliest toothpaste valuation articles for the general public

IF you will say "Pebeco"
to your druggist *now*, you
won't need to say "Ouch!"
to your dentist later.

PEBECO
TOOTH PASTE

Ten-Day Trial Tube mailed Free upon request.
Address Lehn & Fink, 126 William St., New York

A 1916 copy for Pebeco, a paste that was long popular but is now long gone.

appeared in the pages of *Consumer Reports* in 1936. It was at a time when the practise of teeth cleaning with a brush and dentifrice was just becoming a widespread habit. More and more people had access to indoor plumbing, which made brushing more convenient. Reminiscing 50 years after that report the magazine noted that some products were downright dangerous then. For instance, some contained strong acids that whitened the teeth beautifully but ruined tooth enamel. Others contained substances that were toxic or irritating. Given the ad copy — "A lot of nonsense was spread about the powers and abilities of dentifrices, pandering to social insecurity, others played to fear of pyorrhoea" — and the lack of standards in manufacturing, it came as no surprise to *Consumer Reports* that most of the products in that 1936 report were rated as Not Acceptable.[16]

After branding advertising claims for the dentifrices as "uniformly false" the 1936 report went on to say "brushing of the teeth probably does have some value in preventing decay," but "it is the brush and not the paste or the powder one puts on it which is of chief importance." Among the products rated Not Acceptable were all the tooth bleaches ("even one application can cause irreparable damage to the tooth enamel"), all products containing sodium perborate (because of the danger of boron poisoning), Pepsodent powder and paste ("excessively acid"), Forhan's powder and paste ("expensive"), Ipana toothpaste ("will not prevent or cure pink toothbrush"), and Colgate Ribbon Dental Cream ("contains starch, which may promote decay"). A few products were rated Best Buys, including Ward's Tooth Powder (17 cents for a 3.5-ounce can), Milk-I-Dent Dental Cream (10 cents a tube), and Wrigley's Spearmint Toothpaste (10 cents a tube). Cheaper still were the three formulas CU gave then for home-made tooth powder: precipitated chalk; a mixture of salt and baking soda; and a mixture of calcium carbonate, castile soap, and flavoring.[17]

Baltimore City College bacteriologist Arthur H. Bryan published results of studies he made in 1938 on antiseptic toothpastes. He found they were not strong enough to harm the gums or tooth enamel and while their use decreased the number of bacteria in the mouth for one hour after use, at the end of that hour the number of bacteria increased and at the end of two hours was as high or higher than before.[18]

Another new-style dentifrice launched in the 1930s was the liquid dentifrice. Proctor & Gamble, a huge presence in soaps, but a stranger in drugs, started the liquid dentifrice field in the fall of 1938 when it developed Teel and began to test market it through radio and newspaper ads. A year later Teel was distributed nationally. Second in the field was Pepsodent, which reportedly experimented with a liquid for three years but waited to see how Teel fared. When the answer became clear Pepsodent Liquid Dentifrice got test marketed in half a dozen markets before receiving national distribution in the summer of 1939. It was backed by a magazine ad campaign. To introduce its liquid Pepsodent offered druggists the first free deal in the company's history. With every 12 bottles purchased, druggists got one bottle free. Immediately after Pepsodent came the liquid Flodent, made by the Flodent Products Company. It made a successful debut in Roanoke, Virginia. Then, in October 1939, Colgate-Palmolive-Peet introduced Cue, its new entry in the liquid dentifrice area. Researchers estimated that Americans then spent between $30 million and $40 million a year on dentifrices. Four out of 10 citizens reportedly used powders but because powder lasted longer than paste, powder items were thought to account for no more than 30 percent of the dollar volume. What worried the trade was that very fact that liquid items lasted longer than either paste or powder. Both Pepsodent and Colgate, each having a big stake in the paste and powder markets, were believed to hope the liquids failed but entered the arena themselves because they did not want Proctor & Gamble to get the jump in the liquid business that Dr. Lyon's had gotten in powders. Dr. Lyon's remained the dominant maker in the powder field, with an estimated 40 percent market share. To that point Ipana — which ranked with Colgate and Pepsodent in the big three of toothpaste makers —

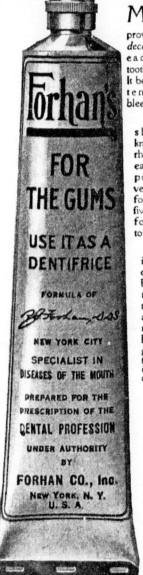
had made no move toward either a powder or a liquid dentifrice.[19]

Albert Ingallis wrote a piece for *Scientific American* in 1940 in which he declared most of the nationally known dentifrices were safe. He added that no dentifrice could keep the mouth germ free nor could any prevent acid mouth as it was normal for the mouth to be acidic. Also, he said no dentifrice could prevent tooth decay nor could any of them treat, cure, or prevent pyorrhea. Bad breath, as well, could not be prevented, or removed, by the use of a dentifrice. All those things were regularly claimed by various preparations in their ad campaigns. "Really insidious are claims for tooth whiteners, since these preparations contain acids — hydrochloric acid, for ex.," added Ingallis. "Nor will they always whiten teeth since some teeth were never white to begin with. Also dentists don't prefer powder over paste [a popular ad slo-

Forhan's advertised itself for many years as curing the gum disease pyorrhea, after stating that four out of every five people suffered from it, as declared in this 1917 ad — another false claim the company was eventually forced to abandon.

gan at the time for a powder] — no difference, except the public seems to find paste more convenient." Like many others from this era he argued the brush was the most important element in oral hygiene and "the dentifrice is its junior assistant." However, he did conclude "a good dentifrice is more than worth to us what we pay for it."[20]

When *Consumers' Research Bulletin* evaluated toothpowders in 1944 it pointed out, as it said it had been doing for some years, that the proper use of the toothbrush was the factor of primary importance in cleaning the teeth, "not what is put on the brush." To get as economical a dentifrice as possible it recommended its own formula for tooth powder — the use of precipitated chalk (at a cost of 30 cents a pound if bought locally, 45 cents by mail). If desired, baking soda could be added in the ratio of one ounce to one pound of the powdered chalk. For flavor, the advice was to add a few drops of oil of peppermint. Said the piece, "The chief function of any dentifrice is to aid the toothbrush in the removal of food and loose debris from the teeth. A dentifrice does not serve any other important function."[21]

What *Consumers' Research Bulletin* worried the most about, and concentrated the most on, was the degree of abrasiveness of the powders. The ADA did not admit to its listing of Accepted Dentifrices any which contained siliceous materials such as pumice or silica for daily use. Many people believed that material used for cleaning the teeth should not be harder than the teeth. In the Mohr scale of hardness, tooth enamel had a hardness ranging from 5.5 to 7.0; with calcium carbonate (precipitated chalk) at 3.0 to 3.5. Other polishing agents included talc, 1.0; magnesium carbonate, 2.5; tricalcium phosphate, 4.0 to 5.0; and pumice, 6.0 to 7.0 (much too hard). When *Consumers' Research Bulletin* rated the powders it did so by establishing a comparison against a standard of precipitated calcium carbonate, used as a control and given an arbitrary rating of 100. *Consumers' Research Bulletin* found the powders it tested ranged from 201 for the Squibb powder to 47 for Craig-Martin (the least abrasive). Sixteen items were listed in the ratings with a price range of from about five cents to 15 cents per ounce. Six of the products had a hardness rating above that of precipitated chalk, Dr. Lyon's Tooth Powder had an abrasiveness rating of 166, for example. In 1939 Pepsodent Tooth Powder was accepted for approval by the ADA. However in April 1941, that approval was withdrawn because of advertising claims made for the product.[22]

And nowhere did the dental profession and the toothpaste industry clash as often or as heatedly as they did over advertising. The U.S. government also had more than an occasional run-in with the toothpaste industry. None of the experts in the area was all that enthusiastic about dentifrices in this

A 1919 ad copy for Klenzo.

period — almost everybody viewed the brush as by far the most important factor even, sometimes, to advocating its use without any dentifrice. It was left to advertising — often with outrageously false claims with respect to toothpastes — to try and turn Americans into dedicated user of commercially prepared dentifrices. And it did.

4

Toothpaste, Advertising and Marketing, 1900–1945

Is Acid-Mouth at work on the teeth of your loved ones?—Pebeco ad, 1920s.

What are your teeth saying about you today?—Listerine toothpaste ad, 1920s.

You'll wonder where the yellow went, when you brush your teeth with Pepsodent.—Pepsodent ad, 1930s.

Researcher Peter Goulding argued in 1957 that advertising had only a nodding acquaintance with dentifrices prior to 1900. But around that year the dental scientist and the advertising copywriter met head on as more and more research was done on dental decay. Each time a possible new lead was reported in a research journal, a dentifrice that contained the new element would appear, a practice Goulding said remained in vogue up to the time he was writing. First it was an alkaline dentifrice — supposed to combat the acids in the mouth which the profession believed caused tooth decay — then it was an acid dentifrice, supposedly to stimulate the flow of saliva in the mouth and thus clear away food debris that combined with oral acids to cause decay. By 1918 the *American Dentist* publication commented, "A long and earnest perusal of dentifrice advertisements might lead one to believe that the manufacturers' efforts went into the development of a slogan and an advertising theory instead of into the development of a useful and beneficial article for the toilet." In the midst of Goulding's piece the editor of *Today's Health* (as *Hygeia* had been renamed in the early 1950s) added his own thoughts, "The advertising of dentifrices, both in the professional and lay press, has reached the stage of transparent absurdity where the sophisticated layman, however uncertain for the reason of his skepticism, smiles in derision." As late as 1931 *The Journal of the American Dental Association* had to warn that hydrochloric acid was still being used in products sold to the public as tooth whiteners. It did whiten the teeth but also had the ability to peel off the enamel. Up to that time, declared Goulding, the copywriter had to depend chiefly on claims of whitening the teeth and sweetening the breath, along with vague allusions to decay-preventing properties.[1]

Originally Colgate sold dentifrices merely as a sideline to its main product line of soaps. With the coming of the collapsible metal tubes for paste Colgate quickly switched to those containers and moved to make toothpaste one of its main product lines. In the very early 1900s Colgate advertised: "We couldn't improve the product so we improved the tube." Its slogan, "Comes out like a ribbon, lies flat on the brush, Colgate's Ribbon Dental Cream," became so well known that it was put to music and sung by college glee clubs, according to journalist Don Wharton. Liquids and powders began slipping in popularity, losing out to the paste, and by 1911 Lyon's was about the only powder advertising nationally.[2]

In the first half of the 20th century, argued Wharton, toothpaste advertising had concentrated on a fear of disease, and a desire for beauty or at least popularity. Pebeco was one of the first of the toothpaste brands to produce a catchphrase, "Acid-Mouth," advertised in the pages of the women's magazines of 1916. Later catchphrases included Ipana's "Pink Tooth Brush," Kolynos's "Germ Mask," Bost's "Smoker's Teeth," and Forhan's "4 out of 5 Have It" [referring to the gum disease pyorrhea]. By 1930 a toothpaste without a scare campaign was rare, believed Wharton. Pepsodent, a commercial sensation was, in the view of Wharton, virtually created by two advertising men, referring to Albert Lasker and Claude Hopkins of the ad agency Lord & Thomas. Once they took on the new Pepsodent dentifrice Hopkins scoured through dental books wherein he encountered references to mucin plaques on teeth. Adopting that to build a campaign around Hopkins decided the name was too awkward and inscrutable and renamed the problem "film." Launched in 1917, his ads for Pepsodent played up the idea that only Pepsodent removed this "clinging film" on the teeth while boosting the product as a creator of beauty. Hopkins believed people were less interested in any anti-disease measures within the product than in attaining "more success, more happiness, more beauty, more cheer." Those were also the themes of his ads with results said to be "spectacular." Pepsodent went on to become the best selling toothpaste even though it retailed at double the price of most other brands. Eventually Pepsodent was bought by Lever Brothers.[3]

Those fulsome and highly exaggerated ads for dentifrices marked a major change from the small, quiet, and usually modest claims made for those products in the first few years of the 1900s. For example, an ad in 1903 for Rubifoam dentifrice said, simply, "Clean, white teeth and Rubifoam are synonymous."[4]

And it was its advertising that was usually given the credit for Pepso-

Even the heavy smoker may have a clean, fresh mouth

Pebeco Tooth Paste restores to the smoker's mouth the clean, fresh taste which makes the first smoke after breakfast so enjoyable.

Pebeco gives instant refreshment to the membranes of the mouth, both in the morning and at night. And it keeps the teeth cleaner.

We do not claim that Pebeco will prevent a smoker's teeth from becoming stained. Teeth should be "scaled" by your dentist at regular intervals.

But Pebeco will keep your mouth fresh. It will keep the teeth clean, and it will check the condition known as "Acid-Mouth," which destroys teeth. The cost of one good cigar will keep a man supplied with Pebeco Tooth Paste for weeks.

LEHN & FINK, Inc.
635 Greenwich Street, New York

Canadian Agents: Harold F. Ritchie & Co., Limited, 10 McCaul St., Toronto

Also makers of Lysol Disinfectant, Lysol Shaving Cream, and Lysol Toilet Soap

Have You "Acid-Mouth"

?

It Is Thought To Be the Chief Cause of Tooth Decay

These Test Papers Will Tell You —Sent Free With 10-Day Trial Tube of Pebeco

There are probably many causes that contribute to decay of the teeth, but dental authorities seem to agree that in the vast majority of cases decay results from over-acidity of the mouth. You can easily tell if you have "Acid-Mouth," and also see how Pebeco tends to counteract this tooth-destroying condition, by the simple and interesting experiment with the test papers, which we will gladly send to you upon request.

Moisten a blue Litmus Test Paper on your tongue. If it turns pink, you have "Acid-Mouth." Brush your teeth with Pebeco and make another test. The paper will not change color, thus demonstrating how Pebeco helps to counteract "Acid-Mouth."

Just send a post-card for Free Test Papers and 10-Day Trial Tube of Pebeco.

False claims abounded in this 1921 ad with Pebeco stating it defeated acid-mouth as well as doing wonders for smokers.

dent's phenomenal success — to move to be market leader in a short number of years in a field that was already crowded wherein few believed there was room or need for a newcomer, and with a product that cost more per ounce than any of its rivals. By 1927 Pepsodent had full distribution in the U.S., along with an export business in more than 50 foreign nations; yet it had relatively few salesmen on staff. With the Pepsodent company more than 90 percent of the total sales cost was devoted to advertising. "National advertising is our sales force," explained an unnamed executive with Pepsodent and "we expect advertising to do the work that the salesman is normally called upon to do." Pepsodent felt its best chance for success rested with the consumer rather than with the jobber or dealer and if they could get people to try Pepsodent and then ask for it at the druggist or other retailer, the jobber and dealer would be forced to carry it.[5]

Soon after Pepsodent began business in 1915 it started to enlist the support and interest of the dental profession both by direct mail and by advertising in publications aimed at dentists. According to the advertising trade journal *Printers' Ink* it was generally accepted at that time that a dentifrice manufacturer had to send out a force of salesmen — called detail men — to solicit dentists' recognition of his product. Free deals and special discounts were looked upon as the only weapons with which the manufacturer could break into the crowded field. Pepsodent, though, broke all those rules. Its campaigns directed to dentists got inquiries from 6.6 percent of the dentists in America in just three months time. The same mail-order tactic used with dentists was then used on jobbers and before the company was two years old it had over 100 jobbers distributing Pepsodent. In 1917 the first consumer campaign began, but only after tests in five or six cities had determined what queries for 10-day sample tubes of the product would cost. Detailed records were kept as to inquiry costs, the pulling power of various types of ad appeals, the pulling power of various newspapers and magazines, and so on. Of course, such tactics have long since been old-hat and common everywhere in advertising but much of it was pioneer work in 1917. The more such data existed the less risk there was for Pepsodent in relying on advertising instead of salesmen. Pepsodent's tactics allowed the new paste to find a spot in an overcrowded field as it overcame the obstacles of not being wanted in the first place by jobbers and dealers who saw no need for a new toothpaste and did not want the headaches of handling yet another brand, and the hurdle of being higher priced than dealers wanted to see in a toothpaste. "So Pepsodent's main effort has been directed at the consumer rather than the trade," concluded *Printers' Ink*. "Salesmen could not have reached the consumer. Advertising that had the advantage of being tested did reach him."[6]

Another researcher who looked at dentifrice ads in this period, from the perspective of 1972, was Fred Danzig in the trade journal *Advertising Age*. In the 1920s, he reported, Pepsodent ads referred to "the new-day dentifrice ... a scientific toothpaste based on modern research, now advised by leading dentists the world over." A coupon offered a 10-day tube free, one tube per family. Ad copy read, "Pepsodent disintegrates the film, then removes it with an agent far softer than enamel. Never use a film combatant which contains harsh grit." Similar messages could be found in ads for other brands. At the time Pepsodent was boasting about its film-removing properties, Pebeco was asking, "Is Acid-Mouth at work on the teeth of your loved ones? Send coupon below for free litmus test papers and a 10-day trial tube of Pebeco ... if it remains blue, there are no unfavorable acids in the mouth.... Pink, then acid-mouth is working destruction on the teeth."[7]

Still around the same time Ipana claimed it contained "Ziratol, a gentle healing antiseptic that makes gums firm and healthy.... Far from harming your gums, Ipana is a toothpaste that thousands of dentists recommend to patients whose gums are soft and spongy. Send for a trial tube." Listerine advertised, "it cleans the teeth a new way." At last, the copy continued, "our chemists have discovered a polishing ingredient that really cleans without scratching the enamel." Its catchphrase was, "What are your teeth saying about you today?" Forhan's Toothpaste "for the gums" declared, "More than a toothpaste. It checks pyorrhea. Four out of five are victims. Will pyorrhea claim you too?" Coupon and free trial offers dominated the ad strategies in the early 1920s; when sales began to dip late in that decade, radio came to the rescue.[8]

On radio Ipana was promoted by the Ipana Troubadours and Fred Allen, for example. In August 1929, Pepsodent sponsored a 15-minute NBC radio program called *Amos 'n Andy*, which had its origins as *Sam 'n Henry* on WMAQ, Chicago. *Amos 'n Andy* was on the radio six nights a week and Pepsodent sponsored it because it wanted to counter the Ipana Troubadours. Soon the program became a smash hit with Americans reportedly stopping whatever they were doing between 7:00 and 7:15 P.M. to listen. Within weeks of the show's debut, Pepsodent sales had tripled. In the late 1930s when sales of Pepsodent began to slip, Edward Lasker (son of Albert and also with Lord & Thomas) suggested a comedian named Bob Hope be used to promote the brand. Even though Hope's earlier radio shows had flopped, Edward felt the talent was there — given better writers. In the years that preceded the 1944 sale of Pepsodent to Lever Brothers for $10 million Hope's Pepsodent shows had become radio's number one attraction and contributed such famous advertising copy as "You'll wonder where the yellow went, when you brush your

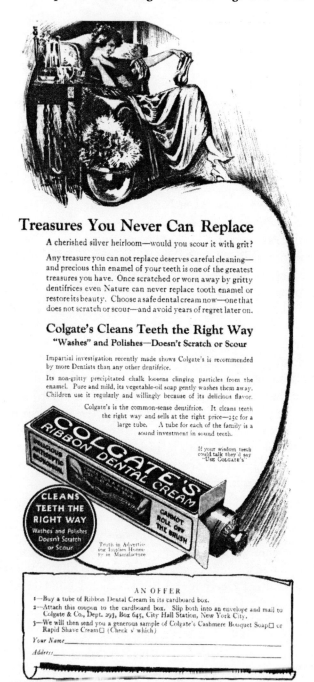

A 1923 ad for Colgate, long the most popular dentifrice in America.

teeth with Pepsodent," and the story of "Poor Miriam" who did not brush with Irium. Albert Lasker reputedly once said, "I invented Irium, tell me what it is!"[9]

When *Printers' Ink* ran a 1925 piece on Forhan's ads it started by saying the public had become conscious of the importance of the proper care of the teeth because the task had been undertaken by the manufacturers of dentifrices, toothbrushes, and so on, to the benefit of those makers, dentists, and the public. Ethical considerations then barred dentists from advertising. "While dentists hold aloof from advertising, manufacturers are busily engaged in showing them the way," declared the article.[10]

That article went on to paint Forhan's ad campaign as an almost altruistic effort to aid the dental profession. Since the start of its consumer advertising, went the piece, Forhan's "has always endeavored to keep before the public the work performed by dentists in guarding public health." Ad copy concentrated on benefits the public would derive from regular contact with dentists, as opposed to waiting until driven there by necessity: "Through the medium of its advertising, the Forhan Company is making the services of the dentist known to his community." According to the article, since dentists hesitated to take the initiative in impressing upon the public the importance of preventing the ravages of decay, the Forhan company had undertaken the task. A perhaps more cogent explanation of the campaign came in the conclusion when the reporter observed, "Of course, this advertising should do much to win the good-will of the dentist, whose endorsement is a valuable asset to the sale of this advertiser's product." And that the copy was especially important because it would help to make dentists familiar "with a proper application of the principles of advertising in educating the public to co-operate more closely with them in teeth preservation."[11]

The cost of sending sample products to medical professionals in 1931 was estimated at $50,000 a year for each of America's drug making firms, with most of those samples going to physicians and druggists. At that time one of the biggest sampling campaigns ever staged in the pharmaceutical field was under way, expected to run for a year and to cost over $100,000. Every month a standard-size tube of Pebeco toothpaste was mailed to 180,000 dentists and physicians. Every third month a couple of dozen sample-size tubes were sent to the same list of people in the hope the professional men would distribute them among their patients. Manufacturer Lehn & Fink was then sending dentists professional jars and tubes of Pebeco Dental Cleanser, which was Pebeco Tooth Paste plus a small percentage of silica. Dentists who received those samples were encouraged to use them in cleaning the teeth of patients after doing their work (this product was only for professionals — dentists —

and was not for sale to the public). Sample-size shipments to dentists included the cleanser with samples of Pebeco Tooth Paste. When dentists wrote in for more of the Pebeco Dental Cleanser, expecting to pay, Lehn & Fink told them it was not for sale but they would send more, for free, whenever the dentist's supply got low; all he had to do was write. The hoped-for result was that dentists would use the cleanser in their work and then recommend Pebeco Tooth Paste to their patients.[12]

Having reached national distribution by 1932, Bost Tooth Paste then embarked on the largest ad campaign in its history. Notwithstanding America was in the midst of the Depression, a $600,000 campaign was launched that featured car cards in 39 cities, reinforced by magazine, newspaper and radio advertising and by store displays. Bost Tooth Paste was an invention of chemist Dr. William Dale Bost, who, after several years of experimenting on the effect of tobacco stains upon enamel, claimed to have perfected a compound for removing the discoloration from teeth. Thus, from its inception, Bost ad copy had always stressed that it worked wonders on the teeth of smokers. In August 1931 the company staged a test campaign in Fort Worth, Texas. When it entered the Southwest Bost was totally unknown there and faced with the competition of many well-known and heavily advertised brands. By March of 1932 Bost claimed it was the best selling toothpaste in that market and it had attained that position through advertising alone. It was that campaign that was then going nationwide with the keynote of the strategy contained in the slogan "Beware of Smokers' Teeth" (the first letter of each word spelled out Bost). Faces of beautiful women dominated the ads with the slogan on a ribbon across their mouths. Women were used in the ads as the company made a determined bid to capture the then rapidly increasing universe of female smokers.[13]

In describing the use of negative ad copy in that campaign, C. H. Lesser, treasurer of Bost, said, "Fear, whether it be of growing age or of anything else, is a tremendous stimulant." Arguing that fear should be used in conjunction with other emotions he added, "Consequently, we scanned the list of feminine emotions for something which would add tone to our copy, and at the same time impart a tempering effect. Out present copy is a combination of fear — and vanity." A point-of-sale display for dealers challenged customers to undertake a test. It showed a young woman blowing a puff of cigarette smoke through a handkerchief, leaving a dark brown stain. The text on the display explained that if the hankie was placed on a hard surface and rubbed with a liberal application of Bost Tooth Paste the stain would disappear. Readers of the text were urged to make the same test using their regular dentifrice. Lesser believed the ad was powerful enough to generalize to non-smokers. "And so, though our message may first appear restricted, it is in truth practically universal."[14]

Edward Plaut, president of Lehn & Fink (manufacturer of Pebeco toothpaste), said, "We have faith in the American Government. We have faith in the American people," and in 1933, before explaining the company was attempting to translate that faith into direct action in the shape of an unusual offer it was advertising in 22 cities. Declared the offer, "In recognition of the present cash shortage [it was the Depression], from now until April 1, dealers will accept personal checks dated July 1, 1933, amounting to $1, in payment for three tubes of Pebeco tooth paste. All checks are to be made payable to Lehn & Fink, Inc." They had been making plans for something similar before the national bank moratorium was declared. On the Tuesday following the moratorium (announced on a Monday) their offer was formulated. Lying behind the offer, said Lehn & Fink was their desire to show the firm "had confidence in the soundness of our Government and business." Also, Plaut felt the firm would benefit from the goodwill generated: "This offer of credit should add to our reputation and prestige." During the time of the moratorium it was thought people were desperately holding on to their cash and going without necessities even though they may have had the cash to pay for them. (Immediately after being sworn in as president Franklin D. Roosevelt ordered all the banks across the country to close their doors while it was determined which ones were strong enough to reopen, and to restore bank customers' faith.) "Our offer of three tubes of Pebeco for $1, on credit, should stimulate business to a certain extent," thought Plaut. When the plan was formulated on Tuesday, March 7, a letter was sent to 5,341 druggists outlining the scheme and the part they were to play in it. For each check accepted, Lehn & Fink credited each druggist's account with $1.[15]

Sales of Dr. Lyon's Tooth Powder for 1933 were double those of 1932. Manufacturer and owner, the Watkins Company, had spent $550,000 for advertising in 1932, $860,000 in 1933, and $1.5 million for 1934. H. A. Weissman, Watkins vice president, claimed that success was achieved because the firm subordinated the advertising of their brand to the more important job of advertising tooth powder in general. Prominently featured in their ad copy was the main theme, "Use Powder," in whatever medium — car cards, radio, magazines, and newspapers. All, with rare exceptions, talked up the advantages of powder. When Watkins had bought Dr. Lyon's the ratio of paste to powder sales was said, by Weissman, to be about 30 to one in favor of paste products. That meant, argued the executive, claiming nothing about a particular brand for, until the general public was convinced that any powder was the best dentifrice they could buy for keeping teeth clean, "we naturally could not expect success with Dr. Lyon's." Also emphasized in their ad copy was, "Do as your dentist does when he cleans your teeth. Use Powder." As a result of that campaign, boasted Weissman, the sales of most powder brands on the market had increased rapidly: "We realize that we have been building powder volume for our competitors as well as for ourselves."[16]

For 1934, observed Weissman, Lyon's messages appeared in every bus and railroad station throughout America where it had been possible to purchase space. In 1933 Lyon's used 38 radio stations for its ads, and 64 stations in 1934; in 1933 200 newspapers were used for ads, and almost 500 in 1934. "We have no free deals, never had any and we stick to a policy of one price for everybody, whether a large volume buyer or a small drug store," added Weissman. Sampling as a strategy was begun by Lyon's in 1928 with a test in Pennsylvania, with New England added in 1929 and by 1934 the firm sampled "practically every dentist in the country." In addition to sending a sample every month the company also, on request, supplied dentists with all the powder that they could use the year round — to clean the teeth of their patients. Out of 65,000 dentists on Lyon's mailing list there were over 30,000 to whom the concern sent samples at times in between the automatic monthly samples. Six times a year Lyon's made a sample offer over the radio to the general public. The one made in January 1934 brought them 310,000 requests. Another point stressed in Lyon's ads was that "people who have been to dentists know that they use powder in teeth cleaning."[17]

In an effort to better control pricing, discounts, and so on, Pepsodent reduced the number of wholesalers who carried the product to 350 from 700 in 1936. Those remaining agents had to agree to place a cash deposit with the company and to act as selling agents "in conformity with company policies." Despite the official rationale the real reason for the change likely had to do with overall sales and profits as the retail list price on the 50 cent tube of Pepsodent toothpaste was reduced by the firm to 40 cents with, reportedly, no change in the size of the tube or contents, while the company also introduced a new size to retail at 25 cents.[18]

In 1935 Pepsodent sponsored a contest that was considered to be "outstandingly successful" after it closed with 1,546,000 entries. A year later the firm sponsored a contest that was even more successful — it drew 2,253,125 entries. Each entry, in 1935, had to be accompanied by proof of purchase of a tube of Pepsodent toothpaste; that was changed to proof of purchase of any Pepsodent product in 1936. For the 1935 contest entrants were required to write a letter not more than 50 words long on "Why I like Pepsodent toothpaste" while in 1936 entrants only had to suggest a name for the baby born to two of the characters on the hugely popular *Amos 'n Andy* radio show.

The Price You Pay

For dingy film on teeth

Let us show you by a ten-day test how combating film in this new way beautifies the teeth.

Now your teeth are coated with a viscous film. You can feel it with your tongue. It clings to teeth, enters crevices and stays. It forms the basis of fixed cloudy coats.

That film resists the tooth brush. No ordinary tooth paste can effectively combat it. That is why so many well-brushed teeth discolor and decay.

Keeps teeth dingy

Film absorbs stains, making the teeth look dingy. Film is the basis of tartar. It holds food substance which ferments and forms acids. It holds the acids in contact with the teeth to cause decay.

Millions of germs breed in it. They, with tartar, are the chief cause of pyorrhea. Thus most tooth troubles are now traced to film. And, despite the tooth brush, they have constantly increased.

Attack it daily

Careful people have this film removed twice yearly by their dentists. But the need is for a daily film combatant.

Now dental science, after long research, has found two ways to fight film. Able authorities have proved their efficiency. A new-type tooth paste has been perfected to comply with modern requirements. The name is Pepsodent. These two film combatants are embodied in it, to fight the film twice daily.

Two other effects

Pepsodent also multiplies the starch digestant in saliva. That is there to digest starch deposits which otherwise may cling and form acids.

It multiplies the alkalinity of the saliva. That is Nature's neutralizer for acids which cause decay.

Thus every use gives multiplied effect to Nature's tooth-protecting agents in the mouth. Modern authorities consider that essential.

Millions employ it

Millions of people now use Pepsodent, largely by dental advice. The results are seen everywhere—in glistening teeth.

Once see its effects and you will adopt it too. You will always want the whiter, cleaner, safer teeth you see. Make this test and watch the changes that it brings. Cut out the coupon now.

Pepsodent had a long-running campaign about how it removed film from the teeth, 1922.

Commenting on why there were more entries for the 1936 contest Pepsodent vice president of advertising Stuart Sherman remarked the second contest "did not frighten inexperienced writers." Added Sherman, "Theoretically, writing a letter about the product forces people to give considerable thought to its merits and thus stimulates repeat sales. Actually, however, there is considerable doubt about such a letter having any great effect on repeat sales of a comparatively simple product such as tooth paste." Other differences included the fact the second contest ran 10 days longer than the first (27 versus 17) and prize differentials. For 1935 14,493 cash prizes totaling $30,985 were awarded with prizes going to the public amounting to $12,850 of that total (dealers got the rest). Whereas in 1936, 2,832 prizes amounting to $34,000 were awarded, all to the public. Entrants in 1936 were 76.42 percent female, 23.58 percent male.[19]

Malcolm Hart, Pepsodent sales manager, announced in 1938 that the company was then carrying out the most extensive advertising and sales promotion program in its history. It was being built around the new Mickey Mouse radio program that was supported by advertising in 27 magazines and in 3,700 newspapers. The *Mickey Mouse Theater of the Air* (that included other characters such as Donald Duck and aired nationwide for 30 minutes every Sunday) succeeded the *Amos 'n Andy* show, which had served Pepsodent so well for eight years.[20]

Charles Luckman, vice president and general manager for Pepsodent, explained his firm's marketing philosophy in a long account in 1939, when it had been advertising dentifrices for over

For its long-running campaign Ipana focused on the scare tactic of mentioning the dreaded pink toothbrush, 1923.

Does your tooth-brush "show pink"?

ALL TOO OFTEN men and women hold back from giving their teeth the good brushing needed because their gums are soft or irritated.

A "pink tooth-brush" is a sign of tooth trouble to come —a warning to restore your gums to a healthy condition.

In this, Ipana Tooth Paste can help you. For it cleans the teeth thoroughly and exercises a gentle healing effect upon soft and bleeding gums.

Ipana contains Ziratol, long used by the profession in the treatment of soft, spongy or bleeding gums

And flavor! Ipana is smooth, snappy and delightful.

IPANA TOOTH PASTE

Bristol-Myers Co., 69 Rector St. New York, N Y

Kindly send me a trial tube of IPANA TOOTH PASTE without charge or obligation on my part.

Name

Address

City

State

20 years. Pepsodent's dental products were described by Luckman as "habit items" with the major problem being to get people to change brands. As a result of its long experience the firm then based its advertising on a seven-point program that each campaign was expected to address. Point one was to convince users of other brands that Pepsodent was a better product. The appeal had to be specific, with emphasis on features not possessed by the other brands. Point two was to offer some incentive for making an immediate brand switch or at least as soon as the consumer's present brand was used up. "The principal incentive is bright teeth, made possible by Pepsodent's exclusive ingredient, Irium," explained Luckman, but since many people needed a little extra push, the offer of a sample helped and at various times Pepsodent had used other incentives such as contests and premiums, and the one cent sale (buy one at the regular price and get the second for one cent).[21]

Point three was to reach present users of other brands and reach them often enough so that the urge to buy would at some time coincide with need for the product. "Sporadic advertising for a product of this kind would be inefficient," said Luckman with the consumer having to be reminded when she was ready to buy and "this means consistent, continuous advertising." Point four was to persuade current users to continue to buy Pepsodent while point five was to appeal to younger people who had not formed fixed dentifrice habits and were "more easily influenced." Much of Pepsodent's advertising was directed to that younger audience. Point six was to win the goodwill of dentists so that they would recommend Pepsodent when asked by their patients, or at least would not condemn the brand. An extensive campaign in dental publications helped accomplish that goal. Point seven was to win the goodwill of dealers so that they would push the product and display it prominently in order to supply the needed impulse for an actual purchase.[22]

Pepsodent knew, said Luckman, that the market for dentifrices was almost static. It had reached its ceiling some years earlier and since then the total consumption of dentifrices in the U.S. had not fluctuated more than about 8 percent. That meant, said Luckman, that Pepsodent and other dentifrice makers had to strive constantly to obtain a larger share of the total available business and could only do so by taking away business from one or more other brands. "We never attack the claims made for other brands because we don't believe a competitive fight benefits anyone.... So we devote our energies to talking about our own products and let our competitors do the same. We want no negative sales arguments in our copy," Luckman declared. Luckman acknowledged there was a huge latent market among the non-users of dentifrices but felt Pepsodent would not make much of a dent in it all by

WHITE TEETH – *beautifully polished and safe from decay*

Teeth white and gleaming ... a charming smile — you can have these with Pebeco

How your salivary glands can be made to keep your teeth in perfect condition

THE TEETH you admire can be yours. White and shining, healthy teeth.

Cleansed and protected by nature's own method.

Nature intended the alkaline fluids of your salivary glands to neutralize the mouth acids as they form. But today, in spite of careful brushing, your teeth decay because your salivary glands are no longer doing their work.

Modern soft food does not give them enough exercise. Their normal, full flow has decreased until it is no longer sufficient to counteract the acids of decay.

In "The Prevention of Dental Caries and Oral Sepsis," the greatest dental authority today says, "Some substance which is a salivary stimulant should be used in order to promote and educate the activity of the salivary glands."

It is only recently that dental authorities have known this fundamental cause of modern tooth decay and have discovered a way to restore the protective function of your salivary glands. Today you can use a tooth paste that gently stimulates your salivary glands to flow normally again.

Pebeco keeps glands active, teeth white and safe

PEBECO is a safe, marvelously effective salivary stimulant. Its effect is accomplished by promoting the flow of your natural, alkaline saliva.

As soon as Pebeco enters your mouth your salivary glands secrete more freely. With regular daily use Pebeco entirely restores the normal, protective action of your glands. Their alkaline fluids bathe your teeth day and night, preventing the formation of bacterial plaques or film. *The acids of decay are neutralized as fast as they form.*

Pebeco polishes beautifully. It keeps your gums clean and stimulated, your whole mouth healthy.

Do not let your teeth grow dull and decay. Learn to cleanse and protect them by nature's own method. Send today for a ten days' trial of Pebeco. Made only by Pebeco, Inc., for Lehn & Fink, Inc., Sole Distributors. In the blue tube, all druggists.

A Division of Lehn & Fink Products Company.

Every smile shows your teeth — are you proud of them?

Free Offer

Send coupon today for free generous tube

Lehn & Fink, Inc., Dept. G-50, Bloomfield, N. J.
Send free your new large sample tube of Pebeco Tooth Paste.
PRINT PLAINLY IN PENCIL

Name ....
Street ....
City .... State ....

Pebeco keeps your salivary glands active — your teeth white

A very wordy 1926 ad from Pebeco, stressing the beauty of white teeth.

itself because, "After all, if the millions of dollars spent in dentifrice advertising in recent years has not increased the total market it would be futile for us to try to do the job alone." He also declared Pepsodent could not increase the amount of toothpaste used by individuals, which all only reinforced the idea there was only one way for Pepsodent to expand its sales — by taking users from other brands. "Every Pepsodent advertisement is designed to get non-users to try Pepsodent just once," observed the executive. Sampling continued to be an important strategy for the firm and, in 1939, it was said, "Practically every consumer publication advertisement contains an offer of a sample."[23]

A 1940 ad for Pepsodent proudly proclaimed that "Of all leading dentifrices ... Pepsodent alone has the American Dental Association Seal of Acceptance" and that "All 3 forms of Pepsodent containing Irium get A.D.A. Seal of Acceptance [that is, paste, powder, and liquid]." According to the ad, which played up the ADA angle, "The A.D.A. Council on Dental Therapeutics checked every formula, every test, every claim made in advertising, Pepsodent passed on all counts." While the seal was granted in 1939, the ADA withdrew it in 1941, not being satisfied with Pepsodent's ad claims.[24]

Pepsodent became a publishing company in 1941 when it published *They Got Me Covered*, the autobiography of Bob Hope (the dentifrice maker sponsored the Hope radio show). First printing was said to be no less than three million copies and sold for 10 cents plus the carton from any Pepsodent product. Containing over 100 photos and cartoons, and only 96 pages, the book was probably a little light on text. Masking its interest the book was said to contain no reference to Pepsodent, not even a publishing credit line. Paramount studios and Pepsodent undertook a joint effort to promote the book and Hope's latest film for Paramount, *Nothing But the Truth*. Both companies arranged local tie-ups among drugstores and theatres. Under one plan, druggists carried theater tickets during the picture's run, while cinemas displayed material featuring the book.[25]

Through this period dentifrice ads had taken huge steps from the early simplicity of Rubifoam in 1903 to Miriam and Irium and Acid-Mouth of the 1920s and beyond. A problem was that those steps were in the wrong direction since the claims made were almost all false and as time passed became even more exaggerated and ludicrous. None of this passed unnoticed as the cries of racket and so on, leveled at the dentifrice industry, grew louder.

5

Toothpaste, Advertising Challenged, 1900–1945

There is probably no single industry, unless it is that of cosmetics, that has allowed its advertising to fall to such a low level as the dentifrice industry. — C. B. Larrabee, 1935.

For years the truth about toothpaste has been completely submerged in the torrent of glittering irrelevancies and misrepresentations sponsored by dentifrice manufacturers in the magazines and the newspapers and on the air. — R. M. Cunningham Jr., 1946.

Journalist Catherine Hackett launched one of the earliest, and longest, articles, under the heading of "The Dentifrice Racket," on the industry and its deceptive advertising practices at the start of 1930. She led the way in writing about the dentifrice market as being wholly false, and of generating ads that were all deceptive. Hackett argued that in the previous five years ads for dentifrices, and mouthwashes, had reached new heights of pseudo-science. With the public then spending over $60 million annually for dentifrices she felt people believed then that toothpaste was as much a necessity as soap. And with it came a variety of absurd beliefs concerning the physiology and chemistry of the human mouth that had been so firmly implanted in the public mind as to be almost impossible to dislodge. Included in those mistaken beliefs was that acid mouth was an abnormal, unhealthy condition that could be corrected by the use of certain toothpastes; that pathological conditions such as pyorrhea could be treated by dentifrices, and that anyone could have pearly-white teeth. What strongly concerned Hackett were two statements from the highest authorities that not only failed to put most of the manufacturers out of business but also caused not the least concern to the trade or to the public. One of those statements came from the American Medical Association (AMA): "Dentifrice has in itself no magical or chemical power to clean, and the best mouthwashes are warm water or a solution of common table salt." The second statement came from the American Dental Association, which stated, "The chief value of a dentifrice is to establish a healthy habit by making tooth brushing a more pleasant process and no dentifrice can be used for so-called mouth correction." Government chemists in the Food, Drug and Insecticide Administration of the U.S. Department of Agriculture, charged with the administration of the Food and Drugs Act, declared that any toothpaste should be considered as much a luxury as cold cream or perfume, and that no so-called antiseptic dentifrice that had so far come into their laboratory had the power to kill germs in the conditions under which it was normally used.[1]

For Hackett, one of the best examples of an absolute misstatement of scientific fact in paste advertising was the contention that acid mouth, "the newly discovered national menace," was an abnormal condition and could be prevented by the use of various toothpastes, each of which had supposedly been designed to cure it. According to the ADA it was well known "but not often admitted in the propaganda of certain dentifrice manufacturers" that the ph level of saliva (a method of expressing degree of alkalinity or acidity) was maintained regardless of the material introduced into it and the saliva was normally slightly acid: "Mouth acidity or alkalinity cannot be controlled by any induced substances."[2]

After a copywriter discovered the popular appeal of removing film from the teeth, added Hackett, dozens more dentifrices began employing the well-known principle of using an alkaline or soapy medium to dissolve mucin, and were put on the market. Some of their ad claims included: Orphism, "dental science's latest miracle"; Pepsodent, "the greatest step made in a half-century's study of tooth-cleaning methods"; Pebeco, "a toothpaste specifically created to correct unhealthy mouth conditions"; Listerine toothpaste, "keeps teeth gleaming white with almost no brushing." All of those products, she said, "offer cheap and common chemical agents under the guise of scientific discoveries to combat film." According to Hackett, the most widely advertised toothpastes were of two kinds: those that claimed to cure pyorrhea or other pathological conditions that only a dentist should treat, and those that modestly limited their claims to cleansing or polishing the teeth. Use the first class at your peril, she warned, and the other group if you preferred "their pleasant taste to table salt or powdered chalk, which are equally efficient as cleansing agents." Those claiming to cure pyorrhea consisted mostly of baking soda or borax.[3]

Advertisements for Ipana, Pepsodent, Orphism, and Pebeco toothpastes, Hackett argued, all featured an apparently magical power to whiten dull or yellow teeth, ignoring that nature gave people the color of their teeth and nothing could change it. Some pastes in this class (containing a whitening claim) employed dangerous chemicals such as hydrochloric acid. When a gov-

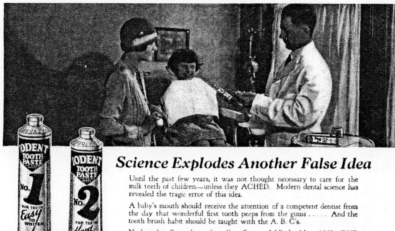

Science Explodes Another False Idea

Until the past few years, it was not thought necessary to care for the milk teeth of children—unless they ACHED. Modern dental science has revealed the tragic error of this idea.

A baby's mouth should receive the attention of a competent dentist from the day that wonderful first tooth peeps from the gums . . . . . And the tooth brush habit should be taught with the A. B. C's.

Neglected milk teeth profoundly affect a child's health—AND THE EVENNESS AND QUALITY OF THE PERMANENT TEETH.

IODENT is an ideal tooth paste for children. They relish its fresh and sparkling flavor. It acts as a gentle tonic to the delicate gum tissues.

And unlike any other tooth paste, it is available in two textures; IODENT No. 1 for teeth Easy to Whiten—recommended for children. IODENT No. 2 for teeth Hard to Whiten—usually preferred by adults.

Buy it at your Naborhood Drug Store

THE IODENT CHEMICAL COMPANY
DETROIT MICHIGAN

IODENT
T O O T H   P A S T E

A 1926 ad for Iodent that featured a model and setting made to look like a dentist and a dental office. This so-called "man-in-white" style of advertising infuriated dentists.

ernment chemist placed an extracted tooth overnight in a solution of one widely advertised brand that declared it removed tartar he discovered the next morning the tooth had the consistency of a well-chewed lump of gum. Tartaroff, a brand described as "the greatest scientific discovery of the age, which transforms teeth immediately into gems of pearl-like beauty" was found by the ADA to consist of hydrochloric acid and water with a trace of aluminum. Also, Hackett pointed out, the term "antiseptic and germicidal" was widely used in dentifrice advertising but that description was then being deleted from actual labels because of the government ruling that no product could be so labeled unless it actually killed bacteria in the conditions under which it would ordinarily be used, "but the law does not touch advertising." That is, such claims could still be made in ads even though these claims had to be removed from product labeling and packaging when such claims could not be proven. No toothpaste that had been analyzed to date by government chemists contained a germicide strong enough to destroy organisms during the few seconds it was in the mouth. The most significant findings in that area were attributed to Dr. Veader Leonard, and other chemical experts, working in the Johns Hopkins laboratories. Forty-one brands of toothpaste, eight of which accounted for 90 percent of total paste sales, were examined for possible antiseptic action and not a single one was found capable of destroying staphylococcus, one of the common microorganisms found in the mouth, after a five minute exposure.[4]

At the end of 1928 the First District Dental Society (of New York) passed a set of resolutions condemning the practice of certain toothpaste manufacturers in making extravagant claims in their advertising copy. Reportedly they were the first such charges putting the dental profession on record against unethical advertising and they met with considerable approval among dentists generally and several other dental societies adopted similar resolutions. In 1930 the First District passed more such resolutions, but also some to praise paste makers who did not make extravagant ad claims. "The pseudo-scientific phraseology which is used to cover this campaign of misrepresentation must be wholly condemned," said the First District statement. "Claims that these preparations are formulae of famous dentists or that the preparation is used or recommended by the dental profession should be shunned by intelligent people and their spurious claims be censured by the dentist," it continued. Ads condemned included advertising that claimed those products if used in time would prevent decay and other maladies. On the other hand the group resolved to support the makers of dentifrices who used an acceptable formula, and who did not claim that their products "possess any curative value, or will prevent decay or diseased mouth conditions, but only act as an aid toward mouth hygiene."[5]

H. H. Bunzell was a science researcher who complained to *Science* magazine in 1931 that a recent advertisement that had appeared in some 250 newspapers and magazines proclaimed that he, Bunzell, had said a certain toothpaste was made from the most effective agents and was to be preferred. And that he agreed with a certain "eminent international scientist" who found that paste to be the best of the 33 he had tested. Yet, explained Bunzell, "I have never made such claims for any dentifrice."[6]

During that same year W. R. Wharton, chief of the eastern district of the Federal Food and Drug Administration, told a radio audience that dentifrices had no value except as cleansing agents; they were not aids in treating disorders of the mouth and they had no antiseptic value. Advertisers of

DENTISTS SAY THIS TO BEAUTIFUL WOMEN
You must protect your charm from the acids which attack The Danger Line

Not only are white teeth and firm, pink gums vital to charm and beauty, but physical well-being often depends upon their soundness.

With the vital fascination of good health depending on them, it is fundamental that you must guard your teeth and gums. But how are you to know which is the most effective method of protecting yourself?

E. R. Squibb & Sons asked the dental profession of America to settle the problem. An investigation was started. 50,000 dentists were asked to state as briefly as possible what constituted the greatest threat to teeth and gums, and what was the best means of combating it. The answers received were amazing in their simplicity and forcefulness.

Beauty, charm, health . . . they are all too precious to risk lightly. This advice from professional men will clear away all doubt as to what constitutes proper oral hygiene:

95% *of the answers agree that mouth acids are the most frequent cause of tooth decay and irritated gums.*

95% *of the answers state that the most treacherous decay and gum infection occur at the place known as The Danger Line, where teeth and gums meet—where a toothbrush cannot reach.*

85% *state that Milk of Magnesia is the best product to neutralize these dangerous acids.*

Squibb's Dental Cream contains more than 50% of Squibb's Milk of

SQUIBB'S DENTAL CREAM

Magnesia in the most convenient and effective form to help ward off the danger of acids attacking your teeth and gums. Each time you use it, tiny particles of the Milk of Magnesia are forced into every pit and crevice where acids can form. There they not only neutralize the acids already present, but remain for a considerable time, to neutralize any new acid that may be formed.

Squibb's Dental Cream combines all the ingredients necessary in a dentifrice. It is a thorough cleanser —leaves the teeth beautifully white —relieves sensitive teeth and soothes sore gums—contains no harsh grit.

Protect your health and beauty. Follow the advice of these authorities. Consult your dentist at least once every six months, and meanwhile use Squibb's Dental Cream. At all druggists—40c a tube.

E. R. Squibb & Sons, New York— *Chemists to the Medical Profession since 1858.*   © 1927

THE "PRICELESS INGREDIENT" OF EVERY PRODUCT IS THE HONOR AND INTEGRITY OF ITS MAKER

A 1927 ad that emphasized beauty and the need to neutralize mouth acids.

certain brands claimed their products would do everything from whitening the teeth and removing the tartar to curing Vincent's angina and pyorrhea, he added, yet toothpastes would do none of that, although he acknowledged a dentifrice did a "real service in cleaning the teeth." Wharton warned listeners never to use one of the whitening dentifrices unless the formula was known to be free of destructive elements — such as hydrochloric acid — that could ruin the enamel of the teeth.[7]

According to S. M. Gordon and E. W. Shand of the ADA Bureau of Chemistry, in 1933, in spite of what the ads said, it was the toothbrush that cleaned the teeth; the toothpaste was of "negligible importance." The merits of the different brands were mostly in the imaginations of the men who wrote the ads, said the chemists, "for all toothpastes are mostly calcium carbonate or phosphate, soap, and flavoring."[8]

Writing in the business publication *Commerce and Finance* in 1933, reporter McCready Sykes expressed amazement at the power of advertising to sell unnecessary items such as toothpaste. He declared that it had been widely known for years that precipitated chalk brushed over the teeth aided in keeping them clean, and that it was inexpensive in that form or it could be more conveniently bought in the form of any of the standard tooth powders. It functioned simply as a mildly abrasive cleanser. Sykes added, "Not so many years ago some advertising agencies came across the idea of toothpaste. Manifestly toothpaste is nothing but toothpowder worked into another form." He added that diseases of the mouth, such as pyorrhea, could not be cured by either paste or powder. Wondered Sykes, "Is there consolation in the new economy that teaches spending for the sake of spending?" Apparently there was for he concluded the making and distribution of "these carloads upon carloads of absurd remedial agents must give employment to hundreds of thousands, if not millions, of men."[9]

Jerome W. Ephraim authored a long piece attacking dentifrice ads in 1934 in *American Mercury*. He began by observing that everybody bought toothbrushes and toothpastes "nearly always with the illusory hope that they will cure pyorrhea, correct acid mouth, check tooth decay, remove stains, stop bleeding gums, purify the breath, or ward off colds and other signs of serious infections. These false hopes are engendered by floods of propaganda based partly on fallacies and superstitions long since abandoned by the medical and dental professions." He pointed out that everybody had acid mouth and that he agreed with the statement of the ADA's Council on Dental Therapeutics: "The sole function of a dentifrice is to aid in keeping the teeth clean by the removal of loose food debris by the mechanical use of the toothbrush." Or, as the ADA's *Journal* had put it, "The claim of therapeutic bacteriostatic virtue in a dentifrice borders on the ridiculous.... To claim tangible therapeutic benefit from the use of a dentifrice is exploitation pure and simple."[10]

According to Dr. Samuel M. Gordon, secretary of the Council on Dental Therapeutics, such claims should be classified as chicanery or outright dishonesty. Relatively only a few dentifrices enjoyed the right of displaying the ADA's seal of acceptance for the main reason that manufacturers refused to comply with the very reasonable requirements of the ADA as to misrepresentation and false advertising claims. Only recently the seal had been withdrawn from two leading makers for consistently misrepresenting and exaggerating the therapeutic value of their products. Said Ephraim, "It is significant that the biggest and most astute exploiters never put such claims on their labels. To do so would bring them with the purview of the United States Food and Drug Administration." Every now and then, however, some concern grew a little careless and repeated some of the old "hocus pocus" from its ads — such as hardening the gums, preventing pyorrhea, checking tooth decay — on the carton or in a circular enclosed with its product. Then the government could and did act. And, continued Ephraim, in several recent cases where the government charged that the claims made for those products were false and fraudulent, none of the makers saw fit to make any defense.[11]

While most ad claims were false, argued Ephraim, he acknowledged that most of the ingredients — with the exception of some found in whitening products — were harmless. He concluded that ordinary toothpastes advertised as film removers and stain removers were mostly harmless but would not do any removing. Nor did any dentifrice have any value in treating bleeding gums, pyorrhea, or other similar disorders of the mouth. A dentifrice, Ephraim concluded, could be said to be an aid in cleaning the teeth and nothing more and as such the two most desirable ingredients were a soft abrasive such as precipitated chalk, and a cleansing agent such as soap.[12]

C. B. Larrabee reported in 1935 that the attitude of dentists toward the advertising of dentifrices was "one of excusable antagonism." In a new book by a dentist that criticized toothpaste ads (*Paying Through the Teeth*) Bissell B. Palmer argued, "Our disagreement is not with dentifrices per se, but with the false claims made for many of them, with the high prices charged for them in relation to their limited value, and with the harmful ingredients contained in some of those products." Larrabee added, "There is probably no single industry, unless it is that of cosmetics, that has allowed its advertising to fall to such a low level as the dentifrice industry" and it was a "fact that an uncomfortably large proportion of dentifrice and mouth wash advertising has sunk to a pretty low ethical standard." Yet Larrabee argued in the very early years of the 20th century the advertising of makers such as Colgate "per-

A good use for that $3 you save

Why not make Junior a present of a nice wrist watch? Or give Dad a tie! Or Mother some perfume or nice handkerchiefs? Any of them can be had for three dollars, which is the average amount you save yearly by the use of Listerine Tooth Paste at 25¢, instead of costlier dentifrices which accomplish no more.

The dentifrice that became a leader in four years

From "scratch" to a position among the leaders in four years! Certainly there is no better evidence of the merit of Listerine Tooth Paste than this remarkable record.

If you have not tried this delightful dentifrice at 25c, do so now. Compare its results to those of any dentifrice at any price. You will find that it accomplishes as much and more than dentifrices that cost sometimes twice as much.

Note particularly how quickly it cleans the teeth. The speediest dentifrice known! This is due to the presence of a remarkable new polishing agent of the gentlest character. Observe how thoroughly it cleans your teeth and heightens their lustre. Note too, that wonderful refreshed feeling of the mouth and gums after the brushing is over. Nothing like it.

Only the most modern methods of manufacture permit such a splendid paste at such a price. Isn't it worth trying? Lambert Pharmacal Co., St. Louis, Mo., U. S. A.

LISTERINE TOOTH PASTE

Large tube 25¢

A 1928 ad for Listerine explained that using its paste saved the average consumer $3 a year — enough to buy Junior a nice wrist watch.

formed a tremendous health service to the country by their teaching of oral hygiene." At a time before the public schools took any interest in the subject those makers, day after day, preached the lesson of oral cleanliness. As a group, dentifrice makers knew their ads annoyed dentists. Answering his own question as to why they did that he explained there was no sales appeal in the simple recommendation "keep you teeth clean. That is not enough for a profit-hungry manufacturer who wants to boost sales. For him the answer is found in scare copy." Radio ads by Dr. Lyon's Tooth Powder had then been modified to say, "Almost all dentists use powder to clean the teeth" (from the implication that all dentists did so). Actually, dentists then mostly used pulverized pumice (dry powder) combined with water (which made it into a paste but with a consistency different from home toothpaste) to clean the teeth of their patients.[13]

On June 9, 1937, the Kolynos concern of New Haven, Connecticut, was ordered by the U.S. Federal Trade Commission (FTC) to cease and desist from allegedly false and misleading representations in its toothpaste advertising. Among statements barred by that order were the following: that Kolynos conquered bacterial mouth, that it removed tartar, that it cleaned teeth better than other dentifrices, that it was a new or totally different product, and that it was "the approved" toothpaste or "the antiseptic" dental cream.[14]

A simple test could be done at home with a nickel and a piece of glass to determine if a favorite toothpaste would scratch the enamel of the teeth. It was a test the United States government required for all the paste it purchased — and it bought a lot. When an order for some 14,000 dozen tubes of toothpaste was contemplated by the U.S. government in 1937, a committee was appointed to write specifications for a safe and effective cleanser for the teeth. First consideration was safety of the tissues of the mouth and the teeth, second was efficiency in removing foreign particles from the teeth, and last was the matter of flavor or perfume. Twenty-five brands were tested against the specifications as adopted for use in government purchasing. More than half failed to meet the requirements with 10 brands failing on the test for scratching. In that test the edge of the nickel was first rubbed over the glass to make sure the metal alone did not scratch. Then toothpaste was spread on the glass and the area again rubbed with the coin. If scratches resulted it was considered a sure indication that a person using that toothpaste could expect scratches on his teeth.[15]

Samuel M. Gordon, in the pages of *Hygeia* in 1937, explained in detail the workings of the ADA's Council on Dental Therapeutics (CDT) after noting it was only in recent years, since the formation of the CDT in 1932, that any real inquiry had been made into dentifrices. The council still considered

Better times are on the way! . . . To show our
faith in our government, our banks, our people

WE WILL TAKE YOUR CHECK
DATED THREE MONTHS AHEAD

● For a three months' supply of Pebeco
Tooth Paste for yourself and your family

The "I Will" spirit of the nation is on the move. Things are happening! And better times are not far away.

To back our faith in the present emergency program, we stand ready to keep millions of America's families supplied with tooth paste . . . on three months' credit.

No need to neglect the vitally important care of your teeth. No need to draw either cash or scrip—

Take Three Months to Pay!

Make out your personal bank check today to Lehn & Fink, Inc., for $1.00. Date your check July 1st, 1933.

Take this check to your druggist or department store. In exchange, you will get three full size tubes of PEBECO (regular retail price $1.50), a full three months' supply for yourself and your family!

Your check will not be cashed by us until July 1st. By that time, all authorities feel that the nation will be on the road

to substantially better times.

This offer will be withdrawn April 1st . . . or sooner, if the local supply of PEBECO is exhausted. Do not delay, get three tubes of PEBECO today and take three months to pay. *Lehn & Fink, Inc., Bloomfield, N. J.*

THIS SPECIAL LIMITED OFFER . . . EXPIRES APRIL 1st

The regular price of PEBECO is 50¢ a tube. Today's price of $1 for 3 tubes (and 3 months to pay) is a special offer made in cooperation with the Government's Emergency Program. This offer ends April 1.

NOTICE TO ALL DEALERS: Please accept personal checks from your patrons for $1.00 payable to Lehn & Fink, Inc., in return for 3 tubes of PEBECO Tooth Paste. Checks must be made payable to Lehn & Fink, Inc. Mail these checks before April 15, 1933, to Lehn & Fink, Inc., Bloomfield, N. J. We will accept them as credit on your account, or for Lehn & Fink merchandise at the regular wholesale prices. This applies to all druggists throughout the country.

PEBECO
GET THREE TUBES TODAY • TAKE THREE MONTHS TO PAY

Another ad for the hard times era, 1933. Pebeco pledged to take a customer's postdated check for $1 to buy three tubes of paste. It was all in response to President Roosevelt's decision to hold brief bank holidays to restore faith in the financial system.

a dentifrice only as an aid to the toothbrush in cleaning the surfaces of the teeth. If the formula of the product was safe and it was advertised in accordance with those limitations, it could be held acceptable and thus could bear the distinction of displaying the council's seal. Dentifrices, to be placed on the accepted list, had to meet certain conditions: (1) a formula giving the kind and amount of each ingredient must be made available and found acceptable to the council (the CDT would not accept potentially poisonous or frankly medicinal ingredients); (2) the product must not be abrasive (Gordon acknowledged no standard test for abrasiveness was then available) and the council would not accept dentifrices containing siliceous material such as pumice and silica; (3) new dentifrices put on the market after 1932 could be named So-and-So's Toothpaste or Tooth Powder but could not carry under any circumstances the title Dr. or D.D.S. as part of its name (a clear slam at Dr. Lyon's and Dr. West's products). Such descriptive names were given an exemption where they had been a brand name prior to the council's formation in 1932 but only with the understanding that they were brand names and not descriptive names. That is, names such as Dr. West's and Dr. Lyon's would never be accepted by the ADA after 1932 and where they existed prior to that time were accepted on the fiction they did not mean what the public took them to mean — some sort of dental involvement or approval of the brand. As a fourth council condition all collateral advertising (away from the tube and its carton, such as on radio and in magazines and newspapers) had to be acceptable and had to adhere to the CDT's definition regarding the limited function of a dentifrice — namely, an aid to the toothbrush in cleaning the accessible surfaces of the teeth.[16]

At the time of Gordon's article the council would not accept toothpastes containing potassium chlorate; drugs related to carbolic acid, such as betanaphthol, which was said to be a constituent of one heavily advertised product on the market; sodium perborate, which could produce burns of the mouth; orris root, to which many people were allergically sensitive; or "inordinately large amounts of sugar." In the case of new substances not previously used in dentifrices, the CDT was said to demand, as a condition of acceptance, tests to show their safety. The Food and Drugs Act of 1906 did not give the Food and Drug Administration jurisdiction over the collateral advertising, which was a problem as the composition of the dentifrices on the market had been much less objectionable than the claims made for them in their advertising. Gordon pointed out that one prominent claim was that dentifrices containing milk of magnesia would cure acid mouth although dentists did not recognize such a condition or disease. "It is an advertiser's disease," asserted Gordon. Other common claims included one that the use of a dentifrice containing betanaphthol, which was chemically related to carbolic acid, would prevent or overcome "pink toothbrush," something Gordon said was "another disease advertisers seek to inflict on us. Dentists do not recognize such a disease." Also attacked in the article were those toothpastes that claimed to whiten teeth, "No one has yet shown that the shade of teeth can be changed, even by the faithful use of a dentifrice three times a day." One advertiser promised to change teeth three shades whiter in three days, a boast described as "combining science and sex appeal, both of which figure prominently in toothpaste advertising." When a group of dentists investigated (acting on a CDT request) that claim it was found that brand did not change the color of teeth "one iota."[17]

Also mentioned by Gordon was the Bost claim that it removed tobacco smoke stains from handkerchiefs. Yet the editors of *Reader's Digest* found that product did not remove tobacco stains from a handkerchief as well as soap did, while the Bost treasurer frankly told his advertising colleagues that his firm's campaign was built on fear, "because fear is a great selling force." With respect to another advertiser's slogan, "Do as your dentist does — use powder" Gordon argued that claim could be dismissed by the statement from CDT that said there was no essential difference in the cleansing properties of a powder over a paste and that it was well known that pumice or silica used for prophylaxis was made into a paste with glycerin or water before application to the teeth (by a person's dentist). Gordon remarked that in 1927 the powder with which that phrase was associated was found to be among the most abrasive on the market and that nothing had since appeared in the literature to show it had been made less abrasive.[18]

The Council on Dental Therapeutics then consisted of ten members, five dentists and five scientists outside the field of dentistry, appointed by the ADA to advise its members and the general public on the composition of dental products and the honesty of their claims. Unfortunately, said Gordon, many of the nationally advertised dentifrices did not appear on the council's approved list and "it may be a bit difficult to obtain council-accepted dentifrices, for not all druggists may carry them." Published by the Consumers' Project of the U.S. Department of Labor, *The Home Medicine Cabinet* (free for the asking) contained the following formula (accepted by the CDT) for a toothpowder: hard soap in fine powder, 50 grams; precipitated calcium carbonate, 935 g; soluble saccharin, 2 g; oil of peppermint, four cubic centimeters; oil of cinnamon 2 g; methyl salicylate, 8 g. Half of that formula made over 16 ounces of tooth powder, enough to last the average family for several months. Suggested as a convenient container for the homemade toothpowder was an empty salt box with a metal spout.[19]

In a 1943 article journalist Blake Clark detailed some of the many run-ins the industry had with the Federal Trade Commission (FTC), the agency whose job it was to protect the public from false advertising. So extravagant were some of the dentifrice ad claims that the FTC had to crack down several times. It had issued complaints against the makers of Ipana, Dr. Lyon's, Calox, Teel, Kolynos, Squibb's, and many others. In some cases the companies, rather than fight the FTC complaints, signed consent orders to abandon their misleading claims; in others they were forced to do so by FTC cease and desist orders.[20]

In a complaint against Bristol-Myers (Ipana) in October 1942 the agency branded as false and misleading such ads as "Keep your teeth clean and white by using Ipana — the yellowish tint on your teeth will disappear." According to the FTC, Ipana would not remove the tint of teeth naturally yellow or stained by tobacco. Also, the agency was concerned over the company's scare advertising campaign about "Pink Tooth Brush." In the words of the FTC that "disease was apparently invented and developed in the admen's offices." Dentists ridiculed the concept and said in their own ADA *Journal* the term "Pink Tooth Brush" was ridiculous "except as an advertising catchphrase." In brushing the teeth, added the publication, a bit of blood could appear on the toothbrush and that may or not be serious but, in any case, Ipana could do nothing for it. FTC experts also declared Ipana had no therapeutic value in the prevention or treatment of gum diseases. Ipana admen claimed the gums needed exercise — "When you massage with Ipana you can actually feel its stimulating effect upon your gum tissues as lazy gums start to waken and circulation speeds up." Observed by the agency was that you could not exercise your gums "any more than you could exercise your toenail."[21]

The R. L. Watkins Company (Dr. Lyon's Tooth Powder) spent $4.21 million over a period of seven years in an intensive campaign to make "Do as your dentist does — use powder" a byword. According to Clark dentists vehemently protested against the implication that the powder they used was similar to Dr. Lyon's, and the FTC investigated. It found Dr. Lyon's powder was in no sense comparable to the kind dentists used; Lyon's was a chalk powder while dentists usually employed a pumice or silica paste (more abrasive and not to be used frequently). Also found by the FTC was that Lyon's was very similar to the toothpastes it belittled in advertisements with the chief difference between powders and pastes, as determined by the agency, was that whereas most pastes were harmless, some powders occasionally contained particles of grit. In view of those and other facts the FTC stated that the firm's representation that Dr. Lyon's Tooth Powder "is free from grit" and "cannot possibly injure or scratch the tooth enamel" was exaggerated and misleading;

a cease and desist order against such claims was issued by the FTC against Watkins in October 1942.[22]

Calox Tooth Powder (made by McKesson & Robbins) said it was different because of sodium perborate and because Hollywood stars used it, "Hollywood has no patent on beautiful teeth. You, too, can have teeth that 'Shine like the Stars.'" In the FTC's opinion the product did not make teeth shiny or whiter and destroyed the claim that sodium perborate "in combination with other ingredients" caused Calox to release newborn, foaming oxygen that penetrated spots other dentifrices missed. The agency said the "marvelous" foam released from Calox was not caused by oxygen but by soap. McKesson & Robbins was ordered to cease and desist from any advertisement representing that Calox would accomplish results that could not be accomplished by competing products.[23]

During the controversy between pastes and powders Procter & Gamble began promoting Teel, a liquid dentifrice. Theirs was another scare campaign warning Americans that their teeth were being irreparably damaged by pastes and powders because of the abrasives they all contained. In April 1943 the FTC charged those representations were not only false and deceptive, but they also unfairly defamed and disparaged competing products. Added to the complaint was that since Teel had no abrasive qualities it could not clean teeth as effectively as many of the pastes and powders. Moreover, the ADA's CDT was told by practicing dentists that Teel itself might even discolor teeth. Even the Teel ads themselves admitted its users could find a mild abrasive necessary: "Once a week brush teeth with plain baking soda." For a time Kolynos' advertising was riddled with exaggerated claims, among them that the product would make teeth three shades whiter in three days. Tests by dentists showed it did no such thing. A further boast was that Kolynos toothpaste could kill 190 million germs in 15 seconds. After receiving an FTC cease and desist order the firm mended its advertising ways and made its way to the ADA's list of Accepted Dental Remedies.[24]

Clark also pointed out that dentists had long been annoyed at ads picturing white-gowned male models posed beside a dentist's chair with accompanying captions such as, "Thousands of dentists agree that one type of dentifrice is the most effective" (Squibb's Dental Cream) or, "Dentists warn against gritty dentifrices. If you're using one to fight tobacco stain, stop at once, and try this safe, modern way" (Listerine Tooth Paste) or, "Dentists urge you to employ the special dentifrice known as Pepsodent." At a CDT meeting held in Chicago a few years earlier, members of the profession registered their protest against these anonymous dentists dreamed up by the admen. Not one of the advertisers using such phrases as those quoted above "had the slightest authority from any dentist or reputable dental society to give voice to their expressions," asserted council members.[25]

By consent agreement with the FTC, E. R. Squibb & Sons could no longer claim that the use of Squibb's Dental Cream or Squibb's Tooth Powder contributed materially to the prevention of tooth decay, and makers of Bost Tooth Paste had to refrain from advertising that it removed tobacco stains from the enamel. For similar and other reasons the manufacturers of Dr. Sach's Dental Cream, Royal Blue Dental Cream, Royal Crown Dental Cream, Hyral, Hi-Ho Toothpaste, Teeth Whitener Formula A, and Teeth Whitener Formula B, had all run afoul of the law that the FTC enforced and had been subjected to criticism and regulation by the commission. The council said an inexpensive, home-made powder could be made from one part table salt and three parts baking soda. With respect to dentifrices, Clark concluded, "none is more than an aid to the brush in cleaning the teeth, none has therapeutic value of any substantial kind, and none stands out as better than the others to any important degree."[26]

Another long attack on toothpaste and deception came in the *New Republic* in 1946, from R. M. Cunningham who complained about false ads — bad breath and Colgate, pink toothbrush and Ipana, bacterial acids and Squibb, Forhan's and pyorrhea. "For years the truth about toothpastes has been completely submerged in the torrent of glittering irrelevancies and misrepresentations sponsored by dentifrice manufacturers in the magazines and the newspapers and on the air," declared Cunningham. Practically all dentifrices were made from three ingredients — a soap, a chalk or abrasive, and a flavor. A notable exception was the liquid Teel, which had no chalk or abrasive. However, he noted, according to the highest scientific authority it would not clean teeth, either. "It has not been demonstrated that Teel adequately performs the sole function of a dentifrice — to aid the brush in cleaning the accessible surfaces of the teeth," said the ADA.[27]

Cunningham felt one of the worst of the current campaigns was for Colgate-Palmolive-Peet's Colgate Dental Cream — "It cleans your breath while it cleans your teeth." Comic-strip ads were featured in which a boy or girl lost a mate because of bad breath, then was set straight by a character who looked like a dentist and said things like, "Colgate's active penetrating foam gets into hidden crevices between teeth, helps clean out decaying food particles, stops stagnant saliva odors, removes the cause of much bad breath. Scientific tests prove that in 7 out of 10 cases Colgate instantly stops bad breath that originates in the mouth." Until 1940, when the FTC ruled against it, Colgate copy stated flatly that most bad breath began with the teeth and that "a safe, sure way to correct bad breath is through the regular use of thorough, cleansing action provided only by the special ingredients in Colgate Dental Cream." Later, in 1944, the FTC told Colgate to stop advertising that any bad breath except that due to food particles in the mouth would be benefited by the use of its product. FTC vigilance resulted in two improvements in this case — an acknowledgment in current copy that only bad breath "originating in the mouth" was aided, and the elimination of references to special ingredients provided only by Colgate's. Commented Cunningham, "Clearly, however, Colgate, like many advertisers, looks on an FTC order not as a warning to stop deceiving the public but as a challenge to the copywriter to duplicate the misleading message without using the forbidden words. The whole implication of the Colgate campaign is still that bad breath come from unclean teeth."[28]

Special-ingredient themes also annoyed Cunningham. Radio ads then said, in awed, hushed tones, "Remember, only Pepsodent contains Irium." But, he pointed out, Irium was simply a name Pepsodent had dreamed up and tacked on to its particular soap substance, or foaming agent. "Exaggerated and misleading claims have characterized the firm's advertising for years," said an ADA report on Pepsodent. It added, "The firm has attempted to endow the word, Irium, which is applied to the soap substitute used in its products with extraordinary virtues which it does not possess." Actually, said Dr. Donald A. Wallace, secretary of the ADA's Council on Dental Therapeutics, Irium was sodium alkyl sulfate — a compound similar to the foaming agent reportedly used in Teel. Irium, according to Pepsodent, "makes teeth brighter."[29]

Forhan's headline had been modified discreetly to read, "Four out of five 'may' have it — gingivitis (inflammation of the gums) leading to pyorrhea." That was after some two generations of ad copy that declared unequivocally that four out of five "did" have it, pyorrhea. An analysis made by the ADA's Bureau of Chemistry failed to reveal a single ingredient that might have been therapeutically significant. But it remained for E. R. Squibb and Sons to hint that its toothpaste might help prevent tooth decay. Squibb Dental Cream, it was maintained, neutralized acid-forming bacteria in the saliva (known to play an important part in tooth decay) and thus helped to forestall decay. According to experts, said Cunningham, "this is nonsense; there is no evidence that the neutralizing properties of Squibb's are strong enough or lasting enough to have any clinical worth. Squibb, then, is guilty of one of the most deplorable practices in the whole field of patent-medicine advertisings: contributing to the buyer's false sense of security." Believing he was protected, explained Cunningham, the buyer of Squibb postponed a trip to the dentist and perhaps allowed things to get worse, as did the user of Forhan's for pyorrhea. "It may even be true that toothpaste advertising sends people to the dentist who would otherwise stay away. But these facts, if they are facts, do not excuse the evils of advertising which seeks profits at the expense of truth," concluded Cunningham. "Millions of people hear Pepsodent's message today because they like Bob Hope; instead of accepting this fact as a public responsibility, the advertiser takes advantage of it to continue a public deception. That is something for the thoughtful businessmen to be concerned about."[30]

In the decade and a half following World War II the dentifrice industry replayed much of what took place in the time before World War II. All kinds of additives were trotted out (more than in the past) and promoted, ads were mostly outrageously exaggerated, the industry clashed with dentists over those claims, and the industry clashed with the government as the FTC was as involved as ever it had been. There was one difference in the immediate postwar period; one additive was introduced that actually worked.

6

Toothpaste, 1946–1960

Despite all the scientific ballyhoo, tooth pastes and powders are still essentially cosmetics. Their purpose is to aid the toothbrush in polishing the accessible surfaces of the teeth.—Consumer Reports, 1949.

Fluoride, furthermore, is a poisonous substance which ... has no place in a toothpaste or powder for home use.—Consumer Reports, 1949.

The modern dentifrice, ammoniated, chlorophylled, anti-enzymed (but basically very much the same product as before), had at last arrived.—Consumer Reports, 1954.

One of the first of the new dentifrices to hit the market post–World War II, containing a new and miraculous additive, was the so-called ammoniated dentifrice. When *Newsweek* reported on that development early in 1949 it remarked that dentistry was moving from treatment to prevention as in its current experiments wherein fluoride was used in drinking water and sodium fluoride was applied to children's teeth to cut down the decay rate. But a newer chemical called ammonium ion had come along that was said to reduce tooth-decay rates in people of all ages by an average of 35 percent. In powder form the dentifrice bore the commercial name Amm-i-dent. The idea for that preventive technique originated in 1934 when a father-and-son team, Doctors Carl J. Grove and Carl T. Grove of St. Paul, Minnesota, found a higher percentage of ammonia nitrogen in the saliva of people naturally immune to tooth decay than in the saliva of the 95 percent of the population subject to caries. Later investigators were said to have shown that ammonium constituent in saliva was nature's way of fighting a micro-organism — a bacteria that generated acids that were held against the tooth enamel by film and gluey deposits of food debris not removed by brushing the teeth. Then researchers were said to have found that ammonia penetrated the gluey deposits and neutralized acid in the mouth, besides halting the growth of bacteria. Amm-i-dent, containing 5 percent dibasic ammonium phosphate and 22.5 percent carbamide, which released ammonia nitrogen or ammonium ions on contact with moisture, was developed in 1946.[1]

By March 1949 ammoniated dentifrices, containing synthetic urea, reportedly accounted for an estimated 20 percent to 25 percent of total paste and powder sales in a market wherein Americans spent $80 million each year on dentifrices while makers spent some $13 million to advertise them. It was such a swift turn in public preferences that the big makers were caught napping; none of the major dentifrice manufacturers had marketed an ammoniated product. Publicity about the discovery — that dentists and the U.S. Public Health Service supposedly had found that synthetic urea and other ammonia compounds helped prevent cavities — appeared in many of the major media outlets and dentifrices with synthetic urea suddenly became in the public mind a sure-fire preventive for cavities. Amm-i-dent (made by Block Drug) was then advertising in 800 newspapers, in magazines, and on the radio. Block spent $400,000 on Amm-i-dent ads in those 800 newspapers in March and April of 1949, with a total of $2 million to be spent by the end of that year.[2]

So spectacular had been the rise of Amm-i-dent Tooth Powder, according to George Abrams, Block Drug Company advertising manager, that four weeks after it had been introduced in a group of test cities it was outselling a leading brand of paste by almost two to one and was outselling all powders combined. Explaining the origins of the product more thoroughly, Abrams said that early in the fall of 1948, Block Drug detail men discovered a growing recommendation by American dentists of ammoniated tooth powder. When those reports reached the management of Block it ordered an immediate study of all scientific research on ammoniated tooth powder. Especially carefully evaluated was the research data from two groups, the University of Illinois, and the Eastern Graduate Research Foundation (New York dentists). Block decided the formula and records of the Eastern Graduate group were the more attractive especially since the New York dentists comprising the Eastern Graduate Research Group had for almost three years been prescribing the Amm-i-dent formula to all of their patients. Many of their fellow dentists who had seen the reports of reduction in dental caries had done the same. Those many prescriptions led to the commercial preparation of the Amm-i-dent formula by Professional Dental Products of Flushing, New York, with Block subsequently purchasing that firm in October 1948 and entering into an exclusive licensing agreement with the Eastern Graduate Research Foundation under which they could produce their ammoniated tooth powder. First editorial comment appeared in the December 1948 issue of *Better Homes & Gardens* wherein an enthusiastic article was headlined, "Slam the Brakes on Tooth Decay." Sales took a big jump.[3]

Abrams boasted, "We all recognized from the first that we had the most powerful advertising story ever on dentifrice. In 60 years of dentifrice advertising, we discovered, the brightening or whitening of teeth and the sweet-

ening of breath were the only two legitimate claims advertisers had been able
to make.... Here we had a toothpowder that not only brightened teeth and
sweetened breath like ordinary, cosmetic dentifrices, but helped prevent cavities as well!" He said the major problems were to present the Amm-i-dent
story to the public so they would believe the message and to get them to discontinue the use of their present dentifrice. Another problem was to emphasize Amm-i-dent was not promising the complete elimination of cavities, but
rather the reduction in the rate of formation of new cavities (said to be a 40
percent reduction on average). When the February 1949 issue of *Reader's Digest*
reprinted the *Better Homes & Gardens* article sales received another boost. An
index of the growth of Amm-i-dent sales during its first five months was as
follows: November 1948, 1; December, 3; January 1949, 20; February, 85;
March, 135. Block Drug said it was then working on an ammoniated paste
product as it acknowledged the public preference for a paste over a powder.[4]

In May 1949 the Magazine Copy Advisory Committee, representing a
majority of national magazine publishers, agreed to follow a set of standards
designed to assure accuracy in the advertising of ammoniated dentifrices.
While no formal code was involved, the committee's recommendations of
acceptability of advertising by member publishers had the weight of one, it
was said. Those standards were drafted in response to a request from the
National Better Business Bureau. A major recommendation agreed upon was
the basic principle that therapeutic claims for ammoniated dentifrices should
be properly qualified to make clear that the products' help in reducing the
number of cavities was not equally effective with all individuals. Much more
research was required, said the committee, before broad statements could be
substantiated. A second important principle laid down was the elimination
of claims tending to create the impression that the ammoniated products were
a panacea, or complete substitute for proper dental care. Such advertising
statements as "Cut Your Dental Bills in Half" was cited as an example. It was
felt that advertisers of ammoniated dentifrices might do well to follow the
examples of some other drug product manufacturers in advising regular con-
sultation with a physician. Meanwhile, another private move toward the self-
regulation of ammoniated dentifrice advertising, by a group of manufacturers,
continued in the negotiating stage, it was reported.[5]

Reportedly, Amm-i-dent was the fourth best-selling dentifrice in America by May 1949, trailing only Colgate, Ipana, and Pepsodent. Little known
Block Drug Company (based in Jersey City, New Jersey) was founded in 1907
and still headed in 1949 by Alexander Block (and then two sons and one son-
in-law). In 1948 the firm grossed $10 million on the sales of 25 dental prod-
ucts (including Polident denture cleaner). Paste then had 85 percent of the

dentifrice market. Even then the ammoniated field was beginning to get crowded as Sterling Drug had brought out an ammoniated version of Dr. Lyon's powder while Rexall Drug had announced AmoRex, a paste. One source commented that 29 firms were either in the ammoniated dentifrice field or were about to enter it.[6]

A little later in 1949 Bernard Tolk reported on a flood of new ammoniated products, many from the majors that had just been placed on the market, or soon would be. Peb-Ammo (Lehn & Fink) debuted as an ammoniated powder in May 1949, with the full line of Pebeco paste and powder to be continued. Others included Colgate Ammoniated Tooth Powder, Kolynos Anti-Decay, and Dr. Lyon's Ammoniated Tooth Powder. Pepsodent had just announced it would soon launch an ammoniated paste, powder, and mouthwash, while other majors had still not made up their minds as to whether or not to enter the field. Calox had reportedly taken out a license but remained

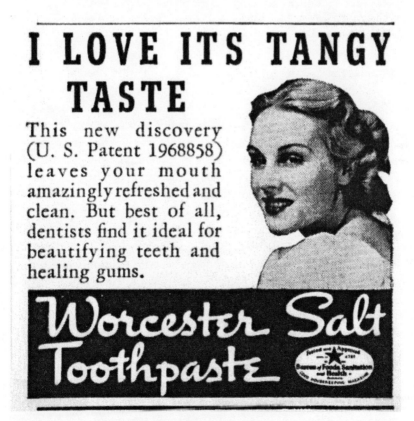

A 1937 ad for a novelty toothpaste.

undecided while Teel had not added an ammoniated substance to its liquid dentifrice and did not plan to do so. Ipana, explained new product coordinator J. J. Clarey, "is watching the situation carefully. We don't know what the ammoniated products are going to do." Squibb Dental Cream declared it had taken a wait-and-see attitude and had no plans to introduce an ammoniated product in the immediate future. Dr. West said it was waiting to see what happened to other companies' advertising and marketing as it felt some of the advertising claims would be disallowed. However, the firm declared it knew how to make ammoniated dentifrices and was ready to jump into the field pending the success of other makers. Alone among the major makers, Iodent (Iodent Chemical Company, Detroit) declined to make any statement regarding its plans to use the new substance. Among other brands on the market were Amion (J. B. Roerig & Company, Chicago), Amorex (Amorex, Chicago), and Amurol (Amurol Products, Chicago). Macy's department store in New York announced an ammoniated powder under its own name. Most of the brands then on the market, manufactured according to three basic formulas, were being sold under license from the University of Illinois. But Block Drug had been licensed by the Eastern Graduate Research Foundation to use its formula, and J. B. Roerig & Company used the third formula.[7]

Speaking at the annual meeting of the American Academy of Dental Medicine in June 1949, Dr. Joseph F. Volker, dean of the University of Alabama Dental School, expressed "sincere doubt" that the ammonia treatment could fulfill the claims made for it. He also worried those products would not only prove a disappointment in the long run but that their wide use before sufficient testing would erode confidence in dentistry and that dentists had been "carried along on the wave" of hype.[8]

That same month, *Consumer Reports* ran an article by Harold Aaron about the new ammoniated dentifrices. First though, Aaron mentioned other much-praised additives that had been recently touted only to disappoint. Sodium fluoride had been excitedly talked about as promising the end of tooth decay. But that excitement had died down as the limitations of the fluoride treatment had become apparent. Its usefulness was said to have been established only for children. More recently the theories of Dr. Bernhard Gottlieb had stirred up controversy after he developed heavy metal preparations (offered to dentists under such names as Impregnol) that originally claimed to banish as much as 90 percent of tooth decay. It soon became apparent there was little or no evidence to support such claims. Both of those two treatments were inconvenient in that they required a visit to the dentist for an application whereas ammoniated items could be bought at the drugstore for home use.[9]

This Family Reduced Tooth Decay with Amazing New Amm·i·dent!

Think what this tooth powder can mean to your family!

The Kovels were among hundreds of families who helped test Amm-i-dent Tooth Powder, during early research, under supervision of dentists. They were delighted with the way it helped them reduce tooth decay. Of course, results vary with individuals. Not every family will get the same high rate of reduction as the Kovels. But your family should enjoy a substantial reduction in its rate of new cavities, with regular use of Amm-i-dent.

You have probably heard of Amm-i-dent already, from your dentist or from friends. You may have read about Amm-i-dent in Time, Newsweek or Parents' Magazine. Here, at last, is a tooth powder that can help prevent formation of new cavities!

First Ammoniated Tooth Powder

Two revolutionary ingredients enable Amm-i-dent to reduce tooth decay—Dibasic Ammonium Phosphate and Carbamide (Synthetic Urea). They eliminate from the mouth large numbers of the acid-forming bacteria which can cause cavities. Now, for the first time, you can help protect against decay with your regular tooth brushing.

Mrs. Kovel says, "My mouth really feels clean after Amm-i-dent and I've never seen my smile look brighter. It's the same with the children. How they love the taste!" Your family, too, will love the clean, minty taste and the bright smiles and sweet breath that Amm-i-dent can bring them.

But remember—nothing can lessen your need for regular visits to your dentist. Seek his care and advice often.

Mothers! Insist that your family start using Amm-i-dent immediately. It costs so little to fight decay the Amm-i-dent way.

At all drug counters. No prescription necessary.

KOVEL
8310-12 35th Avenue,
Jackson Heights, L.I., N.Y.
Used Amm-i-dent during
test research.

Mrs. Rose Kovel (mother):
before using Amm-i-dent:
10 cavities in 12 months
since using Amm-i-dent:
4 cavities in 38 months

Laura (daughter)
before using Amm-i-dent:
3 cavities in 19 months
since using Amm-i-dent:
2 cavities in 38 months

Steven, 8½ yrs.
David, 5½ yrs.
Still have first teeth.
Using Amm-i-dent.
No cavities so far.

Amm·i·dent

FIRST AMMONIATED TOOTH POWDER

The era of the additive was well underway as this 1949 ad touted the ammoniated dentifrice.

According to Aaron, ammoniated dentifrices accounted for 10 percent of the dollar volume of all dentifrices (20 percent to 30 percent in some markets) in February 1949 and by June of that year there were 39 ammoniated dentifrice brands either on the market or soon to be launched. But, said Aaron, those big ammoniated sales were built "on little more than a molehill of evidence that the new products can do what the advertising headlines say or imply they will" and that *Consumer Reports*'s dental consultants were firm in their opinion that "no ammoniated dentifrice has as yet sufficient evidence behind it to warrant more than the hype that it may have prophylactic effects." *Advertising Age* had pointed out that no controlled clinical tests had been completed to show the products had therapeutic value while Aaron observed the National Better Business Bureau told advertisers they were not justified in claiming that ammoniated dentifrices controlled or affected the cause of tooth decay and that dental scientists, who knew most about the subject, made no such positive claims. All the advertising hype was based on the single 1935 research observation that there were marked differences in the ammonia content of saliva between people with tooth decay and those apparently immune to decay. From that it was concluded the presence of ammonia in saliva was the inhibiting factor in decay, but no actual clinical tests were conducted.[10]

Also involved in the issue was the ADA's Council on Dental Therapeutics. A few years earlier the council removed its seal of acceptance from all dentifrices (few actually held the seal) because it considered them cosmetics and held that effective cleaning could be obtained by the use of a home preparation of baking powder and salt. Then in December 1948 the council offered to "accept for clinical trial" new products potentially of therapeutic value, provided controlled tests of the products were actually in progress and other requirements were met. Under that policy the council accepted Amurol for trial. Amm-i-dent was declared to be not acceptable to the council for clinical trials largely because its ad claims that it would aid in the prevention of dental caries were not supported by evidence.[11]

Still in 1949, the ADA was urging people not to expect too much from ammoniated dentifrices because many of the claims made for them were not warranted by scientific evidence to date. A new product was Anti-Cay wafers (made by Purex Products, Baltimore) that bypassed the brushing process. They were about the size of aspirin tablets and when dissolved in the mouth immediately after each meal they were purported to have all the advantages of brushing with an ammoniated dentifrice without the inconvenience. *Consumer Reports* found by analysis that the wafers contained dibasic ammonium phosphate and urea in about the proportions found in many ammoniated toothpowders. According to the manufacturers the rest of the product was composed of sugars, calcium carbonate, flavoring oils and Vitamin D. The value of the wafers in combating decay was said by *Consumer Reports* to be "highly questionable," certainly no better than the ammoniated dentifrices while they had attributes that made them much less desirable. Because a large part of the wafer was made up of sugar, use of the wafers in the mouth introduced a potent decay-producing agent and "by substituting the wafers for brushing the teeth after every meal the user was depriving himself of a possible beneficial action, since there is some indication that brushing the teeth after meals may reduce decay regardless of the dentifrice used." Another product assessed by *Consumer Reports* was the ammoniated Dr. Cornish's Tooth Powder (this product had blatantly ignored the ADA guidelines with regard

Your teeth deserve the best protection!

Amurol your teeth!

—help your dentist fight tooth decay

YES, Amurol your teeth! Give your teeth longer-lasting protection with the dentifrice made *especially* for fighting tooth decay. Amurol has the clinically proved, *balanced* ammoniated formula with twofold anti-decay action:

- *Amurol helps neutralize mouth acids*
- *Amurol checks acid-forming bacteria*

Used as directed, this double action tends to create an ammonia condition in the mouth similar to that found in individuals who are naturally immune to tooth decay. Start the entire family using Amurol—the modern dentifrice named alone in Reader's Digest famous article on tooth decay. Insist on Amurol at drug counters everywhere!

YOUR DENTIST KNOWS

Ammoniated Dentifrice

49¢ and 33¢
New! Giant
Economy Size
Toothpaste 69¢

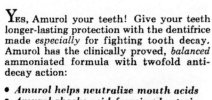

Based on a Formula Developed by University of Illinois Scientists

Another ammoniated product, 1950.

to naming a product after a supposed doctor). It claimed to be successful in correcting bleeding gums, soft teeth, and dental caries. With respect to those claims *Consumer Reports* concluded, "No other dentifrice tested by *Consumer Reports* was so richly endowed with the supposedly therapeutic agents which have become the catchwords of recent dentifrice advertising. And no other dentifrice, of those tested by *Consumer Reports*, have gone quite so far in presenting a jumble of fact and fancy."[12]

In May 1950, three British scientists declared ammoniated dentifrices would not help prevent tooth decay. Doctors G. Neil Jenkins, Donald E. Wright, and T. K. Miller, physiologists and bacteriologists of King's College Medical School at Newcastle-upon-Tyne, had repeated the American experiment from 1935 and found no difference between the saliva from persons with different rates of tooth decay.[13]

In *The Journal of the American Dental Association* in 1950 Dr. Albert H. Kneisner of Western Reserve University, Cleveland, presented a comprehensive review of all the research done till then on ammoniated dentifrices. He pointed out there was no proof of the merits of those products simply because no large-scale study had been done and other contributory factors in the prevention of decay had been ignored (proper brushing technique alone, for example). Added Kneisner, "Names of outstanding men in the dental research field have been prominently displayed in dentifrice ads to the profession. This, despite the fact that the research undertaken by these men was not necessarily devoted to, or in some cases made no mention of the probable prophylactic value of ammonium." And then the craze for ammoniated dentifrices quickly faded away, as people awaited the next miracle additive to appear in dentifrice ad copy.[14]

When *Consumer Reports* evaluated dentifrices in August 1949 it found the area had expanded rapidly, and not just through the addition of ammoniated products. "Despite all the scientific ballyhoo, tooth pastes and powders are still essentially cosmetics. Their purpose is to aid the toothbrush in polishing the accessible surfaces of the teeth," stated *Consumer Reports*. For its report, the organization tested 93 leading brands of popular pastes (44 brands) and powders (49), including 28 ammoniated dentifrices. All items containing particles hard enough to scratch glass were labeled not acceptable (all Kolynos pastes and powders), as were six powders containing sodium perborate or similar substances that had the potential to product mouth burns or lesions (the presence of those chemicals was not noted on the labels of four of them). Pebeco paste was labeled not acceptable because it still contained potassium chlorate (not noted on the label) and had "no business being in a dentifrice." It remained an ingredient although it had been criticized by the

ADA many years earlier. According to *Consumer Reports*, "Few dentifrices are advertised as the simple cleaning preparations most of them are. Instead, their makers talk about alkalizing, sweetening the breath, banishing 'tobacco mouth,' hardening the gums, whitening the teeth, and giving first aid to victims of halitosis, acidosis, gingivitis, bleeding gums, and other ailments for which a dentist or doctor rather than a toothpaste is required."[15]

Average price paid by *Consumer Reports* shoppers for all pastes was 13.2 cents per ounce (a range from 5.8 cents to 25.1 cents) and 11.9 cents for powders (4.3 cents to 23.7 cents). In the evaluation ammoniated items received no special marks for supposed effectiveness; they were treated like all the rest — products with cosmetic value only. Ammoniated pastes cost on average 9.7 cents an ounce more than did non-ammoniated pastes while ammoniated powders cost an average of 7.3 cents an ounce more than the non-ammoniated powders. In its scratch test two brands of paste and 10 brands of powder (eight of them ammoniated) failed to pass that hurdle. Acidity was measured by a product's hydrogen ion concentration, commonly referred to as ph on a scale reading from one to 14 (seven was neutral while higher readings showed alkalinity and lower numbers indicated increasing acidity). Under the U.S. Federal Specifications for toothpastes acceptable ph limits had been set at greater than 5.9 and less than 10.1. None of the dentifrices tested by *Consumer Reports* exceeded the specifications on the acidic side but 16 pastes and eight powders had a ph of 10.1 or higher.[16]

One example of odd advertising cited by *Consumer Reports* involved Iodent, which was marketed in two different strengths — Iodent No. 1 "for teeth easy to brighten" and Iodent No. 2 "for teeth hard to brighten." Formula No. 1 was advertised for "non-smokers and young folks" yet it fell in the high abrasive group while No. 2, advertised as making it possible to "whisk away stubborn smudges," was found to be one of the least abrasive products in *Consumer Reports*'s tests.[17]

Henry Link, president of the Psychological Corporation, conducted polls of consumer buying habits every three months. When he asked people what brand of dentifrice did they last buy he found 78.4 percent had purchased a paste in February 1949, 19.3 percent a tooth powder, and 1.2 percent a liquid. For May 1949 those numbers were, respectively, 73.2 percent, 24.0 percent, and 1.2 percent. When Link looked at buying habits by age he found for those under 30 (paste 78.3 percent, powder 20.6 percent); 30–39 (73.4 percent, 24.6 percent); 40–49 (73.9 percent, 23.9 percent); 50–59 (70.3 percent, 26.1 percent); 60 and over (66.2 percent, 25.9 percent). Link found the use of ammoniated powder to be highest among the younger age groups (under 40) and lowest among those 60 and older.[18]

Another wonder arrived later in 1949 when Dr. Gustav W. Rapp (professor and research biochemist at Loyola University's Dental School) and B. F. Gurney reported to the International Association for Dental Research on the possible reduction of tooth decay by a toothpaste containing chlorophyll (the green substance that gave grass and other green plants their color). Then on the market from coast to coast the paste had been sold during the previous year primarily on the recommendation of dentists. Previously the substance had been chiefly known for its ability to accelerate the healing of various gum disorders but Rapp argued it acted also to prevent the formation of bacterial acids associated with tooth decay and that it retarded the breakdown of the protein part of tooth enamel. Both the formation of bacterial acids and protein breakdown were assumed by dental authorities to be causes of tooth decay.[19]

While scientists had worked on extracting the chemical chlorophyll for years it wasn't until the end of World War II that it became commercially feasible. At that time the Rystan Company in Mount Vernon, New York, was granted patents on water-soluble chlorophyll and began making toothpaste and other products to be promoted ethically (that is, through doctors and dentists). Later other firms got into the business turning out items ranging from chlorophyll deodorant pills to chlorophyll chewing gum. Pepsodent, under license from Rystan, came out with a green-colored toothpaste named Chlorodent. After test sales in four markets in 1951 were said to be sensational, Chlorodent, backed by heavy advertising, went into national release early in 1952.[20]

Lever Brothers (maker of Pepsodent) was the first major manufacturer to market a chlorophyll toothpaste and in just two months its bright-green minty Chlorodent had helped push Lever from third to second (past Ipana, trailing Colgate) in paste sales. So great was that success that by April 1952 Colgate, Bristol-Myers (Ipana), Whitehall Pharmacal (Kolynos) and other big manufacturers were rushing chlorophyll toothpastes of their own onto the market. Rystan had paid a little over $200,000 in 1941 for a patent on all medical and dental compositions of water-soluble chlorophyll derivatives. Lever's licensing agreement brought Rystan nearly $1 million by the time it expired in the summer of 1952. Chlorophyll was then used in many other products and retail counters were full of chlorophyll products that promised to banish halitosis and body odor, and to help heal cuts. On the market were 29 different brands of deodorizing lozenges and tablets, seven brands of chewing gum, four brands of mouthwash, one brand of chlorophyll-impregnated toilet paper, and a cigarette with chlorophyll to take away a smoker's bad breath even while he was smoking. At least nine dog-food makers then added chlorophyll to their products to keep the family dog smelling nice. As well, insoles doused with chlorophyll were available to be inserted in shoes to banish foot odor.[21]

During 1952 Americans spent $187,105,000 on dentifrices. Rystan obtained chlorophyll commercially from green alfalfa. Back in 1940 Colgate and Ipana shared top spot in the paste market, each holding 25 percent of that market with Pepsodent third at 10 percent. By 1950 Colgate was first with 40 percent while Ipana and Pepsodent each had 15 percent. Then, less than one year after its national release Chlorodent itself had 15 percent of the total national market. When the Pepsodent share was added it was felt Lever might be challenging Colgate for first place. Since Chlorodent had launched other makers who had added chlorophyll included Amm-i-dent, Ipana, and Iodent. After Amm-i-dent became Amm-i-dent Ammoniated Chlorophyll in April 1949, its share of the paste market grew from 10 percent to about 14 percent in two months. With respect to the effectiveness of chlorophyll, Dr. J. Roy Doty, secretary of

Here's the new green toothpaste with miracle chlorophyll
you read about in
Reader's Digest...

● The latest *Reader's Digest* report on dentifrices describes a new chlorophyll toothpaste that cleans the entire mouth, including the breath. It tells about tests which show that this new green toothpaste is actually 50% more effective against mouth odors than one not containing chlorophyll.

Chlorodent, and only Chlorodent, produced these amazing results.

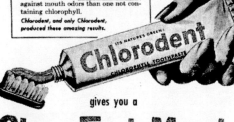

gives you a

Clean Fresh Mouth All Day!

Chlorodent was used in hundreds of tests on people with bad breath. When they brushed their teeth with Chlorodent, their mouth odor disappeared. Two hours later, their breath was still clean in 98% of the cases. Four hours later (end of the tests), 74% were still free of bad breath. By using Chlorodent regularly—preferably after meals—you can be free of mouth odor all day!

Combats common gum troubles

An estimated 50% of all tooth loss can be traced to conditions which start with sore, bleeding gums. Chlorodent promotes the growth of firm, healthy, pink tissue. If you have tender gums, you will want to use Chlorodent for its fast relief of this condition alone!

Fights tooth decay

Chlorodent greatly reduces the mouth acids that "eat" into tooth enamel. It helps combat the bacteria which cause these acids. And it keeps your teeth so clean that bacteria find it difficult to multiply on them. No toothpaste offers better protection!

You'll enjoy Chlorodent's fresh, minty flavor. Try it today!

When your toothbrush bristles are green, you know you are getting the full benefits of chlorophyll*!

Chlorodent gives you this visible proof that active chlorophyll is at work. It tells you that your mouth, breath and gums are chlorophyll-clean! The performance and quality of Chlorodent are unconditionally guaranteed. If you are not entirely satisfied, return unused portion to Lever Brothers Company, New York, N.Y. Purchase price plus postage will be refunded at once.

water soluble chlorophyllins

Chlorodent
The chloro phyll dent ifrice

The chlorophyll craze, 1952.

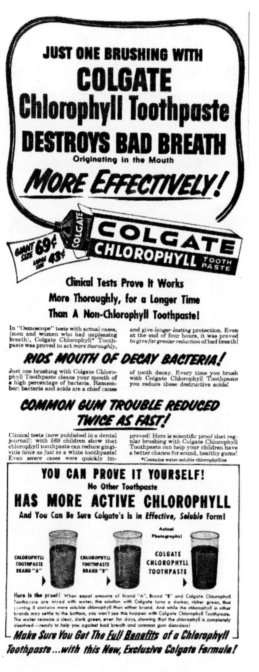

the ADA's Council on Dental Therapeutics, stated, the "evidence presently available does not warrant claims that dental products containing chlorophyll derivatives are useful or beneficial in preventing or curing dental decay." As to its claims to banish bad breath, said Doty, "the evidence as to the usefulness of products containing chlorophyll derivatives is inconclusive." Then the chlorophyll craze faded away.[22]

Nobody knew for sure in 1950 what caused tooth decay. But since acid-producing bacteria were blamed by most researchers, an antibiotic to check the bacteria seemed like a good idea. So that year, with the blessing of the Food and Drug Administration, the Andrew Jergens Company offered druggists just such a prescription item: Dentocillan, a toothpowder containing penicillin. The new tooth powder had been tested first in the laboratory of Dr. Helmut A. Zander of Tufts College Dental School; then schoolchildren in Walpole, Massachusetts, were used as guinea pigs. Reportedly, the new product reduced cavities by 55 per-

When one maker came out with an additive, all the rest followed, 1953.

cent, compared to a control group using a powder with exactly the same ingredients except for the penicillin. Still, many doctors and dentists were convinced it was not a good idea to use penicillin indiscriminately in the mouth. That fact combined with the requirement that consumers first get a prescription before they could buy the new powder probably explained why Dentocillan died a very quick death.[23]

When the American Dental Association surveyed the dentifrice-buying habits of people (81.4 percent of 3,000 families surveyed responded) in 1953 it found that 18.5 percent of consumers said taste was the reason for selecting the dentifrice they used with another 9.0 percent citing aftertaste as the reason. One out of 18 used a particular dentifrice because the dentist recommended it; 23.4 percent thought an ammoniated product was best for the teeth; 20.2 percent thought a chlorophyll dentifrice was best; 16.3 percent thought a plain dentifrice was best; and 36.8 percent said, "It doesn't make much difference what kind is used." Of those answering the question, 69.1 percent used toothpaste, 21.8 percent used tooth powder; 0.8 percent used a liquid product; 8.3 percent used baking soda, salt, or something else. While 60.1 percent said they knew teeth should be brushed after each meal only 29.1 percent said they actually did. The most common practice was twice-a-day brushing.[24]

Toothpaste makers began telling the public about another breakthrough in the summer of 1953, anti-enzyme action. Reporter Albert Maisel explained that at the core of the excitement lay the theory — accepted by most dental experts — that refined sugar was the villain causing most tooth decay. The sugar was rapidly converted by mouth bacteria into acids strong enough to react with the tooth enamel and dissolve calcium, with the result being that another cavity got its start. Enzymes were catalysts produced by the mouth bacteria that sped up the conversion of sugar into acids. Thus if the chain — from sugar to bacteria to enzymes to acids to destruction of enamel — could be broken at any point a lot of decay would be eliminated.[25]

Maisel admitted that penicillin, chlorophyll, urea, and even the detergents that had replaced soap in most pastes then on the market all slowed down enzyme action but the drawback with them and most enzyme inhibitors was that they did not remain in the mouth long enough to be effective. So research on the problem was conducted by Dr. Leonard S. Fosdick, professor of chemistry at Northwestern University Dental College. It was research that lasted four years. Out of 381 compounds tested only 10 were effective but eight of those were eliminated because they were either antibiotics (which could not be taken continuously) or were potentially poisonous. Fosdick was satisfied with two compounds being suitable for paste use. One was sodium

Ipana came out with a product with both wonder ingredients, 1953.

lauroyl sarcosinate (synthesized in the laboratories of Colgate-Palmolive-Peet); the other was sodium dehydroacetate (from the Lambert Pharmacal Company, maker of Listerine toothpaste). Two years earlier Fosdick started clinical trials with the Colgate compound on 3,450 subjects, mostly university students. Reportedly, subjects who used an ordinary toothpaste (control group subjects individually used whatever brand they preferred) averaged almost 2.5

times more new cavities than those who used the sarcosinate paste (another problem with the research was that only 2,200 completed the experiment, the other 1,250 dropped out). From all that work came the "established fact," said Maisel, that Listerine Antizyme and Colgate Ribbon Dental Cream's ingredients had been shown to have a lasting effect in keeping mouth acid low and a year's clinical tests of Colgate's "have indicated its effectiveness — even when used only twice a day — in actually reducing the formation of new cavities." Over all, Maisel's article was very positive and enthusiastic; it was also very uncritical with no negative words and no mention of the array of wonder additives that had arrived so recently in such profusion to such ultimate disappointment.[26]

In January 1954 the American Dental Association announced that new evidence on the so-called anti-enzyme toothpastes did not support claims made for their effectiveness in preventing tooth decay. The ADA's Council on Dental Therapeutics unanimously approved a resolution stating that it had reviewed the evidence on the dentifrices in question and had "found no satisfactory clinical evidence of their effectiveness against tooth decay." And another miracle vanished from sight.[27]

When *Business Week* surveyed the dentifrice industry in 1954 it mentioned the fierce competition and that the toothpaste field was then the scene of a furious race "to invent more miraculous additives and more startling properties." Additive battles got hot in 1949, said the account, when ammonia was added to paste to improve its cleaning properties; and then came chlorophyll, advertised largely as a deodorant. Then there were chemicals said to neutralize harmful enzymes; then came detergents. Lever Brothers was then heading in another direction with the firm test-marketing a new brand of paste called Shield, which contained an antibiotic drug. For 1953 sales of dentifrices in the U.S. were estimated at $150 million. *Business Week* felt that every time a new additive was announced many citizens bought some of the new product even though they were not yet finished with their old tube: "When new additives come along fast, and when they are skillfully advertised, a good deal more dentifrice is bought than is actually used."[28]

Drug companies made the first pastes to be marketed on a big scale, toward the end of the 1800s, observed *Business Week*, but then the soap companies moved in and with their knowledge of mass merchandising, and their willingness to spend huge sums on advertising and promotion, they eventually took the lead. While sales figures were secret, estimates in 1954 were that Colgate-Palmolive was first with 40 percent to 45 percent of total industry sales, and Lever Brothers next at 10 percent to 20 percent (the two soap firms). Next came two big drug companies: Bristol-Myers with 12 percent to 15 per-

THERE IS ONLY ONE ANTIZYME TOOTH PASTE

Each brushing protects 12-24 hours—No other type of tooth paste protects more than ½ hour

Reader's Digest names ANTIZYME by name in reporting this exciting development.

STOPS THE MAJOR CAUSE OF TOOTH DECAY

EVERY MINUTE OF EVERY DAY

New scientific discovery

Here's your chance to try

ANTIZYME

FREE!
TRIAL OFFER

Reducing Bacteria is not the answer

The anti-enzyme fad, 1954.

cent and Block Drug Company with 10 percent to 12 percent. Proctor & Gamble, which ranked with Colgate and Lever as one of the big three soap firms, was then trying to join the other two as a high-ranking dentifrice maker. Proctor's Gleem, featuring a detergent, was the company's first serious effort to get a big piece of the industry and it reportedly spent between $15 million and $20 million in the initial promotion of Gleem.[29]

When *Business Week* published its piece the anti-enzyme phase was still fairly hot with Lambert Pharmaceutical Company (maker of Listerine) having called its new product Listerine Antizyme (one of the two compounds supposedly approved by Dr. Fosdick) while Colgate launched its Gardol, trade name for the other Northwestern chemical. "Today, every important toothpaste maker plugs anti-enzymes or ingredients with similar properties," said the article. Toward the end of 1953, so-called surface-active detergents began to make a name for themselves as ingredients. They were said to give teeth the same kind of protection as anti-enzymes. Ipana then contained a detergent, as did Gleem. There were side effects to the additive race, though. One was the enormous expense involved. A second was that it had drawn some vocal opposition from medical men and government agencies charged with watching activities in the field of drugs. Many medical people were, also, leery of any overuse of antibiotics.[30]

When Walter Goodman, writing in the *New Republic*, surveyed the additives in the field, in 1956, he declared that since all dentifrices were mostly alike it was only advertising that caused a differentiation. Americans then spent an estimated $150 million annually on dentifrices. Early on their success came, thought Goodman, due to the novelty of nationally advertised brands that tasted better than baking soda and were more conveniently packaged. Between World War I and World War II the paste makers discovered a great number of foul ailments, explained Goodman, tongue-in-cheek, which had heretofore been neglected by the nation's medical men: acid mouth, pink toothbrush, germ mask, smoker's teeth, gingivitis, pyorrhea, and halitosis. At the end of World War II one of Colgate's more popular slogans was, "It cleans your breath while it cleans your teeth." Then the post-war wonders began with Pepsodent and its discovery of irium, about which the ADA remarked, "The firm has attempted to endow the word 'irium' which is applied to the soap substitute used in its products with extraordinary virtues which it does not possess." When Procter & Gamble entered the dentifrice market with Gleem it announced, "Just one brushing destroys decay-and-odor-causing bacteria. After one Gleem brushing up to 90 percent of bacteria are destroyed. Only Gleem has GL-70 to fight decay." GL-70 was a surface-active detergent of the type used to brighten clothes and dishes. Ipana then (recently possessed of dibasic ammonium phosphate, carbamide, and chlorophyll) said it contained a new ingredient, WD-9 (another of the surface-active detergents), and declared, "Ipana destroys decay bacteria best of all leading toothpastes." Not wanting to be left behind in the detergent race Pepsodent added its own, called Imp, to the irium-laced product.[31]

Consumer Reports evaluated dentifrices again in April 1954. It noted what was true then, and had been right back to its first evaluation in 1936, was that the dentifrice was an adjunct to the brush, and nothing more, a position it had shared with the American Dental Association over that 18 year period. Because *Consumer Reports* determined pastes commanded the bulk of the market — with powders a very poor second — it limited its evaluation to toothpastes only, a total of 49 in all. Eleven of them had particles of grit in them hard enough to scratch glass and were all rated as not acceptable. No potentially poisonous substances were found — Pebeco had been unacceptable on that ground in 1949 but was no longer being marketed in 1954. Ten brands were slightly more alkaline than the upper limit of the Federal specifications (ph 6.2 to 10.5) but, in the opinion of *Consumer Reports*'s consultants, all remained within the safe limits for products such as toothpaste. Calculated on a per ounce basis, the average cost of the 49 brands was 15.4 cents. Of the 38 brands rated acceptable the average price was 16.0 cents (with a range from 6.4 cents to 25.0 cents per ounce).[32]

   Consumer Reports noted that when it had last tested dentifrices in August 1949 the age of ammoniated pastes had just begun, with chlorophyll entering the paste field in 1950 and "Nature's own deodorant" had already been credited with $45 million in toothpaste sales. Added *Consumer Reports*, "Three short years later, the industry hit bingo with antienzyme action. The modern dentifrice, ammoniated, chlorophylled, anti-enzymed (but basically very much the same product as before), had at last arrived." An editorial in the February 1954 issue of the *Journal of the American Dental Association* stated that with so little clinical evidence available to that date "the anti-enzyme dentifrices may well turn out to be not a miracle but a mirage — which, according to Webster, is an optical phenomenon produced by a stratum of hot air."[33]

   One other additive of note of this era was, of course, fluoride. That ingredient began to appear in dentifrices in the late 1940s but did not receive much of a reception at that time. When *Consumer Reports* evaluated dentifrices in 1949 it rejected two brands of powder precisely because they contained a fluoride additive, a substance *Consumer Reports* felt to be poisonous. Rejected were the brand Flurea (made by K-R Lab, Seattle, and containing sodium fluoride) and Dr. Cornish's Tooth Powder (fluoride). That latter brand promoted itself more as an ammoniated item but sometimes pushed its fluoride connection in some of its ads. In its 1949 conclusion on the additive fluoride *Consumer Reports* argued, "Fluoride, furthermore is a poisonous substance which CU and its consultants believe has no place in a toothpaste or powder for home use. All studies to date as to the effectiveness of fluoride-containing dentifrices in reducing decay are negative."[34]

   Early in 1955 it was reported that a new decay-checking toothpaste was expected to come on the market soon, one that depended for its anti-decay action on fluoride. A year's trial of the new paste by schoolchildren resulted in a reported decrease in the tooth decay rate of 50.6 percent for the 209 children who got the fluoride paste, compared to the 214 subjects who got an identical paste except that it had no fluoride. In part that study was supported by a grant from the Procter & Gamble Company and was conducted by Doctors Joseph C. Muhler, William H. Nebergall, and Harry G. Day of the School of Dentistry and chemistry department of Indiana University, Bloomington, and Doctor Arthur W. Radike of Ohio State University College of Dentistry, Columbus. Putting a fluoride into a dentifrice followed the earlier discovery of the tooth decay checking power of fluorides occurring naturally in drinking water. Fluoride was then added to the water of many communities to give the benefit of its anti-decay action to children as their teeth were forming. Additionally, fluoride was applied to the teeth of schoolchildren by many dentists as an anti-decay measure during a child's regular visit, as a topical application.[35]

On February 15, 1955, Procter & Gamble (P&G) announced that it would introduce, on February 21, a new paste containing a fluoride compound. P&G said the toothpaste, Crest, would be sold at first in three cities — Columbus, Ohio, and two yet to be determined, one in Oregon and one in New York State — as test markets. Unlike fluoride in drinking water, the fluoride in the toothpaste — called a stannous fluoride — worked directly on the exterior enamel of the tooth.[36]

When *Newsweek* ran a small piece on the new paste it treated the subject mostly with skepticism as it listed the various miracle additives that had been launched in the previous few years only to all fall flat. It placed fluoride at the end of that long list noting that the ADA was among those awaiting additional confirmation of the fluoride paste's effectiveness. Also noted was that P&G itself had underwritten the study that showed its paste to be effective in decay reduction.[37]

Reporter Bruce Bliven wrote an enthusiastic article about the new development that was published in *Colliers* at the start of 1956. He gave Joseph Charles Muhler, associate professor at the Indiana University School of Dentistry, credit as the developer of fluoride toothpaste, specifically stannous, or tin, fluoride. "And the new toothpaste works," declared Bliven. A more recent study, one of the largest of its kind in dental research, showed the paste cut the rate of tooth decay almost in half for the 3,600 Bloomington, Indiana, residents (children and adults) who participated in the study. "But there is no doubt at all that the toothpaste really does reduce decay," he reiterated. Reportedly the paste's stannous fluoride, like the sodium fluoride most dentists used, combined with the surface enamel of the teeth and made it considerably more resistant to the mouth acids that caused decay. Muhler agreed his fluoride toothpaste was no substitute for fluoridated drinking water but some cities were slow to take that step and the topical application given by dentists was expensive. From the new and larger study (started in May 1952 and lasting three years) it seemed that adults also benefited from using the paste. In the children's test reduction in the caries' rate was 50.6 percent at the end of one year while for the adult group (subjects ranged from 18 to 38 years, with a median age of 20) the reduction in decay was 41.6 percent after one year. Muhler had started research work on fluorides in 1945. P&G was then the only company producing Muhler's compound (under license from Indiana University through the foundation that owned the patent). Reportedly nearly every major toothpaste maker was then making, or was about to make, a fluoride paste. There were then four on sale, all of which had been developed in their respective companies' laboratories according to their own fluoride formulas: Colgate's Brisk, Bristol-Myers's Sentry, Block Drug's Super Amm-i-dent, and Lambert's Antizyme.[38]

Skepticism about the fluoride pastes remained. Walter Goodman observed in 1956 that no sooner had several million households used up their sample tubes of Crest than they received sample tubes of Brisk through the mail. For the later brand Colgate copy declared, "Only Brisk has Fluoride/85 ... hardens tooth enamel, makes teeth stronger, starts working instantly to defeat decay." Dr. Harold Hellenbrand, ADA secretary, was cited as having said, "The American Dental Association is not aware of evidence adequate to demonstrate the claimed dental caries prophylactic value of Crest.... Published evidence to support the usefulness of adding a fluoride in other dentifrices is even less convincing. The Association therefore believes that all fluoride dentifrices are being marketed prematurely."[39]

Journalist Peter Goulding, in the American Medical Association's official publication, *Today's Health*, argued early in 1957 that there was more real evidence to back up the claims for the new fluoride dentifrices but the dental profession and much of the general public "have been understandably skeptical" after prior claims for many miracle additives. Goulding said one of the soundest statements had been made 50 years earlier by dental scientist Dr. G. V. Black who said simply that the real value of a dentifrice was to help the brush do its cleaning job and to induce people to brush their teeth more often.[40]

All those additive miracles, of course, led to much exaggerated advertising copy and to some long-running feuds with dentists, among others.

7

Toothpaste, Advertising and Marketing, 1946–1960

The hucksters' puffs of dental creams and dental powders are deplorable, exasperating and embarrassing. — American Dental Association, 1953.

[Toothpaste false ad claims are] "almost criminally deceptive and misleading." — Dr. O. J. McCormack, 1955.

The R. L. Watkins company, a division of Sterling Drug (Dr. Lyon's Tooth Powder) entered the paste market for the first time in 1947. For some time the firm felt the saturation point for its powder was close at hand and recognized the paste field was much more fertile. "More people prefer tooth paste," said D. H. Williams, divisional vice president, "than tooth powder. It's just a matter of consumer preference. We have reached the point in the tooth powder field where we are selling Dr. Lyon's to our quota. Now we are out to corner our share of the toothpaste business." After working for three years to a goal of developing a paste the company announced it had one that polished teeth 2.5 to 5.5 times brighter and four times faster than other toothpastes. It decided the two products would not be linked at all in ads and that the word "Dr." would not appear on the new item (supposedly to lessen customer confusion). Thus the new item was christened Lyons Tooth Paste (with no apostrophe). An introductory ad campaign ran in 70 newspapers and cost $300,000 for that 10-week newspaper campaign. Additionally, some ads were run on some of the 11 radio programs that Sterling Drug then sponsored. Radio commercials, like newspaper copy, stressed the ability of the new product to "get teeth 2½ to 5½ times brighter than any other toothpaste." Window and interior displays were set up in 25,000 outlets and mail solicitations were sent out to a list of 75,000 drug outlets. Each of those 75,000 outlets was mailed a gift display whether they ordered any of the new product or not. It consisted of an easel-type counter display to which were attached three packaged tubes of the new product; two of the 25 cent sized tubes and one of the 50 cents size. Each outlet could keep the items for personal use or sell the three and keep the whole $1. Preceding the gift mailing were two solicitation mailings that also went to all 75,000 outlets. The first mailing was a teaser type to alert the reader to watch for a special new product that was coming soon while the second was a specific announcement of the new product along with details such as its advantages, pricing, and so on.[1]

According to D. H. Williams Sterling started thinking about producing a paste in 1943 and began the actual research in 1944. That research led it to select aluminum hydroxide as the best available cleansing agent; it had never before been used as a dentifrice, he said. Lyons Tooth Paste was distributed in three different sizes, retailing at 10 cents, 23 cents and 43 cents, under fair trade laws (a remnant of World War II) then in effect in 45 of the 48 states. The 10 cent size had a list price of 85 cents a dozen to retailers; the 25 cent size had a list price of $2 a dozen and the 50 cent size listed at $4 per dozen.[2]

Writing in 1948 Don Wharton remarked that toothpaste ad campaigns aimed at the greatest horror copywriters could imagine: deficient sex appeal. Reportedly the average person stuck to the same brand less than 18 months while the average household contained at least three different brands. By his figures a tube of toothpaste retailing for 41 cents represented roughly four cents worth of ingredients placed in four cents worth of tube and given eight cents worth of advertising with the manufacturer left about 11 cents for overhead and profit, and the retailer 14 cents.[3]

An editorial in the January 1950 issue of the *New York Journal of Dentistry* looked at the current crop of dentifrice ads and declared "the dentist experiences a feeling of degradation. To add to his injury, some of the advertisements state that they have been licensed by a dental college, while others quote freely and copiously from the works of Famous Dental Scientists, and from the dental press." Unfortunately, thought the editor, not only were manufacturers attempting to exploit the dentist, dentistry and dental literature, "but also that the latter allow such exploitation to prevail." Noted was that one dentifrice maker boldly displayed the University of Illinois as the licensor of his magic formula even though the researchers involved said themselves their sample was too small for conclusions, the control group was not properly controlled and they did not know how much credit to give the brushing and how much to give the dentifrice." Also observed was that chlorophyll-containing toothpastes were then being sold as a new and more effective way to control dental caries yet such claims were based on the sole finding that chlorophyll was found to have reduced caries in 20 female hamsters but not in males. In the editor's opinion the dentist should make it clear to his patients that to that date there was no chemical method of stopping tooth decay and that the best that could be expected was what seemed to be a reduction at most of only 40 percent of the annual increase in dental decay by the use of topical applications of sodium fluoride.[4]

At a meeting of the Greater New York Dental Society in 1951, Dr. Harry Lyons, dean of the School of Dentistry at the Medical College of Virginia (Richmond) blasted the advertising campaigns of "confectionary" dentifrices that he said generated a false reliance on dentifrices and a resulting neglect of early diagnosis and preventive care. Such ads, he said, preyed on the human emotions of fear, vanity and love as well as on the public's reluctance to seek professional advice and treatment. Massaging of the gums had no value, with or without paste while the value of ammoniated, chlorophyll and penicillin dentifrices had not been proven. Lyons added that proper brushing was a major factor in published test successes of medicated dentifrices and maintained that a 50-50 mixture of table salt and baking soda was as good as any dentifrice on the market. To be fully effective, Lyons argued, brushing the teeth should take place within minutes after every meal and "carrying toothbrushes around ought to be just as acceptable as carrying combs, lipsticks and powder because there's a lot more sense in it."[5]

The editor of the *Journal of the American Dental Association* attacked dentifrice ads in 1953 when he declared, "The hucksters' puffs of dental creams and dental powders are deplorable, exasperating and embarrassing" to the 77,000 association members. "Many of these puffs and superclaims are on the same low level as those made for discredited cancer cures and arthritis remedies," he maintained. The ADA's Council on Dental Therapeutics continued to assert at that time that no dentifrice offered to the public had been found to have any usefulness beyond helping the brush in cleaning the accessible surfaces of the teeth.[6]

Later that same year at its convention the ADA reiterated its claim that no therapeutic dentifrice on the market was a definite safeguard against tooth decay or gum disorders. Claims that chlorophyll derivatives were effective against human tooth decay were called "pure speculation" by the dental scientists. Said Dr. John W. Hein, chairman of the Department of Dentistry and Dental Research at the University of Rochester, regarding chlorophyll, "never has a substance been so exploited and prostituted by ridiculous applications."[7]

At the close of that 1953 ADA convention, in a resolution approved unanimously by its house of delegates (representing 70,000 dentists in the U.S.), the group was urged to advise the public "in the strongest possible terms of the serious danger to health which arises out of the present flood of inaccurate and untruthful claims in advertising for dentifrices and other dental products." In addition, the resolution called on dentifrice makers to cease "practices which tend to destroy the confidence of the public in the integrity of all advertising."[8]

Reporter Howard Rusk covered that 1953 ADA convention and felt the biggest news out of it was the charge that the dentifrice makers were undermining the nation's dental health by misleading advertising; that no genuinely therapeutic dentifrice had yet been developed (one proved to prevent gum disorders or tooth decay) and included specifically in that category were the ammoniated, chlorophyll, antienzyme and penicillin (sometimes called medicated dentifrices) ones. Rusk said that was the strongest action taken by the ADA since medicated dentifrices came into vogue. Its attitude in the past had been that although there had been no recognized scientific proof of the value of such products, they were harmless. One reason behind the more aggressive stand, thought Rusk, was the perceived increasing tendency of the public to put too much faith in the dentifrices' ingredients rather than on its cleansing value. Also, the ADA strongly reiterated its stand taken in 1950 that the fluoridation of public water supplies was a safe and effective procedure for reducing the incidence of dental caries and they urged all communities to adjust the fluoride content of their public water supplies to the recommended level.[9]

Another major annoyance to the ADA, as contained in a 1953 resolution, was that "much of the advertising for these products untruthfully suggests that members of the dental profession are participating in the advertising and promotion of these products of alleged health significance." One example was the antienzyme research conducted by Dr. Leonard Fosdick. Although he made no positive assertion that the enzyme inhibitors he had studied assured definite promise of preventing tooth decay, the ads for such products often pretended otherwise. "During the past 10 years, the American public has been led to believe that by brushing the teeth with various types of preparations dental caries could be prevented," said Fosdick. "Unfortunately, the expectations aroused by clever advertising have not been fulfilled." Responding to such charges a spokesman for Bristol-Myers (Ipana) said they would continue their current ads while a spokesman for Lambert Pharmacal (Listerine) declared, "We can prove our ad claims no matter what the ADA says. We certainly won't change a line of our copy."[10]

Writing in the *New York Times* in 1953 reporter James Nagle argued that the nature of the toothpaste business was such that as soon as one maker announced he had added a new ingredient to the base found in all pastes, all the other manufacturers soon reported they had done likewise. Or, they announced their product had contained an ingredient that accomplished the same result but they had never bothered to advertise it. Examples he cited were chlorophyll and antienzyme. The net result was to make advertising the key to success in the sale of dentifrices. Nagle estimated the big four in the field — Colgate-Palmolive (Colgate's Dental Cream), Lever Brothers (Pepsodent and Chlorodent), Bristol-Myers (Ipana regular and Ipana A/C), and Block Drug (Amm-i-dent) — spent over $20 million for advertising dentifrices in 1953, at a time when the market was worth about $104 million annually at wholesale prices. At Bristol-Myers Ipana and Ipana A/C (ammoniated and chlorophyll) each had its own specific advertising manager. They competed against all other dentifrices and against each other. Ipana regular (then in existence for over 30 years) received 75 percent of the overall dentifrice ad budget with the product being sold mostly in the rural areas. Originated some 18 months earlier and most popular in urban markets, Ipana A/C received the other 25 percent. Reportedly Bristol-Myers stood by the accuracy of its ad claims saying that all copy was reviewed by its own doctors, a dentist, company lawyers, and an outside legal firm that specialized in the field.[11]

Robert Flood, an assistant editor with the advertising trade

More outrageous ad claims, these were about stains on the teeth from smoking, 1948.

THE TELL-TALE "HANKY" TEST...
Blow a thin stream of smoke through a hanky. See that brown stain? That's what dulls smokers' smiles!

SMOKE AND SMILE, TOO!

IODENT No. 2 Toothpaste

A Special Formula Made By a Dentist To SAFELY Remove "Smoker's Smudge"!

Start *today* using Iodent. See how its *longer cleaning action* quickly, safely removes smoke smudge. You'll smile with *confidence* — you'll like Iodent's delightful mint-leaf flavor. Refreshing! Sweetens the breath!

For teeth *easy* to brighten—non-smokers and young folks — use Iodent No. 1, a lighter texture. *Get Iodent today!*

publication *Printers' Ink*, stated in 1954 that in spite of the avalanche of criticism directed at paste makers there was a valuable net benefit to the public: "The incidence of dental care is higher in the United States than it is in any other country in the world." His argument seemed to be that advertising was somehow responsible for that condition. Commenting on Bristol-Myers's ad strategy Flood remarked that Ipana and Ipana A/C were then both running ads in the print media. Ipana A/C made an appeal for readers to switch to antienzyme toothpaste with prolonged anti-cavity action while Ipana boasted it contained the acid-inhibitor WE-9 and that its users could enjoy sweets and still protect teeth from cavities. Both products aimed their pitches at women as they bought most of the toothpaste in America. Ads for Ipana appeared in women's magazines, shelter publications, and comic sections of Sunday newspapers; the brand sponsored *Nora Drake* a daytime radio soap opera and two television shows, *Man Behind the Badge* and *Pride of the Family*. Ipana A/C favored weekly magazines and it used Sunday supplements as well, especially in its early days. Also, it was one of the sponsors of the CBS daytime television program the *Garry Moore Show*.[12]

During the annual convention of the Greater New York Dental Society late in 1955, Dr. O. J. McCormack, president of the Dental Society of the State of New York, agreed that despite all the advertising claims, no therapeutic paste or powder had been accepted by the dental profession. Such false claims, he declared, are "almost criminally deceptive and misleading." A tragedy of the situation was to rely on a wonder product and deny one's self proper scientific treatment and to invite serious dental disorders. "The last five years in particular have seen a succession of so-called magic ingredients introduced to the public through shrieking headlines and alluring text in printed and televised commercials," he added. "The manufacturers of such products must answer to their own consciences and ultimately to the public for their advertising claims based more on sales enthusiasm than conclusive scientific research."[13]

Marguerite Higgins, a Pulitzer Prize winner, was engaged in 1957 by the ad agency Benton & Bowles to write a series of advertisements for Crest Toothpaste. Higgins won the top journalistic honor in 1951 for international reporting. At the time she was engaged by Benton & Bowles she was assigned to the Washington, D.C., bureau of the *New York Herald Tribune*. Victor Bloede, Benton & Bowles copy chief, explained, "It was a case where we need a reporter's reputation for examining facts and setting them down objectively to make truth believable." He added that one of the frustrating problems of ad copywriting happened when "you get a product that actually is so good the superlatives have a hollow ring. Often a way out is the testimonial. But we believe it is even better than a testimonial to engage an outsider with a reputation for integrity and recognized reportorial ability. Such a person lends validity to a factual story." Ads produced by Higgins for Crest contained her name and described her as a "noted journalist and Pulitzer Prize Winner." According to Bloede, "Miss Higgins was given complete authority to write her feature text about Crest as she saw fit." One of the most famous Crest slogans from this era (although not from Higgins) was "Look, Mom — no cavities!"[14]

Around the same time Higgins was settling in with Crest, Bristol-Myers introduced its new Ipana Plus. Described as having a "flowing formula," it was packaged not in a tube but in a plastic squeeze bottle. The company credited one of its secretaries with the idea — it had been looking for a new entrant in the dentifrice field. One day the secretary came back to work after having lunch in a Madison Avenue cafeteria where she had used a squeeze bottle to apply ketchup to her food. She wondered why not package toothpaste in the same way? Although the basic formula for Ipana Plus was the same as for regular Ipana, company chemists had lowered the paste's viscosity, which resulted in a "flowing paste." Reporter Carl Spielvogel wondered why a company would go to all that expense and trouble. Bristol-Myers explained to him that it was because tubes became unwieldy when their contents exceeded six ounces and large cans were difficult to wedge into medicine chests. Another reason, said the reporter, was that in the dentifrice business it was important to regularly come up with something new. The company planned to spend more money promoting Ipana Plus than it had on any new product it had introduced, although it would not specify the amount. Ad copy, explained Bristol-Myers, was to be based on the convenience of the squeeze bottle and the economy the product offered.[15]

A few months after that Lever Brothers had a new pink and white toothpaste called Stripe out in a few test markets, and it soon was available nationwide. Stripe emerged from the tube in five pink and white stripes, had a spearmint flavor and, according to the company, "is the first toothpaste to contain hexachlorophene, well known bacteria killer" It was promoted by a large advertising budget and it was expected that Stripe would have special appeal for children.[16]

Kolynos paste (made by Whitehall Laboratories, a division of American Home Products) took a different advertising approach in November 1958 when it told the ADA it would make no harsh or untruthful claims in its advertising. In response, the ADA said that Kolynos would be allowed to advertise in the ADA *Journal* and could also attend ADA meetings. Taking advantage of that Kolynos ran a four-page ad in the June 1959 issue of *Coro-*

net magazine headlined, "Let's stop cheating our children" and that also said Kolynos was "the only toothpaste accepted for advertising by the American Dental Assn."[17]

Kolynos was banking on ADA approval to put its paste back in the running while the ADA was banking on Kolynos to help put an end to all therapeutic claims, and false ones in general, in the dentifrice industry. But according to a spokesman for Bristol-Myers, there was practically no hope for either outcome. The campaign theme for Kolynos, "the only toothpaste accepted for advertising by the American Dental Assn." was the result of an agreement it made in November 1958 with the ADA. In return for its ads being accepted in the ADA *Journal*, it would submit its ad copy to the ADA for approval. Some of the ADA–approved copy, which had appeared in popular general magazines included, "Make sure your child brushes with a toothpaste offering cleaning protection rather than miracle protection. Do miracle ingredients exist? The American Dental Assn. states: 'Adequate scientific evidence has not yet been produced in support.'" Reprints of the four-page ad in *Coronet* were sent by Kolynos to all of the 75,000 dentists in the U.S. An ADA spokesman added that while no other toothpaste maker had yet requested ADA acceptance for advertising, he hoped the Kolynos ads would bring that about. An account executive for Ipana at the ad agency Doherty, Clifford, Steers, and Shenfield grumbled, "No toothpaste of any size would consider suiting ad copy to ADA requirements. They'd have to pull all the teeth out of a campaign. The ADA would not permit any claims of superiority over other brands." Industry observers felt that since Kolynos had steadily lost market share and was then only a very tiny player in the market that it had nothing to lose from its strategy.[18]

Late in 1959 a spokesman for the ADA charged that some television toothpaste commercials were just as rigged as the quiz shows exposed by the U.S. Congress (a major scandal of the time happened when television quiz shows, one of the most popular genres on the tube, were discovered, in many cases, to have been phoney). Dr. Harold Hellenbrand, ADA secretary, said much of the toothpaste advertising on television and in print actually discouraged proper dental care as it provided a false sense of security. Hillenbrand reiterated the ADA position that the organization recognized dentifrices "solely as helpful adjuncts in cleaning the teeth."[19]

With such a storm of controversy aroused by much of the toothpaste advertising it was almost inevitable that the government would be drawn into the middle of the issue.

8

Toothpaste, Advertising Challenged, 1946–1960

One after another of these [therapeutic] dentifrices has been promoted with unsupported advertising claims of great promise. None has survived the test of time and use.—Dr. Harry Lyons, 1958.

[Colgate's invisible shield campaign was] "a false, misleading and deceptive portrayal of the true properties of Colgate Dental Cream with Gardol."— Federal Trade Commission, 1960.

The United States Marshal's office seized 132 cartons of toothpaste at the New Haven, Connecticut, warehouse of McKesson & Robbins, wholesale drug company, in 1949. It was a seizure made upon information issued by U.S. Attorney Adrian W. Maher, charging the paste was mislabeled. According to the warrant, claims made on packaging and on a circular accompanying each tube were misleading. Those claims pertained to the supposed healing properties of the dentifrice for gum infections.[1]

Later in 1949 the Federal Trade Commission (FTC) ordered the Bristol-Myers Company of New York to discontinue certain alleged misrepresentations as to the therapeutic value of Ipana toothpaste and the extent to which it was used or recommended by dentists. The order required the company to stop advertising that the use of Ipana with massage would prevent "pink tooth brush," that the toothpaste had any therapeutic value in the treatment of mouth, tooth, or gum diseases, or that massage with Ipana stimulated circulation in the gums or prevented gum trouble. A further requirement was that Bristol-Myers discontinue advertising claims that Ipana was used personally by twice as many American dentists or recommended by more of them to their patients than any other two dentifrices combined.[2]

During the late 1950s the issue received more government attention when hearings were held before a U.S. House Government Operations subcommittee on legal and monetary affairs. At a hearing in July 1958 the ADA said some major toothpaste makers were endangering the health of millions of people with false paste advertising and the group urged Congress to make the manufacturers prove the "reckless claims" rather than leave it to the government to disprove them. One ADA witness before the subcommittee, Dr. Sholom Pearlman, secretary of the ADA's Council on Dental Therapeutics, said using toothpaste to remedy bad breath was in many cases "like using perfume when you need a bath." Pearlman told the committee the ADA was unaware of any scientific evidence to back the advertised therapeutic claims for Super Ammi-dent with fluoride, Crest toothpaste with fluroistan, Gleem with GL-70, Ipana with WD-9, Brisk fluoride, Colgate with Gardol, and Stripe with hexachlorophene. He called them all misleading. Procter & Gamble (maker of Gleem) issued a statement to the effect there was nothing misleading about the Gleem ads. Several ADA members referred to toothpaste as a cosmetic and that reliance on those false claims could result in neglect of the teeth and the later possible emergence of serious problems. "The brushing is what counts," Pearlman told the hearing, with the dentifrice being "only an aid to the toothbrush." He showed the U.S. representatives a Gleem ad depicting a happy family eating outdoors and advising that Gleem will protect teeth with only one brushing a day if you could not use it after each meal. Pearlman called that ad "misleading and deceptive" and accused the ad of promoting the breakdown of important oral health habits. A Procter & Gamble spokesman countered, "There is no question about the validity of these claims." One Super Amm-i-dent ad proclaimed "test after test by dentists" proved it worked in decay prevention yet Pearlman observed the ADA did not know of a single test by even one dentist that had been made on the product's alleged decay-fighting properties.[3]

That House Government Operations subcommittee was investigating cigarette and toothpaste advertising with committee chairman, Representative John A. Blatnik (D-Minn.), charging the tobacco and dentifrice industries were flooding the nation "with bunk and junk" about their products. At the hearing was FTC chairman John W. Gwynne who promised the FTC would crack down if Congress would provide money to do the job. Blatnik showed Gwynne an ad for Super Amm-i-dent toothpaste that stated "Saves your teeth from decay" and "Test after test by dentists proved it." Describing that ad as "a flat lie" Blatnik told Gwynne what the ADA's Pearlman said about it and wanted to know why the FTC could not prevent that sort of thing. Gwynne replied the FTC would have to prove with clinical tests that the Amm-i-dent claims were untrue. He suggested that if the ADA had any such proof it should submit it to the FTC.[4]

Members of the ADA urged the House subcommittee to enact legislation that would permit federal agencies to control "reckless claims in advertising." Dr. Ralph Creig, a member of the ADA's council on legislation, told the subcommittee, "The burden of demonstrating the validity of therapeutic claims in advertising belongs morally, ethically and logically with the party asserting them. The current concept that such claims must be considered true and unchallengeable until disproved by the public is fallacious and demonstrably ineffective." Also, he felt it was hopeless to expect the FTC with its small staff and limited resources to evaluate the claims for thousands of proprietary drugs then being marketed. Pearlman attacked one by one claims made for various toothpastes — Brisk (Colgate), Crest (P&G; results were not yet sufficient to back up its claims), Gleem (P&G), Ipana (B-M), Colgate with Gardol, Pepsodent (Lever Brothers), and Stripe (Lever Brothers). Gwynne recalled that three times in the previous 10 years the FTC had considered a trade practice conference for the dentifrice industry (to try and impose order and/or regulation through voluntary consensus and compliance) but each time the idea was abandoned "by reasons of industry opposition and the diversity of expert scientific opinion."[5]

In August 1958 the House Government Operations subcommittee, in a report based on its hearings, stated the FTC had failed in its duty to halt the false advertising of toothpaste. According to the subcommittee some $25 million was spent in 1957 to advertise the 12 largest toothpaste brands and that the three main advertising themes then used in paste ads were untrue and lulled people into an unwarranted sense of security. Those three themes were identified as: stops tooth decay, eliminates bad breath, and needs to be used only once a day.[6]

When he testified at the hearing Dr. Harry Lyons stated, "Within our own time, we have witnessed promotions of therapeutic dentifrices on the alleged merits of peptic digestants, antiseptics, sulphated detergents, wetting agents, urea, ammonium compounds, chlorophyll, antienzymes, and compounds of fluoride." He added, "One after another of these dentifrices has been promoted with unsupported advertising claims of great promise. None has survived the test of time and use." With respect to the makers promoting once-a-day brushing in their ads, Lyons declared, "There are no shortcuts to dental health, and to mislead the public in this regard is to work deliberately against the public welfare."[7]

Dentists continued to agitate for the government to put curbs on those false paste ads. Dr. Paul H. Jeserich, dean of the University of Michigan's School of Dentistry and president-elect of the ADA in November 1959, urged the federal government to curb the "reckless claims" of many of the major dentifrice makers. He noted the history of "miracle dentifrices had been an unhappy one as one after another those products had been promoted with unsupported claims of great promise for preventing dental decay or diseases of the gums. None had lived up to their claims. Jeserich repeated the ADA position that no therapeutic dentifrice on the market did what it said it did. However, Jeserich did pay tribute to dental scientists who had discovered that a trace of fluoride in drinking water supplies was related to a low rate of dental decay.[8]

A week later U.S. secretary of Health, Education and Welfare Arthur S. Flemming declared that dentifrice advertising that was false or misleading did a great disservice to the public by keeping people from seeking proper dental care. He called attention at a news conference to criticism of such ads voiced a few days earlier by Jeserich and remarked that he agreed with those criticisms.[9]

In the following month, December 1959, Jeserich (then ADA president) revealed his group's attack plan for false ads. It called for legislation by Congress permitting federal agencies to eliminate such advertising, and for a code of fair practices to be set up with the cooperation of the FTC or the Food and Drug Administration. A third component called for scientific proof of advertising claims to be submitted to the FTC so the burden of proof would be shifted from the government to the manufacturers. During 1958 the U.S. public spent $230 million on dentifrices.[10]

Around the same time the chairman of the FTC, Earl W. Kintner, asked Arthur Flemming to send him any proof of false and misleading advertising of dentifrices he had. In an interview Kintner made public the text of a letter he had written Flemming. That letter was a reply to the secretary's press release of November 9 that warned against such advertising. Kintner also announced that he was asking for the cooperation of all other federal agencies with experts and testing labs to help him gather evidence against persons deceiving the public with false claims. He named the Bureau of Standards and the Department of Agriculture as two other agencies whose help he would seek. On the basis of expert evidence, contended Kintner, the solution to the problem of false advertising claims by dentifrices was the enforcement of the present law, rather than the enactment of a new law that would put the burden of proof on the advertiser. According to Kintner the FTC had started negotiations with the ADA more than a year earlier, at the conclusion of hearings before the Blatnik subcommittee. Kintner said the FTC had expected the dental association to furnish the expert testimony necessary to prove the complaints against the manufacturers. "But despite our hopeful waiting, little was forthcoming from the association except more criticism of this agency," explained the agency chairman.[11]

In response to the Kintner interview an ADA spokesman said, "I regret to report that, with one or two exceptions, nothing has been done, and the

Now! ONE Brushing With
COLGATE DENTAL CREAM
Removes Up To 85% Of Decay And Odor-Causing Bacteria!

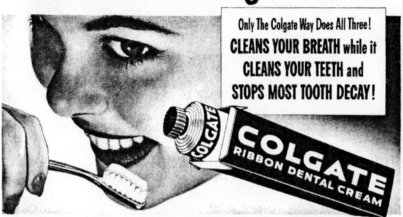

Only The Colgate Way Does All Three!

CLEANS YOUR BREATH while it
CLEANS YOUR TEETH and
STOPS MOST TOOTH DECAY!

Just One Brushing with Colgate's Stops Bad Breath Instantly!

Your very first brushing with Colgate's each morning removes up to 85% of the bacteria that cause bad breath! Yes, scientific tests prove that Colgate Dental Cream stops bad breath in 7 out of 10 cases that originate in the mouth! Every time you brush your teeth with Colgate's you clean your breath while you clean your teeth!

Just One Brushing with Colgate's Removes Up to 85% of Decay-Causing Bacteria!

Every brushing with Colgate Dental Cream removes up to 85% of the bacteria that cause decay. But—if you really want to prevent decay, be sure to follow the Colgate way! Scientific tests showed that the Colgate way of brushing teeth right after eating stopped more decay for more people than ever before reported in all dentifrice history!

Brushing Teeth After Eating Stops Tooth Decay Best!

Scientific tests over a 2-year period showed a startling reduction in tooth decay for those who brushed their teeth with Colgate's right after eating! In fact, X-rays showed no new cavities whatsoever for almost 2 out of 3 people. Yes, the Colgate way of brushing teeth right after eating is the best home method known to help stop tooth decay!

Gives You A Cleaner, Fresher Mouth All Day Long!

A false claim from Colgate in 1953 about removing bacteria while it also slipped a "man-in-white" into part of the ad. No dentifrice ever did anything for bad breath.

public continues to be deceived by the unsupported claims of manufacturers." He added there was no sound reason why advertisers who chose to make representations as to the health benefits of their products should not be called upon to substantiate those representations with scientifically acceptable evidence.[12]

Perhaps stung by criticism directed against itself the FTC lumbered into action and entered the dentifrice advertising field with a complaint near the end of November 1959, charging that Colgate-Palmolive protective shield ads for Colgate with Gardol toothpaste in magazines, newspapers, and on television, fooled the public and hurt competitors. That complaint was issued two weeks after a barrage of criticism was leveled at the agency, especially by the ADA and by Flemming. While Colgate's protective shield television commercials were prominently mentioned in the FTC's announcement, the complaint was concerned with therapeutic claims, rather than television techniques. That complaint was seen as a signal there could be other challenges issued on other dentifrice ads. According to the FTC, Colgate with Gardol "does not completely protect the user from tooth decay or the development of cavities by forming a 'protective shield,' as claimed in the company's advertising." In addition to misleading the public, argued the commission, the ads "unfairly divert trade from competitors and substantially injure competition in violation of the FTC act." Few formal complaints had ever been made in the dentifrice field by the FTC. One complaint was issued in 1943 when the FTC claimed that Forhan's toothpaste statements that the product guarded against gum disease were not accurate. In 1952 a cease-and-desist order was issued against the makers of Forhan's.[13]

Responding to the complaint the Colgate-Palmolive Company of New York denied the FTC charge that it falsely advertised toothpaste and went on to accuse competitors of deceptive claims. While denying any misrepresentations on its part Colgate asserted the claims of its competitors for their dentifrice products "have not been and are not based upon, nor warranted by clinical or laboratory tests and have been and are false, misleading and deceptive." It asked the FTC to dismiss the complaint.[14]

Colgate also charged that its competitors would get an unwarranted advantage if the FTC pressed ahead with the complaint. It denied that its protective shield ads represented or implied complete protection against tooth decay or cavities and, in any case, no good purpose would be served in pursuing the complaint since the company said the protective shield commercials had been permanently discontinued voluntarily by the company at great expense.[15]

An examiner for the FTC ruled, on August 4, 1960, that Colgate-Palmolive had to stop saying that its Colgate with Gardol provided complete protection against tooth decay. Colgate announced it would appeal the ruling. After the formal complaint had been issued the previous November 19 Colgate had discontinued its invisible, protective shield campaign at what it said was a cost of $100,000. Leon R. Gross, the examiner, ruled the invisible protective shield advertising prepared by the Ted Bates & Company ad agency for Colgate had been "a false, misleading and deceptive portrayal of the true properties of Colgate Dental Cream with Gardol." He cited Colgate's television ads in which things such as a coconut or a baseball were thrown or hit toward a person in the foreground of the scene. The objects in the advertising, however, bounced off a transparent glass shield at the last second with the announcer then saying that Colgate with Gardol formed a similar invisible protective barrier around the teeth. Gross rejected Colgate's argument that the FTC charges should be dismissed because it had voluntarily eliminated the invisible shield theme from its advertising after it had been served with the complaint. "The evidence in this record does not support a finding that the respondent will not, in the future, unless restrained by this commission, misrepresent the true properties, and caries-inhibiting value, if any, of Colgate Dental Cream with Gardol," he explained.[16]

On January 4, 1960, the FTC charged four television ads (one was for a dentifrice) used false props to support their ad claims. That represented the first large-scale action by the FTC against purportedly exaggerated advertising claims on television. It issued formal complaints against the makers of the four products and also cited their advertising agencies. In each of the four instances, said the FTC, the demonstration on television did not prove what the announcers said it proved. One complaint was against Lever Brother's Pepsodent toothpaste. Those four complaints stemmed from the intensive monitoring of television begun by a special unit of the commission on November 11, 1959. Three monitors watched commercials all day with one assigned to each network — NBC, CBS, and ABC. Three others watched for misleading advertisements on evening television at home. In the Pepsodent ad, the complaint stated a demonstration of a cigarette-smoking machine's depositing yellow smoke stain on an enamel dinner plate (cleaned off by Pepsodent) did not actually prove that toothpaste was effective in removing tobacco stains from the teeth of all smokers.[17]

Lever Brothers responded by issuing a confusing statement wherein it claimed the FTC did not say Pepsodent would not remove yellow smoke stains, nor did it claim that the television demonstration in any way misrepresented what actually occurred. It only charged that the visual method used to demonstrate that Pepsodent removed smoke stains from teeth did not prove it. Added Lever Brothers, "We are confident that we will be able to prove to the commission's satisfaction that the demonstration used is in all respects appropriate to convey properly Pepsodent's ability to remove yellow smoke stains."[18]

When a two-day hearing was held on the FTC complaint against Pepsodent toothpaste in July 1961 lawyers for Lever Brothers contended that almost any toothpaste could remove smoke stains from teeth or from enamel in general.[19]

FTC hearing examiner Harry Hinkes ruled in February 1962 that Pepsodent did not use deceptive advertising and dismissed the complaint against Pepsodent, Hinkes, in his ruling, declared the television audience was sufficiently sophisticated to realize what Pepsodent meant when it limited its claims to being able to remove yellow stains. Pepsodent defended itself by saying that all along it had only been talking about the ability of the product to remove freshly deposited tobacco stains on the teeth, not a long-accumulated build-up. Yet it used the term "yellow" stains instead of "fresh." Lever Brothers argued "yellow" was the color of freshly deposited stains while brown or even black was the color of the long accumulated build-up and everyone knew the difference between the two and everyone knew that no toothpaste (including Pepsodent) could remove the latter.[20]

Unhappy with the Hinkes ruling the agency submitted it for review by the FTC. On October 17, 1962, by a 3–2 margin, the FTC dismissed charges that Lever Brothers used a deceptive ad for Pepsodent, upholding the Hinkes decision. The majority said only that the 1960 complaint should be dismissed "because of failure of proof." In their dissent the minority said the earlier dismissal was based on a "wholly unrealistic" interpretation of Pepsodent's claims — that most people knew "yellow" (used four times in the 60-second ad) referred to fresh tobacco stains while "brown" meant accumulated stains.[21]

As this period ended a startling change took place in dentifrice advertising when, in August 1960, the ADA officially recognized Crest toothpaste as an effective decay preventive agent. Even some dentists were taken by surprise. And it changed the face of dentifrice advertising and the relationship between that industry and the dentists. But first a return to toothbrushes. Until the summer of 1960 that lowly, low-tech implement was considered by dentists and most others to be the most important item of oral hygiene, far more important than any dentifrice that was placed upon it.

9

Toothbrushes, 1946–2008

Many persons continue to brush their teeth as a ritual or for the aesthetic benefits. And many use toothbrushes well beyond the time when the bristles are worn out. — American Dental Association, 1958.

The toothbrush market is underdeveloped. There could be twice as many toothbrushes sold as there are now. — Anonymous toothbrush maker, 1975.

A survey conducted by two Chicago dentists, Doctors Allen O. Gruebbel and J. M. Wisan, discovered that four out of five of the toothbrushes in use in American families in 1948 were so badly worn or in such an unsanitary condition that they were no longer useful for oral hygiene purposes. A sample of 1,929 U.S. families was selected; they submitted a total of 8,176 toothbrushes to the two dentists. Of those brushes, 1,580 (19.3 percent) were found to be in satisfactory condition, while 6,596 (80.7 percent) were determined to be unsuitable because of bent and broken bristles, matted bristles, unsanitary condition, or a combination of faults. Gruebbel and Wisan concluded that few Americans followed the oral hygiene practices recommended by dentists and "the remedy for this situation can be found only in an aggressive campaign to inform every individual of the value of the frequent use and renewal of the toothbrush." Brushes were sent in as a response to an advertising campaign that offered a free toothbrush in exchange. By that time 80 percent of all toothbrushes were nylon but, reportedly, the argument over natural versus nylon bristles, as to which was better, was still prominent among dentists.[1]

In response to a campaign sponsored by the Du Pont company, in cooperation with the ADA, toothbrushes were sent to Dr. Robert G. Kesel at the University of Illinois College of Dentistry in 1958. Brushes were then classified according to bristle and sanitary condition. A total of 2,032 brushes were sent in; 700 of them were rated usable; 1,219 unusable; 90 were described as doubtful; 23 (1 percent) were not toothbrushes at all but were miscellaneous items such as vegetable cleaning brushes. The largest proportion of unusable brushes were found among the age group 45 to 50; next most likely to be unusable were the brushes of children aged 1 to 5; next, those of 25 to 30 year olds. Boys and girls between 10 and 15 had the highest percentage of usable brushes; 42 percent of women had usable brushes, and 38 percent of men. In the decade between the two surveys the percentage of unusable toothbrushes had dropped from 80 percent to 67 percent. Commented the ADA, "Many persons continue to brush their teeth as a ritual or for the aesthetic benefits. And many use toothbrushes well beyond the time when the bristles are worn out."[2]

When *Consumer Bulletin* evaluated toothbrushes in 1959 it recommended the straight-trimmed, straight-handled brush with a comparatively small brushing surface (one inch to 1.25 inches long, $\frac{5}{16}$ inches to $\frac{3}{8}$ inches wide) with medium textured bristles. Fifteen brands were tested by the organization with six being top rated, or recommended — Dr. West's, 29 cents; Pepsodent, 69 cents, Py-Co-Pay (Pycopay company), 69 cents; Rexall De Luxe, 69 cents (Rexall Drug Company), Tek Deluxe, 69 cents (Johnson & Johnson), Pro Double Duty, 89 cents (Prophylactic) — with an average price of 66 cents. Seven brands were rated as intermediate — Dobson Deluxe, 59 cents (Walgreen); Lactona Multi-Tufted M-39, 69 cents (Lactona); Oral B 40, 75 cents (Oral B company); Arlton, 15 cents (F. W. Woolworth); Dentabest, 10 cents (G. C. Murray company); Tek Short Oval, 29 cents; Dr. West's, 69 cents — with an average price of 46.5 cents. Not recommended were two other brands from Lactona, at 69 cents each. Based on a limited survey of 288 women made by Du Pont a few years earlier, 45 percent of American families had one toothbrush per person while 55 percent had more than one each.[3]

In 1961 annual sales of toothbrushes were estimated at about $64.5 million (retail) while annual sales for dentifrices were $234.8 million (retail). An estimated seven tubes of toothpaste were sold for each brush. Although brush sales were fairly static Colgate-Palmolive had entered the field in 1960 with the result that consumers were presented with what *Printers' Ink* called a bewildering array of choices and "everything from curved, arched or angle contours to natural or nylon bristles to bite-size and other size heads." All major companies then had an 89-cent premium brush, up from the old top price of 69 cents from a few years earlier. Increasingly, drugstores, which once had the bulk of the toothbrush business, were losing out to grocery and supermarket chains. Brush makers saw their main problem as not being one of broadening the base of the market but of getting the present users to buy more brushes with the consensus among the manufacturers being that the American consumer held on to his brush and used it far too long. Most people, reportedly, bought one brush a year while for best results, according to the ADA, they should have bought three or four. Among the advertised brushes the top-seller was thought to be the Dr. West line with second place held by the Pro-phy-lac-tic Brush Company (a subsidiary of Warner Lambert). Actually, though, said *Printers' Ink*, the top seller was from the Fuller Brush organization — a door-to-door operation that did not advertise. Dr. West spent about $1.7 million on toothbrush advertising in 1960, Pro-phy-lac-tic over $500,000. Tek-Hughes (a division of Johnson & Johnson) had a regular line of adult and children's brushes. Py-Co-Pay (from Block Drug Company) had a line of two brushes, 79 cents for nylon bristles, and 89 cents for a natural-bristle product. That company spent $375,000 in 1960 on television ads for its brushes. Pepsodent spent $843,000 on measured media in 1960 on its toothbrush line. Colgate entered the field with a single 89-cent brush. A spokesman for Colgate explained the firm decided to go into the field because "toothbrushes are a natural extension of our efforts to build our image in the oral hygiene field."[4]

Block Drug Company launched a Py-Co-Pay brush with a new shape, in 1962, and promoted it with what

What a peach of an idea! A child's tooth brush with a two-note whistle in the handle! Get one for your youngster today, at your drug counter. Made by the maker of famous Pro-phy-lac-tic Tooth Brushes.

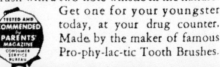

A novelty brush from Pro-phy-lac-tic in 1949.

was said to be the heaviest television ad campaign ever used to advertise a toothbrush. Ads for the new tapered brush proclaimed, "the first anti-cavity design tooth brush, with two cleaning actions your dentist recommends. One — new straight-line design that fights cavities because every bristle reaches every surface. Two — exclusive Py-Co-Pay now comes on a new tapered handle." Television ads went on to say that "more dentists recommend Py-Co-Pay than any other tooth brush." That claim was based on surveys made by Block Drug in which 50 percent of the country's dentists were surveyed each year. In the 1961 survey, 34.3 percent of the dentists queried said they recommended Py-Co-Pay to their patients, while the second most frequently mentioned brand was named by 22.8 percent, according to Block.[5]

With the exception of new brush shapes nothing new had happened in the manual brush field for a long time, not since nylon bristles had replaced natural ones. And marketers seemed to be desperate. Du Pont introduced what it said was a new innovation in manual brushes in 1964, an implement that was said to clean on the surface and between the teeth and to gently massage the gums all at the same time. Bristles in the middle row were slightly longer and stiffer than those in the adjoining rows. They were described as being set in two tiny hinged springs so they would give and move up and down as well as sideways when slight pressure was applied. Du Pont proudly considered its new Denta-Flex toothbrush to be the first significant innovation in non-automatic toothbrushes since the arrival of the nylon bristle.[6]

A 1964 survey done by Dental Survey Publications involved sending a questionnaire covering 18 product groups to a random sample of 5,000 dentists with results based on the answers of the 780 (15.6 percent) who returned the questionnaires. In the category of manual toothbrushes Py-Co-Pay was recommended by 38.8 percent of the respondents, Lactona by 32.8 percent, and Oral B by 27.1 percent of the responding dentists.[7]

Approximately 144 million manual toothbrushes were sold in 1964 for an estimated total of $72 million, the same totals as in 1963. Sales of automatic brushes were expected to be about five million units for $60 million in 1965, plus another $10 million spent for the replacement brushes for those units. The Pepsodent line of manual brushes was thought to be battling it out with Pro-phy-lac-tic for top spot in the manual market. Those two were followed by Tek, Dr. West, Colgate, and Py-Co-Pay. Other brushes in the field were Oral B (from Weco Products, as was Dr. West), Lactona, and Squibb Angle. Admen for companies that produced both manual and automatic toothbrushes felt the manual market had not been, and would not be, affected by the automatic items.[8]

A 1967 survey of Americans' tooth brushing habits was sponsored by

Colgate-Palmolive's Cue toothpaste brand. For that survey every dentist in the nation was contacted and 4,206 responded by questioning all the patients they examined (54,727) on a single, specified day. Of the families with annual incomes estimated at less than $5,000 only 41 percent brushed their teeth twice a day or more often; for families with incomes between $5,000 and $10,000 the figure was 51 percent; and in families with incomes over $10,000, 63 percent brushed twice a day or more often. For households with a grade school education the figure was 35 percent; 48 percent for high school; 65 percent for college-educated. A regional breakdown indicated 50 percent of households in the Central U.S. brushed twice or more a day, 52 percent in the West and 55 percent in both the South and the East. Among children, 34 percent of those under seven brushed twice a day or more frequently, 40 percent of those aged seven to 12 and 50 percent of those aged 13 to 18.[9]

Consumer publication *Changing Times* published a vague guide to choosing a toothbrush in 1971, although

Get a new Tek 29¢

NEW no-slip grip! NEW sleek tapered handle!

No better brush at any price

1953.

no brand name was mentioned. It gave no preference for nylon over natural bristles and said size and shape were mostly personal preferences but then cited the ADA's long-standing recommendation for the head of a brush for general adult usage, "the straight-trimmed, straight-handled brush with comparatively small 1" to 1¼" long, ⁵⁄₁₆" to ⅜" wide brushing surface." For texture choice the article opted for the safe choice of medium. Also, it cited one estimate that Americans on average still bought only one toothbrush a year. *Changing Times* recommended having two brushes so the user could alternate them when one was still too moist to be reused, and to replace brushes every two to three months.[10]

Somewhat earlier, in 1960, a study by N. J. Dudding suggested that a substantial proportion of the population objected to brushing their teeth without a dentifrice. That study was prompted by an initial attempt to test the anti-decay effects of good toothbrushing technique in the absence of a dentifrice. It was found that those subjects selected to brush daily with no dentifrice would not take part in the study for more than six weeks. The significance of that behavior was considered worthy of a follow-up, which was done in 1971. Students were asked to participate in a comparison of brushing with water as against brushing with a paste or powder dentifrice. Fifty subjects consented after about 280 had been asked. By the end of 14 days, 38 percent of the subjects using toothbrush and water refused to continue in the study if they had to refrain from using a dentifrice. That figure was 46 percent at the end of five weeks. An additional 40 percent of the subjects expressed a dislike for using no dentifrice; only four percent of the subjects favored water-brushing. When subjects used the equivalent of a home-made preparation, a salt and soda powder, 20 percent withdrew from the study and an additional 31 percent expressed a dislike for using the mixture. At the end of the five-week period only 5 percent of those using a paste dentifrice had withdrawn.[11]

The FTC and Chemway Corporation settled their dispute over ads for Dr. West's Germ Fighter toothbrush with a consent order in 1971 that omitted the FTC's original demand for corrective ads. The settlement required Chemway to notify each direct customer that he could exchange remaining inventories of Germ Fighter brushes treated with phenylmercuric acetate for untreated brushes. Compared to that was the order proposed by the FTC late in 1970 that would have prohibited Chemway from advertising any toothbrushes for one year unless 25 percent of the space or time of the advertisement consisted of a disclosure that previous advertisements for the Germ Fighter were false. According to the agency the chemicals in the Germ Fighter brush had no medical significance in killing germs likely to cause infectious mouth conditions. Also, the settlement prohibited Chemway from using any dangerous substances in toothbrushes or making any therapeutic claims unless it could show it had adequate and controlled studies showing the product did not endanger users.[12]

A spokesman for a major toothbrush maker remarked in 1975, "The toothbrush market is slipping away from drug stores — and it's their own fault" while another said, "The toothbrush market is underdeveloped. There could be twice as many toothbrushes sold as there are now." According to the trade publication *American Druggist* the drugstore share of the toothbrush market had decreased from 51 percent in 1969 to less than 45 percent in 1974. One reason for the decline was because many other types of retail outlets were handling brushes but the publication believed the main reason drugstores were losing out was because they were not being aggressive enough in displaying and promoting toothbrushes. That, despite the fact drugstores were felt to be ideal outlets since customers could receive professional advice on oral hygiene, and brushes, from a pharmacist. Toothbrushes were described as good items to handle since the gross margins of 40 percent to 60 percent were higher than for just about anything else. Remarked a spokesman for brush maker Oral B, agreeing with most in the field who considered toothbrushes to generally be impulse buys, "Unless the customer is specifically coming from the dentist I can't think of a toothbrush as a planned purchase — unless someone has just lost his toothbrush." *American Druggist* argued that toothbrushes should be used only once every 24 hours, should be rinsed after each use to remove bacteria, should be replaced every three months, and that flossing was a necessary adjunct to brushing. According to the publication retail sales of toothbrushes, in millions of dollars, were as follows: 1968, $66.3 (of which $33.9 was drug store volume); 1969, $70.1 ($35.9); 1970, $73.4 ($37.1); 1971, $77.8 ($38.2); 1972, $82.4 ($39.4); 1973, $88.2 ($40.5); 1974, $92.6 ($41.5).[13]

Replacement of worn brushes remained a sore spot with the industry. Richard Hyman, vice president of Iowa City–based Owens Brush Company, believed, in 1982, that about two-thirds of the toothbrushes in use at any one time were in need of replacement with that failure to replace not based on price — the range was then generally 79 cents to $1.89. "It's a matter of gradual wear, " said Hyman. "When you get a hole in your shoe, you fix it. When your razor's dull, it's terrible. But your toothbrush wears so gradually you're not conscious of it." The result of such a long, slow wearing-away process was that consumers replaced toothbrushes only 1.3 times a year, according to Hyman's data, despite the fact the industry urged replacement be done every three to four months. With the toothbrush market then at $170 million in

annual sales at retail, the industry could only mourn the market was not three times higher, where it would be if consumers replaced their brushes in accordance with industry recommendations.[14]

Reporter Jennifer Alter reasoned that advertising would be the logical way to inform the public of the importance of replacement but then observed that most companies did not do much brush advertising anyway. In 1981, $10.2 million was spent in support of tooth-brushes, more than half of that came from Johnson & Johnson. Top-selling brushes were then, in order, Reach (Johnson & Johnson), Oral B (Cooper Laboratories), and Pepsodent (Lever Brothers). In Alter's view the ADA was then less interested in toothbrushes than it was in toothpastes. Said an ADA spokesman, "We are not involved in helping the toothbrush industry market its products, except in the sense that we encourage consumers to brush their teeth and periodically buy a new tooth-

A combination offer in 1955 to buy a brush and paste.

brush." One toothbrush marketer who did not advertise explained, "The market itself is fairly small and it really doesn't warrant a high level of advertising." Introduced nationally in 1978 by Johnson & Johnson, the angled Reach brush was soon joined by Reach Plus and in 1982 by the Reach Child Brush. Lever Brothers launched DX, a brush with slanted bristles in 1981, supported with a $3 million campaign, but by late 1982 the brand was no longer being advertised. One reason for less advertising of brushes was that many of the makers concentrated more on getting the aid of dentists in marketing toothbrushes. Dentists regularly gave brushes away to their patients, or sold them cheaply, and could buy those brushes direct from the maker, usually in the range of $3.50 per dozen.[15]

A study done in 1987 by dentist Dr. Richard T. Glass, chairman of the department of oral pathology at the University of Oklahoma College of Dentistry in Oklahoma City, was a throwback to the 1910s and 1920s and was right in keeping with those times. He claimed toothbrushes harbored bacteria that could prolong sore throats and other oral infections. And a warm steamy bathroom was the perfect environment for the growth of those organisms. Besides removing your brush from the bathroom he recommended starting a new toothbrush every two weeks, since it took less than three weeks for bacteria to heavily infect the bristles. But he conceded that was not likely to happen because "the average person gets very attached to his or her toothbrush." Glass's conclusions were based on a pilot investigation of 30 brushes: 10 used by people with healthy mouths; 10 belonged to patients with oral disease; and 10 pre-packaged, unused implements. Reportedly, not only did he discover bacteria on all the used toothbrushes but, more alarmingly, on four of the brand new toothbrushes as well. Although the idea that toothbrushes were unsanitary and caused all sorts of health problems had once been popular and believed — with some justification at the time — it was an idea that had been discredited and dead for some 60 years prior to the Glass study. Despite that, a few media outlets featured the story.[16]

When journalist David Born examined the oral hygiene sections at full service drug stores in 1987 he remarked that a customer would find at least five or six different brands of manual brushes, each with a choice between hard, medium or soft bristles; child, junior, or adult sizes; three, four, or even five rows of tufts; six to eight colors; at least that many shapes, and also two or three electric brushes. If you were like many people you would not even bother to choose, he thought: "You'll wait until your next dental visit and hope for a free toothbrush, trusting that he or she will pick the right one for you." Born declared that 90 percent of all brushes sold in the U.S. had nylon bristles with just 10 percent having natural (hog) bristles, and that a toothbrush lost its effectiveness after only three to five weeks of use. In picking a brush dentists were said to favor soft or medium soft implements, bristle tufts of equal height, and for adult brushes to have six to 10 tufts in each of three to four rows. Born argued that a thorough brushing should take between two and three minutes.[17]

With a bewildering array of choices in toothbrushes available in retail outlets *Consumer Reports'* dental consultants could offer no advice in 1989 except to say they believed any brush could be as effective as any other if used conscientiously. At the same time the ADA said, despite the myriad of claims made by brush marketers, no specific toothbrush could then be recommended as superior for removing dental plaque. Three years later *Consumer Reports* reported on some of the ad claims made by toothbrush manufacturers. Viadent's Jordan V declared the handle was "like [a] dental instrument" while on the AquaFresh Flex implement the flexible neck worked like a "shock absorber" to reduce pressure and to "prevent gum disease." Copy for the Colgate Plus brush said it "works like a dental tool to fight bacterial plaque at home"; the Crest Complete brush stated that "Because teeth aren't flat," its "crinkle-cut" profile allowed it to "get further between teeth."[18]

Of 500 people surveyed in a study sponsored by brush maker Oral B in 1992, 97 percent said they would not borrow someone else's toothbrush if they forgot to bring their own on an overnight trip. Fifty-five percent of those surveyed admitted they left the water running when brushing their teeth. In other trivia matters it was found by this survey that the leading choice of brush color was blue (23 percent) followed by red (20 percent) and yellow (16 percent); least popular colors were purple and pink (5 percent each). Forty-seven percent of respondents said they used their old toothbrushes as household cleaning tools.[19]

Sales of toothbrushes were estimated at $620 million for 1993 with more and more makers getting involved with more and more different models, special grips, special bristle arrangement and configuration, fancier colors, and brushes that changed color. Dep Corporation introduced one in the summer of 1992 (the firm's first brush) that changed color when held for two minutes, about the time it took for a recommended proper brushing—and that was the point; it was a reminder. Colgate-Palmolive had introduced Colgate Precision in 1992 as a premium-priced implement and launched three other new brushes in 1993. Reportedly Colgate spent $6.1 million on the promotion of its brushes in 1992. According to business reporter Pat Sloan the top 10 toothbrush sellers were as follows: Oral-B, 20.0 percent; Reach, 16.4 percent; Crest Complete, 15.8 percent; Colgate Plus, 15.5 percent; Private Label, 6.3 percent; Colgate Precision, 5.6 percent; Aqua-Fresh Flex, 5.2 percent; Butler,

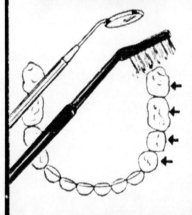

4 out of 5 CAVITIES

STRIKE YOUR

BACK TEETH

PROTECT your teeth by careful brushing with the brush that's bent like your dentist's mirror to reach those hard-to-get-at places.

SQUIBB ANGLE

TOOTHBRUSH

LOOK FOR IT AT YOUR DRUGSTORE

A 1955 ad that stressed the brush head angle.

3.9 percent; Colgate, 2.1 percent; Pepsodent, 1.5 percent; and all others, 7.7 percent.[20]

Around the same time reporter Trish Hall remarked that dozens of new models had turned up in stores in the previous 18 months, many with curved or twisted handles. She thought they were aimed at the growing number of people who had reached their 30s and 40s, the age when gum disease began to strike and keeping gums intact was more of a challenge than keeping cavities at bay. Many of those new brushes promised to do more than keep teeth clean; to brush under the gum line and between the teeth where plaque lurked. Advertising for toothbrushes reached $59 million in 1992 while total toothbrush sales that year amounted to $560 million in 1992, according to Hall. Replacement recommendation remained at an advised three to four months but Americans bought on average just 1.8 toothbrushes per year; Japanese consumers complied with 3.1 purchases per person per year. Procter & Gamble entered the brush market for the first time in 1992 when it launched the brand Crest Complete. Colgate started selling its Precision brand in October 1992, contending that it did a better job of removing plaque because the bristles were at different heights and were arranged in rows of varying densities.[21]

When Maryanne Thumser did an advice piece on how to pick a toothbrush, for *Good Housekeeping* in 1995, she suggested the softer the bristles the better. As for size, she recommended a brush that covered three to four of your teeth when you set it against them. "Stick to the old-fashioned straight handle. Curved and angled handles may look jazzier, but they're unnecessary," she added. Thumser was also partial to flat-head bristles and heads that tapered in width toward the top (diamond or boat shaped). While she recommended a brushing last for two minutes she admitted that most people spent 30 seconds or less on each brushing.[22]

McCall's did a small advice piece that same year, mentioning the days of "the bland, boring toothbrush are over. You can now buy brushes that bend, buzz and even change color when it's time to toss them out."[23]

Pat Sloan reported in 1996 that toothbrush sales were then at $550 million yearly. Two new products out that year, Colgate Plus Ultra Fit Compact Head, and Reach Plaque Sweeper (Johnson & Johnson) were supported with a total of $30 million in promotion. The former brand was said to be aimed at adults and teens with smaller mouths. Leading toothbrush makers then were Oral-B, 22.8 percent; Colgate, 22.2 percent; Johnson & Johnson, 15.5 percent; Crest, 12.8 percent; and SmithKline Beecham's Aqua-Fresh, 5.8 percent. Colgate had introduced Colgate Plus Ultra in 1996 and was expected to spend $40 million in total in 1996 marketing its toothbrushes. Johnson & Johnson was expected to spend $20 million on brush marketing that year.

Steve White, Colgate's toothbrush marketing director, commented, "Super premium toothbrushes and kids toothbrushes are driving category growth. In response to that, Colgate Plus and Colgate Total are introducing line extensions incorporating those benefits that are driving growth."[24]

When someone spoke of the U.S. as being an overly litigious nation he might have had the following in mind. A class action lawsuit was commenced in Chicago in 1999 by Mark Trimarco who alleged that eight toothbrush makers (including Colgate) and the American Dental Association were negligent because they did not warn consumers about toothbrush abrasion. Trimarco declared in the suit that he and "all others similarly situated" were suffering from what the complaint called "a disease known as toothbrush abrasion," which was "a distinct clinical entity caused by toothbrushes of the following bristle types: firm, medium and soft, both natural and synthetic." According to the complaint people suffering from that injury were consumers who were not "informed or warned about the danger of toothbrush abrasion." Moreover, toothbrushes were unsafe and unreasonably dangerous for their intended use in that their packaging contained no warning as to the risks of toothbrush abrasion or instructions on how to brush to avoid the injury. ADA was listed as a defendant because it gave its seal of approval to the brushes of the makers named in the suit. More than a year later, in July 2000, Trimarco's third amended complaint was dismissed by the Cook County (Illinois) Circuit Court. ADA general counsel Peter M. Sfikas commented, "The court dismissed the case when it became apparent that the plaintiffs lacked a sound theory for their claim."[25]

For the year 2000 toothbrush sales were estimated to be $1.2 billion.[26]

In a 2003 survey conducted by the Massachusetts Institute of Technology, adults and children were asked which invention they could not live without. And it was the venerable toothbrush that emerged as the number one invention in the opinion of those surveyed; the invention Americans could least live without. Closely behind, in the number two position, was the automobile.[27]

According to a 2005 Japanese study people who brushed their teeth more often stayed slimmer. In a survey of the everyday habits of nearly 14,000 people whose average age was in the mid 40s, Dr. Takashi Wada, a Tokyo university professor, found that people who managed to stay slim tended to brush their teeth after every meal. In America, around that time, dentists were recommending people brush their teeth twice a day, for a maximum of two minutes each time. However, people where also advised not to brush for more than three minutes at a time as excessive abrasion could damage the teeth or gums.[28]

Data collected in Chicago from more than 400 dentists just in advance of the Chicago Dental Society's 141st annual midwinter meeting revealed that only 30 percent of the surveyed dentists continued to use a conventional, manual toothbrush on their own teeth, down from the 60 percent registered two years earlier in 2004. It was, of course, the electric toothbrush that drove the numbers down.[29]

The old idea that the toothbrush, harboring as it did various micro-organisms, was little removed from an instrument of death surfaced once again in recent times. A popular medical journal wondered in print in 2003 if a person's toothbrush could be making that person sick, before replying to its own query, "probably not." The piece went on to say that experts at the American Dental Association declared that while toothbrushes might harbor potentially harmful bacteria after a person recovered from a cold or other infectious diseases, the organization stated the detergents found in almost all toothpastes killed the micro-organisms that might linger on the brush between brushings. Still, the association continued to recommend that toothbrushes be replaced every three to four months or sooner if the bristles became worn. An American Dental Association seal of acceptance could be found on worthy toothbrushes.[30]

Despite such assurances, this time around the idea of a killer toothbrush gave rise to a new product. A Mr. Pinsky was the founder of Violight, a company based in Hartsdale, New York, that made a toothbrush sanitizer — a cup-sized device retailing for $49.95 in 2005 that used ultraviolet light to sterilize toothbrushes. A 10-minute exposure to the light was deemed sufficient; such light was also used to sterilize hospital instruments. "Toothbrushes carry various organisms in the bathroom environment. When you flush the toilet, the spew lands on it, even though you can't see it," said Pinsky. When he first thought about marketing such a device, back in 2002, he started to talk to people about their toothbrush care. Though he found several people who either immersed their brushes in Listerine or gave them time in the dishwasher, most people did not give the issue of toothbrush care much thought.[31]

Within a few months it was reported that at least three manufacturers of toothbrush sterilizers had items on the market. A business reporter by the name of Robert Davis observed that many scientists said there was no evidence that toothbrushes transmitted disease and that brush sanitizers were unnecessary if a brush was handled and stored properly. However, Davis added, "If you want to go further and buy a toothbrush sanitizer it can't hurt. But don't swallow the hype that it's necessary to stay healthy."[32]

At the beginning of 2008 a piece in a trade journal argued there was a growing realization that washing a toothbrush with hot water was not enough to rid it of bacteria and that fact had given rise to a new market segment, a niche market in toothbrush sanitizers. It was also observed that it all happened at the right time for a product category in dire need of innovation. One battery-powered sanitizer, from Violight, had a suggested retail price of $20. Reportedly, it used a 10-minute dose of the light to remove up to 99.9 percent of the micro-organisms that accumulated on a brush between uses. Other manufacturers were active in that market and had created a variety of low-tech and high-tech devices to tame the killer toothbrush.[33]

Writing at the very end of 2008, journalist Eddy Ramirez delivered another warning about the fact that toothbrushes could become infected with bacteria, with attribution being from the American Dental Association. That was apparently a twisting of their position in which they acknowledged bacteria was found on the brushes but stated, also, that it was no problem. Ramirez then summarized some of the things people could do to keep a toothbrush clean over its ADA recommended life span of three to four months. Some people, it was said, advised running the toothbrush through a microwave oven on high for 10 seconds to kill germs while other sources recommended running the brush through a dishwasher. However, the association cautioned that either of those two methods could damage a toothbrush. Ramirez declared that a better way of caring for a toothbrush was to use sanitizers. But, he added, "There is no need to be paranoid. Studies haven't confirmed that the bacteria that grow in a toothbrush are harmful to your health." Despite the ADA's consistent recommendation to get a new toothbrush every three to four months most people changed their brushes less frequently, and often much less frequently. To assist the public the makers of Oral-B, one of the leading brands of toothbrushes, had products featuring bristles that faded or changed color to indicate it was time to replace the toothbrush.[34]

As of 2005 the toymaker Hasbro, Inc., had been trying for more than six years to find a use for its invention of a pea-sized device that transmitted sound through enamel and bone. At first, the firm tried marketing the technology in a lollipop that, when sucked, would play a catchy tune. But parents balked at the $10 price tag and the product was discontinued. Unwilling to give up, Hasbro considered items such as forks and spoons that would play a song in the mouth but none of those ideas made it out of the lab. So, in 2005, Hasbro had a musical toothbrush that rendered a recorded riff from a pop star that lasted two minutes exactly — precisely the amount of time dentists recommended a person should spend brushing their teeth. Hasbro liked the idea because It was generally believed children did not spend the recommended amount of time brushing and thus the new item would appeal to parents who would buy it to ensure their children brushed longer. Calling its new product Tooth Tunes, Hasbro was then in talks with major recording artists and labels to acquire songs. The two-minute recording was stored on a microchip no bigger than the dot on top of the letter i. Pushing a button on the brush caused a minicomputer to start playing the song. Sound waves were transported through the transducer to the front teeth, traveling from there to the jawbone and then to the inner ear. Music produced by Tooth Tunes was said to be, for the user, a cross between the sound of music coming out of a stereo speaker and the sound of humming to oneself. The transducer's sound waves did not travel efficiently through air, so someone standing near the person brushing heard only a hum, similar to the sound of a Walkman in use on a fellow passenger in a train. As envisioned then, each Tooth Tunes brush would come with just one song. When the brush wore out, the whole brush had to be replaced at a cost of another $10. Hasbro planned to launch Tooth Tunes in late summer of 2005, in time for the start of the new school year. Reportedly, retailers were interested. CVS Corporation, the nation's largest pharmacy chain then sold 116 different types of toothbrushes, including 88 manual models and 28 battery-powered items.[35]

Unexplained problems apparently surfaced because Hasbro, at the very end of 2005, announced Tooth Tunes would launch in the spring of 2006. But by then there was another competitor. OraWave announced in 2005 its Tuned Musical 2-Minute TwinSpin. It played one of eight short tunes through a handle speaker after the user reached the two-minute mark in brushing as a reward for proper brushing. It was a product aimed solely at children. Late in 2006 OraWave expected to introduce the $35 Tuned Musical MP3 Twin-Spin, which would download songs into the toothbrush handle through a water-protected USB port.[36]

Finally, in the fall of 2006, came from Tiger Electronics (a division of Hasbro) the $10 manual, musical toothbrush. According to reporter Warren Buckleitner, who tried one of the devices, "The feeling is a bit eerie. The sound is transferred through the brush tip, into the teeth, and right into the inner ear, so you feel the music. Because volume is related to pressure, you can turn up the volume by applying steady pressure to your teeth. Unfortunately, you can also hear better when not brushing, which children can soon learn." As of the spring of 2007 Tooth Tunes were being sold nationwide in stores or at www.toothtunes.com. Those brushes featured 17 artists including the Black Eyed Peas, Hilary Duff, and Kiss. There was even a brush that played *Y.M.C.A.* (Village People). Supposedly, the switch on the brush was "slime-proof" and batteries that provided power for up to six months were included. When the batteries ran out the item had to be thrown away.[37]

The toothbrush was described as a mature market, that is, one in which everybody already had one or more. It made increasing market share a difficult matter for a manufacturer. All that was left was so-called innovation. In the five years leading up to the end of 2007, Colgate had launched a total of 14 manual toothbrushes. Oral-B typically introduced one electronic brush a year, the result of the work of more than 300 designers and engineers over three to five years. Said Timothy Dowd, a senior analyst with the research firm Packaged Facts, "This rush for innovation is all madness. If you didn't have product innovation the market would rise or fall with the population because everybody brushes his or her teeth." Stephen Wilcox, a principal at Design Science Consulting in Philadelphia remarked, "The toothbrush has been around forever. We've quit improving it. Now we're just competing for the consumer's attention, so we're seeing a lot of mindless tweaking." Despite makers' claims their toothbrushes offered superior cleaning there were relatively few large, well-controlled studies demonstrating a clear advantage for one brush over another. How methodically a person brushed was far more important than the brush he or she used, most experts agreed. "A meticulous brusher can remove plaque with a bit of wood as well as with a state-of-the-art toothbrush," commented Dr. Susan Karabin, a periodontist in Manhattan.[38]

For the 52 weeks ending November 4, 2007, sales of manual toothbrushes through the mass market (drugstores, supermarkets, and discount stores — except Wal-Mart Stores) totaled $501,755,100 from unit sales of 187,783,200. In drugstores only the totals were $166,150,800 from 58,640,650 units. Top three selling models (drug stores) were: Oral-B Pulsar, $15,642,690 (9.41 percent); Oral-B Indicator, $13,762,120 (8.28 percent); Colgate 360, $12,100,160 (7.28 percent). Of the remaining seven models from the top 10, five more were Oral-B (Procter and Gamble) models.[39]

Given the low-tech nature of the toothbrush and its relatively inexpensive price it was inevitable that the industry would push for something much more expensive. And so the electric toothbrush arrived.

10

Electric Toothbrushes, 1940s–2008

[The electric toothbrush] will become one of the most widely accepted consumer products in the American household.—Advertising Age, 1964.

The toothbrush is a clear example of a product where the machine has failed to replace the hand tool.—Stores, 1995.

Electric toothbrushes did not arrive to stay until the early 1960s, but a few earlier efforts to electrify the brush had taken place. An account in *Scientific American* in 1921 told of a new invention — an electric toothbrush that could be attached to any bathroom wall and driven from any lamp socket. The apparatus was described as 6.5 inches wide and 8.5 inches long.[1]

Motodent, Inc., of Los Angeles launched a magazine campaign in 1937 for an electric toothbrush to retail at $10 for the basic unit, with individual cleaning arms, separately numbered (one for each family member) priced at $1.50 each, including brush. Replacement brushes cost 50 cents each.[2]

Electric Motor Corporation (EMC) of Racine, Wisconsin, was promoting its electric toothbrush, Toothmaster, in 1941. *Business Week* commented, "Electric toothbrushes have been invented by the dozen, tried out — and forgotten." But until that time, explained the piece, none had advertised in major media outlets as Toothmaster was then doing. From December 1940 to March 1941 some 1,200 Toothmasters had reportedly been sold to people who tore the coupon out of magazines and mailed it to Racine with $7.50. Major retailers were said to then be starting to stock the item. Toothmaster was developed by Dr. R. L. Lasater, a dentist in Chicago's prosperous North Shore. He designed it not for cleaning teeth but specifically as an instrument for massaging the gums of his patients after cleaning up their pyorrhea with a course of office treatments. Then Lasater turned the manufacture over to a small shop in Racine (EMC). Electric Motor was trying both sales appeals in its promotion — pyorrhea prophylaxis and easy brushing with the usual dentifrice. The apparatus was described as looking much like an electric shaver with a toothbrush attachment (for cleaning teeth) and a rubber-pronged device of the same approximate shape (for gum massage).[3]

None of the above-mentioned items, of course, lasted very long but the device arrived for good in April 1961 when E. R. Squibb & Sons (a division of Olin Mathieson) brought out a plug-in brush named Broxodent (brox was German for brush, oxo was Greek for electricity, dent was a derivation of the Latin word for tooth). General Electric (GE) announced in the summer of 1961 that it would shortly market a cordless, battery-operated electric brush. Squibb had chosen to introduce Broxodent through trade and medical journals (that is, not promoted directly to consumers through the mass media) so that those who might balk at putting something electric in their mouth might hear about Broxodent first from their dentists. Both Squibb and GE had by then applied to the American Dental Association for an endorsement of their products. A competitor of both, noting that if such endorsements should happen the whole industry might benefit from the publicity, commented, "The ADA has made a lot of noise in Crest's behalf; it's about time they did something for toothbrushes."[4]

In doing tests for an upcoming report on electric toothbrushes *Consumer Reports* came across one brand in 1962, Vibra-Dent (made by Chase Manufacturing Company of New York City), which presented a potentially lethal shock hazard. It had been on sale less than two months when *Consumer Reports* discovered its fault. It was so constructed that if it were accidentally dropped into a basin of water anyone attempting to retrieve it might be electrocuted if he were touching a ground at the same time (for example, a faucet, or a water-splashed floor). In view of the seriousness of the situation, *Consumer Reports* informed the U.S. Food and Drug Administration (FDA) and Chase of its findings and then issued a public warning in the form of a news release. However, "Most of the press withheld any mention whatsoever of *Consumer Reports*'s warnings," complained *Consumer Reports*. A week or so later Chase informed *Consumer Reports* it was redesigning Vibra-Dent to eliminate the hazard. Although the FDA began an investigation of the incident, *Consumer Reports* found the old Vibra-Dent still on the market. According to Chase, its production had been halted but, noted *Consumer Reports*, its sale was still being promoted as a cut-price feature in a number of chain drugstores.[5]

When GE introduced its brush late in 1961 it was a time when a conventional toothbrush could be had for 50 cents while GE marketers had to figure out how to sell one for the high price of $19.95. Work on the item began in GE labs three to four years earlier. Powered brushes had been sold, with varying success, for some 30 years, observed advertising trade journal *Printers' Ink*, and while at least two then current makes had been on the market longer than General Electric's, the latter's implement seemed to be the only one ever powered by a rechargeable nickel-cadmium battery. Others had used flashlight batteries or had been powered directly by an electric cord. Several GE laboratory models were produced before the final one was chosen, some with cords. Fully charged the brush provided 15 two-minute brushings. Various motions were tried in the lab for the brush with a controlled back-and-forth motion selected as the best, with a speed of 2,000 strokes a minute — 33 a second, each 3/16 of an inch long. Four snap-in brushes came with a unit, each colored differently. In tests done by GE the electric brush was said to have removed 20 percent more food debris than was done by manual brushing. The name chosen for the product was the General Electric Cordless Automatic Toothbrush. Test marketing began in Chicago in October 1961, backed by a press conference and newspaper and television ads as well as by a mailing to dentists. Next came an introduction of the product into the New York metropolitan area in March 1962, which included department store demonstrations. Soon thereafter the General Electric Cordless Automatic Toothbrush went into national distribution.[6]

Three months after its first report on the problem with the Chase product *Consumer Reports* noted that despite repeatedly being informed by Chase that its product would be promptly altered for safety, the firm continued to market the hazardous model. Then, early in June 1962 an appearance change was found in the samples on retail counters in New York City when it was found that a plastic head had replaced the old metal one. But the alteration was not meaningful, declared *Consumer Reports*, and "The plastic-headed version was just as dangerous as its predecessor." Even after the FDA, alerted by *Consumer Reports*, had seized the product in New Orleans as misbranded because its label failed to warn users of the potential danger, the essentially unaltered Vibra-Dent continued to be sold with its sales no doubt helped, believed *Consumer Reports*, by a full-page ad in *Life* magazine just before the seizure, but some six weeks after *Consumer Reports* had issued its public warning. Besides *Life*, two other magazines, *Parents*, and *Good Housekeeping*, were to carry full-page ads in their June 1962 issues. However, those ads did not appear as both magazines rejected the ads. *Good Housekeeping* stated specifically that its rejection was due to the fact the product was unsatisfactory.[7]

As a recent mechanical innovation, the electric toothbrush prompted one reader of *Consumer Reports* to write, "For the average family the electric can opener is silly enough, but the electric toothbrush is stupidity on such a magnitude that it reflects a new all-time low in the intelligence level of our American way of life." Many were said to be worried that a whirling, motor-driven brush pressed against the teeth and gums might harm the surfaces of the teeth and lacerate gum tissue. As to the value of electric toothbrushes, reported *Consumer Reports*, the consensus of dentists seemed to be that an attitude of hopeful waiting was called for. *Consumer Reports* looked at five brands but ran tests on only the two brands it found to be safe. They were both rated acceptable; the GE at $19.95 (though heavily discounted with as much as $5 or $6 off that list price), and Broxodent at $19.75. Those prices were considered to be high, by *Consumer Reports*. All three of the remaining brands were judged to be not acceptable — Vibra-Dent with its potential lethal shock hazard; Riam (made by Riam Ltd., a division of Pinco Inc., Chicago, $9.95) because of the possibility of gum and lip irritation (reported by some test users) and considered not suitable as a substitute for manual brushing; and Toothmaster Model V (the Toothmaster Company, Racine, Wisconsin) sold largely through dental supply houses. It did not meet *Consumer Reports*'s electrical safety requirements for an appliance of that type but was described as presenting a far less serious hazard than the one from the Vibra-Dent.[8]

Entrants in this new field continued to mount as *Advertising Age* reported three newcomers in the fall of 1962. Chemway Corporation introduced its Dr. West's automatic toothbrush priced at $19.95 with an ad copy theme that proclaimed "now your teeth can feel dentist-clean every day," with additional copy stress on the safety of the battery-operated unit. Several exclusive attachments were available with the Chemway brush; a gum massager, a tooth polisher, and a stain remover. Another entry came from Landers, Frary & Clark (subsidiary of J. B. Williams Company), who announced their Universal Handy Hannah automatic toothbrush with a suggested retail price of $19.95. The third new entrant was really a re-entry, the Chase Manufacturing Company (a subsidiary of Ross Products). Chase had replaced the Vibra-Dent with two battery-operated models. One was the Ross automatic toothbrush priced at $7, battery included. The second, called Chase, was sold in a simpler package, without battery, for 50 cents to 75 cents less than the Ross. According to Squibb the sales of its Broxodent continued to do "very well" although *Advertising Age* said GE dominated the market, and one survey conducted in Chicago showed it outselling Squibb by a margin of 10 to one.[9]

Business reporter Goody Solomon, writing in *Barron's* magazine in October 1962, declared that some 250,000 of the automatic devices had been sold since they first came to market nationally early in 1961. Popularity was growing at such a rate that unit sales for 1962 were believed to have the potential to top one million. Until a few months earlier, said Solomon, five firms monopolized the field but seven more companies joined in during the last part of 1962. Enthusiastically, Solomon argued that with an automatic brush the job of correct toothbrushing was done efficiently, without effort, and in 45 seconds, in contrast to the three minutes required for comparable results by the conventional manual method. Squibb had been the first company to achieve nationwide retail distribution — in April 1961 — with its Broxodent (made in Switzerland), after three months of detailing dentists throughout the nation and advertising in professional journals. To that point only two brushes, Broxodent and GE's, had submitted any information at all to the ADA's Council on Dental Therapeutics. Products from other companies ranged in price from $5 to $19.95.[10]

Testament to the growth in the area could be seen when *Consumer Reports* evaluated electric toothbrushes in April 1963, just eight months after its initial look. Fifteen brands were rated in the latter report, compared to five models the first time. Only five of the brands were rated as acceptable; Val-Dent ET-100 (Valco Inc., Chicago, $14.95), Broxodent (Squibb, $19.75), Electra-Dent 200 Model ED-200 (Samson United of New York, $19.95). General Electric 5101 (GE, Ashland, Massachusetts, $19.95), and Universal 7003 (Landers, Frary & Clark, New Britain, Connecticut, $19.95). Most of the new brands ran on batteries (not rechargeable) and most of those 10 brands rated not acceptable were so rated because of power deficiencies such as very short life, stalled easily, and so on. Not acceptable were Brushmaster Model A (Brushmaster, a division of Seaman Industries, Los Angeles, $9.95), Chic 595 (Morris Struhl Inc., Jersey City, New Jersey, $5.95), Dr. West's MK-1 (Chemway Corporation, Wayne, New Jersey, $19.95), Jaguar (National Silver Company, New York City, $7.98 — made in Germany), Rensie (Rensie Import Company, New York City, $9.95 — made in Japan), Riam (Pinco Inc., Chicago, $9.95 — made in Switzerland), Ross Automatic Toothbrush (Chase Manufacturing, $7.98 — made in Japan), Toothmaster Model V (The Toothmaster Company, Racine, Wisconsin, $17.95), Vibra-Dent (Chase, $12.95 — apparently still for sale and still with a current hazard), and Whirlee (Whirlee Inc., Long Island City, New York, $2.98 — made in Japan). *Consumer Reports* summed up by reiterating that electric toothbrushes were good for those with neuromuscular disorders, invalids, and so on, but that the jury was still out on its efficiency for regular toothbrush users.[11]

Late in 1963 *Changing Times* reported that GE had 40 percent to 50 percent of the market with several dozen companies also competing for a share. Second was Squibb with 30 percent. According to this account between 900,000 and one million of the devices were sold in 1962. Also agreeing that the jury was still out on the effectiveness of these electric brushes, this publication recommended that a consumer not buy a power toothbrush without the help of his dentist.[12]

Early in 1964 *Consumer Bulletin* ran its evaluation of the new product, after observing, "Effective brushing of the teeth does not require a dentifrice; brushing with water only is probably as effective as brushing with toothpaste." In research reported to the ADA's Annual Session in 1963 Dr. M. Ash Jr. of the School of Dentistry of the University of Michigan found that manual brushing and brushing with an electric toothbrush were about equally effective. Estimates were that between 1.5 and 2.0 million units were sold in 1963 and "there are said to be 44 companies making electric toothbrushes, which range in price from $5 to $20." Some models imported from Japan sold for as little as $3. By this time there were at least three different types of brushing actions used by the implements as well as a great variation in the speed of the products (2,100 cycles per minute, 3,600, and so on). *Consumer Bulletin* declared it was not then possible to give a firm recommendation on any model on the basis of the type of its motion or speed. The ADA's Council on Dental Therapeutics was still studying the matter although the ADA's *Journal* was then accepting ads for at least two power brushes, the Broxodent and the GE model.[13]

When the power brush was three years old, in April 1964, business journalist Lydia Wallack observed that consumers had purchased a total of three million units, with annual sales having reached $33 million. Reportedly, no one was then sure exactly how many electric toothbrush makers existed. Manufacturers' lists of their competitors ranged anywhere from 40 to as high as 81, depending on whom they considered their competition to be. Yet still more makers were entering the field with Johnson & Johnson, and Block Drug — both big names in manual brushes — each putting out new power items. Wondering why the electric toothbrush was so popular Wallack argued three factors accounted for the growth: parents' concern over healthy teeth and gums for their children as well as for themselves, dentists' approval, and "heavy advertising and promotion." At the beginning, said a Squibb spokesman, druggists were skeptical about handling the product because they were not sure they could sell a $20 brush. But, explained Squibb, "Heavy advertising convinced them to stock our product."[14]

When GE started its campaign to win over individual dentists to its brush, related Wallack, GE mailed 16-page brochures containing some of its research findings to over 95,000 dentists. The ADA still had said nothing official on the subject but it had attacked the ad claims of one electric toothbrush maker (Ronson) when it headlined an illustration that in effect claimed the conventional, manual toothbrush was obsolete. According to the ADA's Council on Dental Therapeutics that claim was "exaggerated and misleading" and needlessly disparaged a device useful in oral hygiene programs. Wallack said that Squibb and GE accounted for 75 percent of the market with most industry observers giving the edge to GE; that company claimed it had 50 percent of the market. Far behind in third place was thought to be Universal. Rumors circulated then that Chemway Corporation (Dr. West) had already dropped out of the electric brush market. However, the company denied those rumors. Carl J. Wolff, Chemway director of new products, said, "Due to the confusion within the electric toothbrush market, plus constant price-cutting tactics, Dr. West has temporarily reduced its promotional activities in this field."[15]

More evidence that the electric toothbrush had made it as a permanent member of American society could be seen when John Avery Snyder wrote a short, humorous piece for the *Atlantic Monthly* in 1964 mocking "America's newest practical gadget — an electric toothbrush." Ironically, he wrote, "Being one of the laziest people in the world I had always considered it a major imposition to have to brush my teeth in the violent back-and-forth shimmying motion my dentist had recommended."[16]

A major breakthrough for the electric toothbrush came on August 27, 1964, when the ADA Council on Dental Therapeutics granted recognition to two models, General Electric's and Squibb's Broxodent, as "effective cleansing devices." That marked the first time the association had given such recognition to any electric toothbrush. The council gave the GE product a Group A classification and authorized the statement that the product "has been accepted as an effective cleansing device for use as part of a program of good oral hygiene to supplement the regular professional care required for oral health." It gave Broxodent a Group B classification, which was a "provisional acceptance as an effective cleansing device." Group A consisted of accepted products listed in *Accepted Dental Remedies* published annually by the council while Group B encompassed products that, because of their newness, lacked sufficient evidence for regular listing in *Accepted Dental Remedies*, but for which there was good evidence of usefulness and safety. One caution from the ADA was that claims for the brushes should be limited to oral cleanliness and stressed there was no proof that one type of motion in a powered brush was superior to another (Squibb's brush used an oscillating motion while GE's was up and down). Data from other power brush makers was then under consideration by the ADA. With the recognition, thought *Advertising Age*, the electric toothbrush would become "one of the most widely accepted consumer products in the American household."[17]

When Dental Survey Publications conducted a survey in 1964 they sent a questionnaire covering 18 product groups to a random sample of 5,000 U.S. dentists, with 780 (15.6 percent) returning a completed questionnaire. Of the dentists who recommended electric toothbrushes to their patients, 50.4 percent recommended Broxodent, 38.8 percent touted GE, and 10.9 percent pricked Oral-B.[18]

When *Consumer Reports* evaluated power brushes in August 1966 it reported that by then seven brands had been given recognition by the ADA's council, and they were all included among the 25 models tested by *Consumer Reports*. Two levels of recognition remained within the ADA program. A maker of a Group A brush was permitted to advertise it "has been accepted [by the ADA] as an effective cleansing device for use as part of a program for good oral hygiene to supplement the regular professional care required for oral health." The manufacturers of a brush that had received Group B recognition could make the same claim, except that they had to put the word "provisionally" before "accepted." Ordinarily the status of a Group B product was reviewed every year, and the model's maker generally was expected to submit additional data within three years to raise the status of his product to Group A. Promotion of any item achieving ADA recognition had to comply with carefully specified restrictions. Prices for the 25 brands tested by *Consumer Reports* ranged from $7.95 to $21.95. Of the seven accepted by the ADA, General Electric 5104 and Broxodent D1 were both in Group A while General Electric 5108, Py-Co-Pay 1165 (Block Drug), Sunbeam CT-7 (Sunbeam Corporation), Tek HB 60 (Tek-Hughes Company), and Westinghouse HB20 (Westinghouse Electric Corporation) were all Group B.[19]

Several years later, in 1969, when *Consumer Reports* revisited the product again it declared its key finding was, "There's no good evidence that electric brushes clean teeth any better than a properly wielded manual brush. But if motorized brushing appeals to you, *Consumer Reports* believes a model recognized by the American Dental Association is a better choice." At that time *Consumer Reports* tested 16 models, of which only six had ADA recognition. Most of those implements used what was called an accurate brushing motion — the bristle ends followed an arc as they moved up and down. The rest of the brands used either an orbital (they moved in a circle, more or less) motion or combined side-to-side movement with accurate up-and-down motions. ADA–recognized models were General Electric TB1 (Group A), Dominion 2716 (Dominion Electric Corporation, A), Presto TB3 (National Presto Industries, B), Broxodent 2502 (Squibb, A), Westinghouse HB16 (Westinghouse Electric Corporation, A), and Ronson 71002 (Ronson Corporation, B).[20]

Little of note happened in the field of electric toothbrushes until the latter half of the 1980s when a new — and much more expensive — generation of the items arrived on the scene. Reporter Jane Brody observed in 1986 that

the Dental Research Corporation of Tucker, Georgia, manufactured Interplak, a $99 electric brush said to be specially designed to scrub out plaque
that lodged in between the teeth and in tooth crevices. Its bristles rotated at
a speed of 4,200 times a second, changing direction 46 times a second. By
comparison, manual brushing was conducted at a speed of about 160 strokes
per minute.[21]

Interplak's $99 brush turned out to be a runaway success with sales of
about one million units in 1988, up from 75,000 in 1986. Less expensive electric brushes — aimed at the same market — came from Broxodent at $44 and
Water Pik at $61. The latter model was also an irrigator that featured puls-
ing jets of water.[22]

In its 1992 evaluation of the power brushes Consumer Reports rated 10
models that ranged in price from $30 to $119. A survey of Consumer Reports
readers revealed that nearly 17 percent of them owned an electric toothbrush,
but 72 percent of those people said they usually used a manual brush instead.
Mentioned most often as the reason for the reluctance to use the electric
toothbrush was the time and effort involved in using or maintaining the
device.[23]

Trade publication Stores (for the retail sector) lamented in 1995, "The
toothbrush is a clear example of a product where the machine has failed to
replace the hand tool." Despite decades of marketing the item, said the publication, a nationwide survey of U.S. households revealed that only 3 percent
of U.S. adults had used an electric-powered tooth cleaning device in the previous 24 hours; 88 percent used a manual toothbrush; 9 percent did not
brush their teeth that day. Only 1 percent of respondents said they used an
electric toothbrush daily. Failure of electric toothbrushes to gain a significant
share of the market was reflected, thought the article, in the fact that after
many years on the market, 66 percent of those surveyed did not know the
name of a single brand of electric toothbrush.[24]

On the other hand, Mary Lord reported in 1998 in U.S. News & World
Report that nearly one in eight American homes had at least one of these
devices and sales continued to climb with annual sales amounting to $184 mil-
lion, about 25 percent of the volume of the total toothbrush market. Lord
reported the choice was then among electric brushes with bristles that vibrated
30,000 times a minute, those that flossed gums, those that provided oral irri-
gation, and even an ionic brush that claimed to repel plaque by supposedly
reversing the polarity of the teeth. More than a dozen models were available,
ranging from $50 to $149 in price.[25]

Consumer Reports looked at power brushes once again, in 1998, when it
tested 13 popular models. First Consumer Reports reiterated that a proper

brushing required two minutes but the average American brushed for only 45 to 60 seconds. *Consumer Reports* also declared, "In fact, according to the American Dental Association (ADA), as well as many researchers we contacted, powered brushes aren't any better at cleaning teeth than manual ones." As well, *Consumer Reports* found no compelling clinical studies showing that powered brushes had a side advantage in plaque removal. Those tested models ranged in price from $25 to $130 and had such exotic names as Panasonic Power Floss and Brush EW118WC, SenSonic Advanced Plaque Removal Instrument SR-200W, and Teledyne Water Pik Plaque Control 3000 PC-3000W.[26]

Another development took place in 1998 when John Osher and three colleagues developed the SpinBrush. They wanted to develop a power brush to sell much more cheaply than existing brushes then on the market. Spin-Brush worked on batteries and sold for just $5; it went on within three years to become the nation's best-selling toothbrush, manual or electric. In 2000 Osher and friends sold 10 million SpinBrush units, more than triple the existing three million per year U.S. electric toothbrush market. Then, in a deal that closed in January 2001, the item was sold to Procter & Gamble, and became the Crest SpinBrush. Colgate moved to try and get a share of the low-priced market when it launched ActiBrush, a power unit that retailed at $19.95.[27]

Crest was then the dominant player in the oral hygiene field and had been so for many, many years. It all began in 1960 with official ADA recognition of the value of fluoride in toothpaste.

When reporter Mary Carmichael looked at the electric toothbrush field in 2003 she commented that the power brush had become a prized yuppie item in the 1980s but that the low-cost market had been invaded some three years earlier from when she was writing, in the form of the $5.99 Crest Spin-Brush. Since then the sales of that item had doubled. Yet Carmichael observed that recent data from 29 clinical trials showed that most battery-operated toothbrushes were no more effective at removing plaque than were the plain old manuals. Only the pricier rotation-oscillation models (bristles circled first in one direction, then the other) such as the Braun Oral-B performed better, removing 11 percent more plaque.[28]

That same year it was reported that the Philips Sonicare electric toothbrush led the high-end market — it retailed for $99 to $119. It then launched its first new model in 10 years, the Sonicare Elite ($129–$139) that had such features as timers to ensure people brushed 30 seconds in each quadrant of the mouth, and dual speeds. Frank McGillin, vice president of marketing for Sonicare, exclaimed, "People who use Sonicare are incredibly passionate about it." According to journalist Jack Neff, sales of power brushes more than doubled between 1999 and 2003 to $315.7 million. But almost all of that was in the low end of the market; Sonicare Elite cost up to 20 times as much as the highest-priced SpinBrush Pro. Over that same time period the sales of manual brushes dropped 12.4 percent to $455.5 million.[29]

Gillette announced in 2005 it had created a computerized electronic toothbrush that told users when to stop brushing. The Oral-B Triumph Professional Care 9000 had an "onboard computer" in the handle and a microchip in each brush head, which tracked usage and alerted the user when it was time to change the brush head. It also notified the user every 30 seconds to brush another "mouth quadrant" as well as alerting the user when the two minutes was up. Those pieces of information were displayed in one of 13 languages on an LCD screen on the product, which retailed for $179.99. Asked if the new model would go into every home Ian Chalmers, director of marketing at Gillette Canada, replied, "No, it's not. But there is a definite need out there.... People will pay for performance."[30]

A year later, 2006, in the UK, Procter and Gamble launched an Oral-B disposal electric toothbrush that contained an integrated AAA battery. It was designed to be thrown away after a few months' use. However, it was difficult to remove the battery before disposal and that led to the item being heavily criticized by environmentalists. Oral-B's Pulsar retailed for six pounds Sterling.[31]

For the 52 weeks ending December 30, 2007, the sales of power toothbrushes in the mass market (drugstores, supermarkets, and discount stores— except Wal-Mart Stores) in America totaled $204.3 million (19.9 million units). For drugstores only the totals were $70.2 million from 6.5 million units. Top three sellers (drugstores) were Oral-B Vitality, $9,475,000 (13.5 percent); Sonicare Elite, $7,200,000 (10.3 percent); and Oral-B Crossaction Power Max, $6,887,000 (9.8 percent). Of the seven others in the top ten, three were from Crest, three more from Oral-B, and one other from Sonicare.[32]

11

Crest Toothpaste, 1960–2008

[The ADA's] action [in recognizing Crest] was necessary and wise and substantial benefits will accrue by restoring a greater measure of truth to dentifrice advertising.—Dr. Paul H. Jeserich, ADA president, 1960.

Dentists have no more business in advertising than advertising men have in dentistry.—Dr. Michael Zazzaro, 1960.

Crest toothpaste had been hitting away at the decay preventive theme since it was introduced in 1955 and it finally paid off five years later in 1960. On August 1 of that year the ADA officially recognized the Procter & Gamble fluoride dentifrice as "an effective decay preventive agent," the first and only toothpaste ever to receive therapeutic acclaim from the dental organization. In a statement published in the August 1 issue of the *Journal of the American Dental Association* the ADA Council on Dental Therapeutics reported, "Crest has been shown to be an effective anti-caries [decay preventive] dentifrice that can be of significant value when used in a conscientiously applied program of oral hygiene and regular profession care. Crest dentifrice may also be of value as a supplement to public health procedure." Emphasized by the council was that its endorsement applied only to that specific brand [other fluoride products were on the market], whose principal ingredient was stannous fluoride [some used sodium fluoride]. Procter & Gamble was the sole licensee for that ingredient. No other dentifrice had demonstrated therapeutic value to the council, said the ADA. In 1959 Crest spent over $3 million for network television ads alone, and more than $350,000 for print advertising. According to the council three elements were involved in its precedent-making decision: the maker's willingness to limit advertising claims to those supported by adequate research, the results of clinical studies conducted during a 10-year period, and the safety of the product. The ADA then recognized three methods of obtaining the benefit of fluoride: dietary fluorides (fluoridation of community water supplies), topical application of fluoride solutions directly to children's teeth by a dentist, and through the use of Crest. While the product had to limit its advertising in the manner prescribed above, there was no apparent restriction on making the point that the ADA said Crest prevented cavities.[1]

Crest was launched nationally, after about a year's market testing, in January 1956, although the first fluoride product was Block Drug's Super Ammi-dent. Around May 1956 Colgate-Palmolive came out nationally with Colgate's Brisk fluoride toothpaste. Bristol-Myers continued testing Sentry, its fluoride version but ultimately abandoned it. As of 1960 the only major threat to Crest was said to be Brisk, but that product had never taken off. While it was still sold, it was not then advertised. All fluoride toothpastes had been blasted by the ADA in both 1956 and 1958 for making what the organization believed were unfounded and misleading claims. One attack was directed at a Crest ad headline — "Look, Mom, no cavities" — although the ADA was no longer going to ask the company to modify that headline. Market leaders in the toothpaste field were then Colgate with a 35 percent share of the market; Gleem (P&G), 20 percent; Crest, 12 percent; Pepsodent, 11 percent; Stripe, 9 percent, and Ipana, 7 percent. Thus, the top six selling brands had 94 percent of the market.[2]

In an evident response to the ADA announcement of its Crest endorsement, Procter & Gamble stock on the New York Stock Exchange went up eight points for the day, moving from 118 to a close of 126, an increase of nearly 8 percent.[3]

At the time of the Crest breakthrough the dentifrice industry was worth about $235 million a year with advertising for the products estimated at about $37 million per year. During 1959 P&G spent $3.8 million in measured media on its Crest campaigns. P&G also spent more than twice that amount on Gleem ($8.8 million) stressing that Gleem was "for people who can't brush after every meal." Of that Gleem ad total, $5.4 million went to network television, and $2 million to spot television. Top seller Colgate spent $12.8 million in measured media for dentifrice ads in 1959 with about half of that amount going to network television, one-quarter to spot television; and one-quarter to magazines and newspapers. According to *Printers' Ink*, Colgate had been number one for nearly 50 years. After abandoning its Gardol invisible shield campaign it reverted to an older theme that stressed, "Fight tooth decay with Colgate. Help stop bad breath all day." Lever Brothers spent almost $2.6 million in 1959 to support fourth-place Pepsodent, virtually all of it on network television. Its main theme was downplayed toward the end of 1959 after the ADA publicly blasted the "You'll wonder where the yellow went when you brush your teeth with Pepsodent" theme. The company replaced that with copy that stressed, "Pepsodent cleans your teeth more effectively than any other leading tooth-paste." Also in 1959, Lever spent almost $4.4 million on its red-and-white Stripe toothpaste, more than half of that to network television, to emphasize that Stripe offered "toothpaste benefits plus mouthwash benefits in one product." Bristol-Myers spent $4.4 million that year on Ipana to proclaim the brand "kills decay germs best of all leading tooth pastes!" Those previously mentioned top six selling brands — with 94 percent of the market — spent a total of $36.8 million on advertising themselves in 1959.[4]

Stannous fluoride, a compound long used by dentists to protect the teeth from decay, was not patentable. Any manufacturer could use it. What was patented in Crest was the combination of stannous fluoride with other ingredients, licensed from Indiana University exclusively. Other makers had to develop their own combination of ingredients if they, too, wanted a stannous fluoride toothpaste. Then, if they wanted an ADA endorsement, they would have to submit research to ADA to support any therapeutic claims. It was a process that could take years, as it did for Crest. Until that happened it appeared Crest would have a huge advertising edge since only P&G would be able to boast that its Crest had the endorsement of the ADA.[5]

On the second day after the ADA announcement P&G stock rose a further three points for a 2-day gain of 11 points. Off the record, according to *Business Week*, P&G competitors were reported apprehensive and at the same time angry with both P&G and the ADA. A spokesman for one of the main dentifrice makers insisted that some dentists were upset with the ADA action that was virtually unprecedented since professional groups rarely, if ever, endorsed competing brands. He claimed, "ADA has lost face because of the unethical and unprofessional endorsement." When asked about its policies the American Medical Association said it had never endorsed a particular branded drug. A spokesman for another P&G competitor said for years ADA had wanted some sort of control over dentifrice advertising "but manufacturers never would permit it." Now, he added, "P&G has accepted ADA control. They'll have to travel to Chicago to get advertising copy approved and I predict that in a year's time they'll be sorry." In explaining why it decided to announce its approval of Crest, ADA explained, "There is no desire on our part to make money for Procter & Gamble. On the other hand, if a product comes along that is of significant benefit to oral health, we feel a responsibility in letting the public and dental profession know about it." That organization was careful to point out that Crest was no substitute for water fluoridation in preventing tooth decay.[6]

Effects of ADA's endorsement on Crest sales were noted by *Printers' Ink,* still in the month of August 1960, although it was mainly an anecdotal report from wholesalers and retailers around the U.S. as no hard numbers were provided. In some marketing areas the sales of Crest were said to have increased three to four times over the old rate. Speculation was printed that Crest's market share (third place at 12 percent) had shot up and passed second place

Gleem's 20 percent share. "Crest's sales gains, significantly, have come on almost no formal promotion of the dental association's commendation," said *Printers' Ink*. "P&G, one of the nations' ablest marketers, has allowed publicity and word-of-mouth to do the main selling job."[7]

ADA's August 1 announcement received wide coverage in newspapers and other news media. P&G capitalized on this by featuring three of the news articles in its first consumer advertising of the ADA move, later in August. At ADA, Dr. Roy J. Doty, secretary of the Council on Dental Therapeutics, admitted there had been "some limited reaction" to the ADA move with most of the letters to the organization asking for further information. In a few instances, he said, "the persons felt the move was outside the usual dignity of the association." Doty felt many of those complaints arose because patients got the impression from news stories that ADA had "endorsed" or "approved" Crest toothpaste, whereas the council, he pointed out, had only "recognized the usefulness of the dentifrice as a caries preventative agent." He added that Crest was in a classification under which continued recognition was contingent not only on the clinical value of the product, but also on the adherence to ADA standards of labeling and advertising. In the case of Crest, Doty continued, that would relate to the fact that ads should emphasis that the product was effective "only when used as part of a program of oral hygiene." *Advertising Age* did its own spot check of wholesalers and retailers around the country, at almost the same time as *Printers' Ink* did its check, finding sales of Crest up significantly, 10 percent to 50 percent in many, or most, of the areas checked.[8]

Advertising Age then did a small mail survey among 500 dentists drawn from ADA's 95,000 members. It found that by a two to one margin, respondents to the survey approved ADA's endorsement of Crest. Most of those dentists intended to recommend it to their patients. On the other hand, about one-third of respondent dentists felt strongly ADA should not have endorsed Crest, disapproved the endorsement, and declined to recommend Crest to their patients.[9]

In an analysis of August 1960 toothpaste sales it was reported that Crest unit purchases jumped 39 percent over the previous month and the dollar volume increased 60 percent. Thirty-four percent of the purchasers were described as brand switchers: 13 percent from P&G's Gleem; 6 percent from Pepsodent; 5 percent from Ipana; 4 percent from Stripe; 3 percent from Colgate; and 3 percent from all other brands.[10]

Consumer Reports observed that ADA recognition of Crest was tentative with the product having been put into Group B of the association's classification scheme for dental therapeutics. Group A was for fully accept-

Benton&Bowles

It's not creative unless it sells.

You start with a good product. Without it, advertising really doesn't pay.
But given a fine product like Crest toothpaste and a sound marketing strategy, it's not enough
just to be clever in your advertising or to be entertaining.
It's not enough to be talked about or to win awards for creativity. Advertising cannot be called creative unless it sells.

You can't beat Crest for fighting cavities.

Crest ad, 1974.

able products that were allowed to use the ADA Seal of Acceptance. Group B was for products that "lack sufficient evidence to justify present acceptance, but offer reasonable evidence of usefulness and safety." Products placed in Group B were re-evaluated periodically, and usually did not remain there for more than three years. In a further attempt to dampen enthusiasm *Consumer Reports* noted the decay-preventing ability of Crest was limited though significant. Brushing with Crest ranked last among the three methods then recognized for getting fluoride to the teeth. The most effective way was to add the chemical to the diet (through water supplies); second was a topical application from a dentist. For another manufacturer to get the same endorsement from ADA as had Crest would take a minimum of two years, thought *Consumer Reports*, the least amount of time for an acceptable-length clinical trial.[11]

At the ADA's annual convention in late 1960 the organization's president, Paul H. Jeserich, frequently departed from his prepared text when he delivered the president's address to support and make a strong defense of the ADA's endorsement of Crest toothpaste. He said "the association's action was necessary and wise and substantial benefits will accrue by restoring a greater measure of truth to dentifrice advertising." Jeserich went on to explain that for years he had deplored the trend in the media in which false and misleading claims had been made for toothpastes. In his opinion the one-page Crest ad would do much to force other advertisers to be more careful in their claims. At that convention the rumored revolt against the ADA recognition failed to materialize. The main debate in the group's house of delegates was in connection with a resolution of the Connecticut State Dental Association to the effect that the action of recognition be rescinded. That resolution was defeated by a vote of 279 to 94. In the discussion, the principal concern appeared to relate to the manner in which the recognition had been announced. Objected to was the fact that the announcement went out to dentists from P&G, and not from the ADA. According to the group it was done that way because of cost considerations; it was cheaper to let P&G do the mail out. The most vocal opponent of the recognition was reported to be Dr. Michael Zazzaro of Connecticut, who asserted the ADA had lost prestige as a result of the action. "Dentists have no more business in advertising than advertising men have in dentistry," he complained.[12]

Advertising Age reported at the start of 1961 that the cold war between the ADA and several paste makers because of ADA's recognition of Crest had erupted again in unfavorable reactions by the latter to the dental organization's letter to retailers on the subject. Two major makers wanted to know why ADA did not notify consumers as well as retailers that use of the words "endorses" or "approves" instead of "recognizes" was an exaggeration of the facts concerning ADA's recognition of Crest as providing "some" protection against tooth decay.[13]

According to *Advertising Age*, about a month earlier the ADA had written to about 85 food, variety and drugstore chains urging them not to exaggerate claims for Crest in local advertising and displays by using the words "endorsed" or "approved." In addition, the ADA requested that its name not be mentioned in any local promotions (the ADA could control Crest ad copy — if Crest wanted continued recognition — but the ADA had no control over any extra, local ads). Said a spokesman for a major Crest competitor, "It is our opinion that writing to a few dealers is only a relatively minor gesture. Millions of consumers are still under the impression that Crest has been 'endorsed' or 'approved' by the dental profession, and many are using it with this erroneous concept in mind." Speaking for another major competitor a spokesman said they were not surprised the ADA sent out a word of warning, "but we were a little surprised that the ADA limited its words of warning to retailers and did not spread that same warning to the millions of understandably confused consumers." A P&G spokesman declared they were in complete agreement with the ADA letter, perhaps because ADA had emphasized that P&G was in no way responsible for the misleading local advertising. Crest's market share was said to have moved from 11 percent to 20 percent, but the brand remained third behind Colgate and Gleem. In 1959 the toothpaste market totaled $228 million, which meant that each one-point rise in market share was worth $2.28 million to Crest at retail.[14]

In June 1961 renewed criticism of the ADA for recognizing Crest as a decay preventive was voiced by former ADA president Dr. Leroy S. M. Miner. He said Crest advertising caused people to think the dentifrice was a "panacea" and, as a result, they neglected other dental care measures, including visits to the dentist. Miner argued Crest advertising gave the impression Crest was ADA approved when in fact it was only recognized.[15]

When the ADA held its 1961 convention the house of delegates rejected a resolution offered by the North Carolina delegation to eliminate Group B classification for brand name proprietary products. In effect, that would have removed even the partial approval of Crest as an effective anti-caries dentifrice. The vote was as follows: 292 to reject the resolution, 72 to accept, and 52 abstained. It was a vote that came after several days of invective and bitter personal attacks, according to a news account. Prior to the voting, the board of trustees of ADA issued a report, reviewing the allegations made in support of the resolution introduced by the North Carolina delegation. In it, the board for the first time made reference to activities of the Colgate-Palmolive Company, pointing out that for 20 years that firm had an opportunity to submit evidence on therapeutic dentifrices to the Council on Dental Therapeutics. "Not once in this long period," said the board, "has it ever requested such evaluation, so that it might cooperate with the dental profession in advertising its products truthfully and honestly to the public."[16]

In the opinion of the council, continued the report, "advertising claims for the company's dentifrices have been consistently misleading and one claim — the invisible shield — has recently been the subject of a cease and desist order by the FTC." The board also accused Colgate of financing a survey of the house of delegates in 1960 and of sponsoring the press conference of Dr. Miner. Also declared in the report was that Crest ads were following ADA policies. One of the main critics of Crest recognition at that 1961 convention was Dr. W. R. Alstadt, who denied charges he was being subsidized by Colgate. Other critics argued the Group B recognition had "become a tool for exploitation by commercial interest" and that the public did not realize the difference between limited recognition and full acceptance of a product. According to an ADA public relations spokesman, Colgate had one of its public relations executives at the convention city of Philadelphia for a week prior to the convention to help organize introduction of the issue and the resolution from the floor. No one from P&G, it was said, had been in evidence at the gathering.[17]

At the convention the group of delegates that tried to eliminate Crest recognition included six past presidents of the group, according to *Science* magazine. ADA's board of trustees' report charged Colgate had attempted to influence ADA delegates to oppose Crest recognition. Colgate denied it had arranged the press conference by Dr. Miner. Since Crest had been granted recognition, according to this account, its market share had gone from 12 percent to 26 percent, while Colgate Dental Cream went from 33 percent to 27 percent, although it remained number one. Supporters of the concept of recognition argued it was the responsibility of the ADA to lend its authority and prestige to products that were beneficial to the public; those opposed were wary of permitting ADA to be exploited for commercial purposes. *Science* felt the basic issue was whether professional societies should lend their names, and hence their prestige, to commercial products.[18]

At that Philadelphia convention a 64-page booklet was distributed to the Philadelphia newspapers that hammered home the message: the ADA move assailed the dignity of the profession and Crest advertising based on the ADA endorsement was "misleading the public." *Newsweek* felt that while a grass-roots movement against recognition may have started in North

Carolina by the time the issue reached the convention the movement
had been taken over by P&G's top rival, Colgate-Palmolive. "Last week's
press pamphlets were handed out by Colgate at the same time that newspapers all over the U.S. were receiving 'canned' editorials attacking the ADA
stand," explained *Newsweek*. "The editorials referred to a 'spot survey' of dentists that showed 'an alarming number' opposed to the Crest endorsement."
Yet no results were ever published of the number of dentists contacted or what
the actual results were, observed ADA president Dr. Charles Patton. The vote
against the resolution to rescind recognition (292 to 72) was virtually
the same vote numbers that supported the Crest endorsement one year
earlier. Bristol-Myers was then marketing a new, fluoridated version of its
Ipana.[19]

Bruce Bliven Jr. reported in March 1963 that the dentifrice business was
worth $250 million a year and Crest then stood number one with a 30 per-
cent market share. But Bliven wondered why it was not higher given the pre-
recognition share of about 10 percent and given P&G's powerful distribution
system and given ADA recognition. "Could Crest have possibly done worse?
I don't see how," he mused. He thought P&G and their advertising people
were stumped when their dream came true — "a real instance of product superiority" and "what caused them serious trouble was the problem of telling the
truth. And years and years of being insulted (without conspicuous resentment)
may actually have deafened toothpaste consumers beyond hope of recovery."
Noted was that Crest ad copy was constrained by having to be factual and
was vetted by the ADA while its competitors faced no such constraints. They
were free to make the same wild and baseless claims they had made for years,
including about their fluoride-like ingredients.[20]

Researchers Peter Riesz and Abe Shuchman reported on a study of 3,027
households that had not purchased Crest prior to the ADA's 1960 endorsement. Of that group, 800 white and 36 non-white households converted to
Crest and remained loyal in the post-endorsement period (that extended to
April 1963 when dentifrices were deleted from the panel of household purchase records) while 2,014 white and 177 non-white households did not convert to Crest during the post-endorsement period. For white households with
children the rate of conversion increased with increasing household size, generally. In contrast to the whites, the presence of children had little or no effect
on the rate of conversion for non-white households. For whites, conversion
was directly and quite strongly related to education; for non-whites there was
a relationship between education level and conversion, but it was not nearly
as pronounced. The effect of education for whites was general and its association with conversion was seen in households both with and without chil-

dren. Income appeared to have little effect independent of educational level. Conversion rates were as follows: educational level for white households (2,814): grammar school, .190; high school, .291; college, .412; for non-white households (213): grammar school, .151; high school, .157; college, .243; for white households with children (1,663): by educational level, respectively, .211, .331, .483; for white households with no children (1,151): .160, .219. .301; for non-white household with children (145): .129, .145, .250; for non-white household with no children (68): .194, .200, .235.[21]

P&G started a national ad campaign for fluoride toothpaste in the UK in 1975. One of the selling points was that the toothpaste had been officially approved by the British Dental Association (BDA). No other fluoride toothpaste had that endorsement; it was the first such recognition by the BDA. In the summer of 1975 in the course of a routine meeting, P&G suggested to the BDA that it give official endorsement to Crest. The BDA replied that it would, provided the clinical tests were satisfactory and provided the toothpaste got a product license from the medicines commission, an official government body. Crest passed both tests and three months later the national campaign began, after the endorsement was announced in the BDA *Journal* in September. Competitors were said to have been furious because they knew nothing abut the situation until the announcement of recognition in the *Journal*.[22]

Crest continued to move upward in terms of market share and was firmly entrenched as number one in the industry by the early 1960s. Numbers (in thousands) were as follows: 1966, 30 percent market share (total retail toothpaste sales $287,500, Crest sales $86,250); 1967, 35 percent ($300,000, $105,000, Crest ad budget $16,300); 1968, 35 percent ($300,000, $105,000, $15,800); 1969, 38 percent ($320,000, $121,600, $16,000); 1970, 35 percent ($325,000, $113,750, $14,200); 1971, 35 percent ($325,000, $113,750, $15,000); 1972, 38.2 percent ($325,000, $124,150, $14,000); 1973, 38 percent ($350,000, $133,000, $15,400); 1974, 36 percent ($350,000, $126,000, $18,250); 1975, 36 percent ($450,000, $162,000, $17,300); 1976, 36.5 percent ($525,000, $191,625, $23,000); 1977, 36 percent ($525,000, $189,000, $19,250); 1978, 35 percent ($600,000, $210,000, $23,056); 1979, 34.5 percent ($650,000, $224,250, $26,000). Researcher Roger Carlson concluded that 95 percent of the variance in the sales of Crest was explained by the amount of advertising spent on Crest for the current year and the past two years and that a causal relationship existed between sales and advertising.[23]

As of April 1985 market shares for toothpaste were as follows, according to Hercules A. Segalas, an analyst at Drexel Burnham Lambert: Crest, 29.5

percent; Colgate, 28 percent; Aqua-Fresh, 12.5 percent; Aim, 7.7 percent; Close-Up, 6.0 percent; others, 16.3 percent. Yet as of February 1986 they were as follows: Crest, 38.2 percent, Colgate, 21.5 percent; Aqua-Fresh, 11.5 percent; Aim, 7.5 percent; Close-Up, 7.0 percent; others, 14.3 percent. That was in a mature market worth about $1 billion a year in a product category that usually experienced growth of only around 2 percent a year and annual market share changes of no more than one or two points. What had happened in this case was the slow erosion of Crest's market share as its fluoride advantage no longer had the same impact. But then a dramatic turnaround came when P&G launched Crest Tartar Control Formula in June 1985. Ten months later that brand, sold alongside traditional Crest on store shelves, alone had a 14 percent market share. Colgate and other makers were then testing tartar-control versions of their own. Segalas said P&G mailed out 70 million free samples to homes around the country at a cost of $50 million. He estimated P&G supported the Crest line with a total ad expenditure of $90 million in the fiscal year ending June 30, 1985.[24]

Crest's market share in 1992 was, according to reporter Dana Canedy, 35 percent; 1993, 33.4 percent; 1994, 30 percent; and 1995, 28.5 percent. For 1997 market shares were Crest, 26.3 percent; Colgate, 19.6 percent; Aqua-Fresh, 11.2 percent; Mentadent, 11 percent; Arm & Hammer, 7.5 percent; Sensadyne, 3.3 percent; Rembrandt, 3.1 percent; Listerine, 2.8 percent; Close-Up, 2.2 percent; Ultra-Brite, 1.8 percent; others, 11.2 percent.[25]

As of the summer of 2006 Procter and Gamble sold 39 variations of its Crest toothpaste. Crest had stayed on top of the market until Colgate launched gingivitis-fighting Total in 1998. Colgate has been number one ever since. In those intervening years it had rolled out dozens of Crest varieties, from Rejuvenating Effects Gel to Vivid White Night Moonlight Mint, but none had succeeded. In the summer of 2006 Procter and Gamble was set to launch another variety, Crest Pro-Health toothpaste, which was to carry an ADA seal and supposedly had the ability to treat seven common oral-care problems — gingivitis, plaque, tooth decay, stains, sensitivity, tartar formation, and bad breath.[26]

While Crest moved fairly quickly to the number one spot in the toothpaste field after it received recognition it still disappointed many for its highest market share was little different from the highest shares recorded by Colgate in the many years of its market domination. And that was despite the fact that Crest had marketing advantages that no other toothpaste had ever enjoyed. It was as though no item could get beyond around 40 percent, even if its advantages seemed to indicate it should go higher. Reasons included a confusing backdrop of advertising claims by Crest rivals that were not constrained by truth; a perhaps short attention span by the public as fluoride fairly quickly lost its magic in the eyes of the public, if not its effectiveness; and the still almost continuous propensity of the makers to announce new additives to their pastes, all guaranteed, of course, to perform one wonder or another.

12

Toothpaste, New Wonders, 1960–2008

To begin with the bare toothbrush, used with elbow grease, is far more effective than is any toothpaste in removing plaque. — Jane E. Brody, 1986.

Truth is, anti-plaque toothpastes don't do a lot, although the process of brushing does. — Truman Susman, Pfizer, 1988.

We've found that no matter how white people's teeth are, they still want them whiter and that they haven't yet found the product that delivers enough whiteness. — Helayna Minsk, Close-Up toothpaste, 1994.

After Crest received its ADA recognition in 1960 the other major makers intensified their efforts to come up with a winning fluoride toothpaste. Colgate-Palmolive announced in the summer of 1961 that it was market testing a new stannous fluoride paste called Cue in a couple of spots while at the same time Bristol-Myers touted a new Ipana that contained not just hexachlorophene, but sodium fluoride as well. Only Lever Brothers, among the top four makers, was then without a fluoride brand in the market. In its ads for Cue, Colgate called stannous fluoride "the famous cavity fighting ingredient you've heard so much about" and claimed "no other toothpaste gives you more stannous fluoride" than did Cue. For Colgate, Cue represented a re-launch into the fluoride field. In 1955 it debuted Brisk, a sodium fluoride product, right after Crest was launched but it did not do well and while it was still sold in the summer of 1961 it was no longer advertised. Bristol-Myers was also not new to the field as it had launched the fluoride brand Sentry in 1956 but it had never gotten out of test markets. Shares in the toothpaste market were then said to be as follows: Colgate, 27 percent; Crest, 25.9 percent; Gleem, 20 percent; Pepsodent, 10 percent; Ipana, 6 percent; Stripe, 5 percent. For comparison purposes, market shares in 1953 were: Colgate, 45 percent; Pepsodent, 12 percent; Ipana, 10 percent; Amm-i-dent, 10 percent; Chlorodent, 6 percent; for 1954; Colgate, 37 percent; Gleem, 20 percent; Pepsodent, 10 percent; Ipana, 8 percent; Amm-i-dent, 6.5 percent; Chlorodent, 4 percent; for 1956; Colgate, 35 percent; Gleem, 21 percent; Crest,

12 percent; Pepsodent, 11.5 percent; Ipana, 8 percent; Amm-i-dent, 1.5 percent.[1]

Around March 1963 Colgate-Palmolive began a stepped up ad campaign in magazines, newspapers, and on television based on a new clinical study that "confirms Colgate toothpaste a leader in reducing new cavities." The company increased its advertising spending for its toothpaste by 52 percent, from an average of $2.5 million per calendar quarter to almost $3.8 million per quarter. P&G then was spending about $3 million annually to promote Crest.[2]

By 1964 the dentifrice industry was worth $320 million annually with toothpaste ad budgets that year totaling a record $35.5 million. That summer the ADA gave Colgate's Cue the same recognition it had awarded Crest in 1960. Even before the announcement of that recognition Bristol-Myers declared its new fluoride paste — Ipana Durenamel — to be more effective than Crest in reducing tooth decay. Fluoride toothpaste moved from 12 percent of the total market in 1960 to 35 percent of 1964's total toothpaste sales in the U.S. All but 5 percent of that market went to Crest with Cue a very distant second, followed by Bristol-Myers, with Lever Brothers' Pepsodent Fluoride sitting fourth. Almost unnoticed when Cue was recognized was the fact the ADA also upgraded its recognition of Crest from Group B status to Group A. That meant Crest was entitled to listing in the dentists' *Accepted Dental Remedies* publication.[3]

ADA recognized Cue based on three independent (but financed by Colgate) tests. Colgate had been working on that fluoride entry for more than five years. Meanwhile Bristol-Myers announced it was seeking ADA approval for its new fluoride paste, Ipana Durenamel. For Colgate's Cue, and for the Crest upgrade, ADA approval came on July 30, 1964.[4]

Cue was a stannous fluoride product and was assigned to a Group B classification, as had been the case with Crest initially. ADA's Council on Dental Therapeutics explained the difference between Group A and Group B as being related to "time and available evidence, and not to quality or effectiveness." Ipana Durenamel contained sodium fluoride while Cue, Colgate's first stannous fluoride paste, had been introduced in test cities three years earlier, in 1961, in Texas and New Orleans, after Brisk, Colgate's sodium fluoride brand, had failed in the face of the Crest campaign. After the ADA recognition Colgate said it would rush Cue into national distribution. In its ad copy Cue argued it had "a new and improved polishing agent, a highly desirable pure white colorization [Crest was aqua in color] long sought after in fluoride dentifrices, and a fresh and invigorating taste" that was said to make it easier to sell to kids. For 1963 P&G spent $13,183,000 on ads for Crest while

Colgate spent $11,200,000 promoting its Colgate Dental Cream with Gardol (no fluoride) as it said the product, through clinical testing, proved to be the equal of "the most widely accepted fluoride toothpaste." Crest continued to be number one in the market with an estimated 32.8 percent share; second was Colgate with Gardol at 24 percent; third was P&G's Gleem (no fluoride) at 17 percent. The advertising budget for Gleem was $7.1 million in 1963.[5]

On June 1, 1966, ADA bestowed its recognition on Lever Brothers' new Super Stripe toothpaste, a stannous fluoride version that was to replace the old Stripe as soon as remaining stocks were depleted. However, the ADA's blessing had not resulted in a huge number of sales for two other fluoride pastes, Cue and Bristol-Myers Fact, neither of which had been able to make inroads into Crest's share. Unlike its rivals, Super Stripe was "aggressively promoted with a direct appeal to children," according to Lever Brothers marketing vice president Robert McGhee. Crest still had over 30 percent of the dentifrice market then while Cue had less than 1 percent, Fact about 2 percent and Stripe (the old version) had 3 percent.[6]

In 1968 Colgate introduced Colgate Dental Cream with Gardol and MFP. The new additive MFP was sodium monofluoride-phosphate (a sodium fluoride). P&G criticized that move by saying that all its research suggested that stannous fluoride was clearly the most efficient fluoride, that all others, including sodium fluoride, were less effective. Nevertheless, despite that P&G earlier that year started a test marketing in Jacksonville, Florida, for Gleem with Fluoride 700, a sodium fluoride.[7]

One day in November 1968 in Monroe Country, Indiana, in fieldhouses, armories, factories, football stadiums, and high school gyms, more than 29,000 people gathered to brush their teeth for 2½ minutes as part of a mass brush-in to demonstrate the decay preventing qualities of a new dental paste called Zircate. Reportedly, it guarded against cavities for as long as a year — after one application. Developed at Indiana University by Dr. Joseph C. Muhler (who developed the Crest formula) and Dr. George Stookey, the prophylactic paste contained over 20 times the fluoride concentration of toothpastes then on drugstore shelves. "Muhler's new decay preventive will not be sold over the counter," explained *Time* magazine. "Since indiscriminate use of his patent fluoride formula could be damaging it must be applied under the direction of a dentist or a dental hygienist."[8]

Colgate won ADA recognition of its revised formula Colgate with MFP, in 1969, and was the only toothpaste (besides Crest) ever granted the ADA's permission to use its seal in their advertising. After MFP was launched in the fall of 1968, Colgate hired media star Arthur Godfrey to head the ad campaign as he extolled Colgate's "advanced fluoride" formula and the ADA seal.

Also involved in the campaign was children's program star Captain Kangaroo, who lured children with 50 cent Colgate Cavity Fighter Kits complete
with toothpaste, brush, dentist's mirror, and chewable tablets loaded with red
food dye to reveal improperly cleaned crevices. Thirty million sample-size
tubes of the product were distributed to American households, press kits
mailed to 100,000 sources, from an advertising budget that exceeded $20 mil-
lion. Earlier, after Crest inaugurated the fluoride industry, Colgate's Cue,
Bristol-Myers' Fact and Lever Brothers' Super Stripe all went on to win the
ADA seal. But because clinical evidence was deemed insufficient, they were
denied permission to advertise it. Sales were so poor for those Crest follow-
ers that, as of 1969, only Super Stripe was still being promoted.[9]

Seemingly, just having fluoride in a paste generated no enthusiasm or
interest in 1981; it was all old hat to everyone by that time. And seemingly
something new had to happen every so often so a new marketing war took
place between the makers over just who had the best fluoride product, that
is, the best new and improved fluoride paste. At the time market shares in
the industry were as follows: Crest (P&G), 35 percent; Colgate, 19 percent;
Aqua-Fresh (Beecham), 13.5 percent; Aim (Lever), 10 percent; Close-Up
(Lever), 7.3 percent; Gleem (P&G), 3.3 percent; Ultra-Brite (Colgate–
Palmolive), 3.2 percent; Pepsodent (Lever), 2.7 percent; Macleans (Beecham),
0.5 percent; others, 5.5 percent.[10]

P&G got the new competitive campaign underway in March 1981 when
it brought out Advanced Formula Crest, citing its own tests showing the new
Crest to be 78 percent more effective in fighting cavities than the original
Crest. One P&G spokesman said that reformulating Crest "was perhaps akin
to writing a new ending to the Bible" as the company touted its new Crest
as a scientific breakthrough. It was the firm's assertion that since 1955, Crest
had prevented an estimated 400 million cavities. But, declared Geoffrey Place,
vice president of research and development, "Had Advanced Formula Crest
been available for the past 25 years, 300 million fewer cavities would have
developed." Place added that the ADA seconded P&G's claim that the new
Crest "has been clinically proven to fight cavities even better than before."
However, reporter Sandra Salmans pointed out that the ADA's council, which
had given its endorsements to fluoride pastes such as Lever Brothers' Aim and
Beecham's Aqua-Fresh, had scrupulously refrained from rating the rival brands
in any way.[11]

Responding to the challenge, Colgate-Palmolive, citing its own tests —
which it also highlighted in an advertisement it took out the previous year in
the ADA *Journal*— stated that Colgate was superior to the original Crest and
had not been overtaken by the new Crest. "No toothpaste can claim greater

effectiveness against cavities than Colgate," said Reuben Mark, an executive vice president at Colgate. A spokesman for Lever Brothers expressed concern that P&G ads for Advanced Formula Crest implied its superiority to all other fluoride toothpastes. "Our concern is that consumers are going to believe that the new Crest is better than Aim," explained the spokesman. "We know that Aim is unsurpassed in preventing cavities. If the new Crest is better than it was, that suggests that the old Crest was less effective than other brands." To reinforce its point Lever Brothers had just sent Mailgrams to all ADA members in which it stated, "While the new Crest should be better than the old Crest, there is no reason to expect that it is better than Aim." It went on to suggest that, at best, the new Crest would only be doing what the old Crest should have been doing all along. For its part P&G called on the Council of Dental Therapeutics to review its rivals' claims to having unsurpassed toothpastes. After years of standing by stannous fluoride as the only type to use, Crest joined the other makers in using sodium fluoride — thus the change of trademark to Fluoristat from Fluoristan. Also added to the new Crest was hydrated silica, an abrasive element already present in Aim and Aqua-Fresh. Caught in the middle of the battle was the ADA. "This marketing battle is no place where we want to be," said an ADA spokesman. "The manufacturers are generating this war." He added the ADA *Journal* had accepted the aforementioned Colgate ad because it did not actually mention Crest by name, but referred to "the leading stannous fluoride dentifrice."[12]

Even some very old items made a return to the dentifrice industry. For example, the very old homemade baking soda dentifrice returned, albeit in a commercially prepared form. At the ADA's 1960 convention when the main issue was whether or not the group should rescind the Crest recognition, representatives of the Church & Dwight Company passed out samples of Arm & Hammer baking soda dentifrice. The company quietly pointed out that baking soda had the ADA's okay as a dentifrice since 1932 and that it was under Class A in *Accepted Dental Remedies*. Crest was then still in Class B. Arm & Hammer dentifrice had also been advertised in the ADA *Journal*.[13]

Baking soda toothpastes continued to enjoy at least a limited success into the 1990s. Dr. Clifford Whall, assistant director of the Council on Dental Therapeutics said, in 1994, that based on what evidence the makers themselves had submitted to his group, "Toothpastes with baking soda have not demonstrated that they do anything beyond what normal fluoridated toothpastes do." As recently as 1997 Arm & Hammer Baking Soda toothpaste had an estimated 7.5 percent of the toothpaste market. Some industry observers thought the popularity was due to a nostalgia factor because many people remembered baking soda as a natural substance for cleaning teeth used by their parents and grandparents.[14]

During the summer of 1966 P&G was trying out a new mint-flavored Crest in several cities while Colgate-Palmolive was then expanding the number of test market cities it was using to try out Ultra-Brite, "the greatest thing to happen to kissing since mouthwash," said the ad copy. Ads also described "new extra-strength Ultra-Brite" as "the cavity-preventive toothpaste that ultra-brightens your breath as it ultra-brightens your teeth." Dazzling white smiles were featured in all the ads. Beecham's Macleans toothpaste (in fourth place with 6 percent of the total market) had one of their ads declare, "In the fashion business, sales executive Hilde Wendt is almost unfair competition with her Macleans-white smile." And the fad for "whiter-and-brighter" teeth had begun. The craze for dentifrices that whitened the teeth could last for decades as it waxed and waned.[15]

Those cosmetic-approach toothpastes (the ones that promised whiter-and-brighter teeth and to make your mouth lovelier and more kissable) quickly became an important part of the dentifrice market, accounting for over 18 percent of total toothpaste sales by 1966. Industry executives believed that about 30 percent of the toothpaste market was interested in the cosmetic aspects of toothpaste while the other 70 percent of the market was interested in the decay-prevention aspect of toothpaste. In the early 1960s, the trend was to the fluoride products due to Crest's spectacular success, leaving the cosmetic field relatively open to little known (at least in the U.S.) Macleans. It started in America in 1960 with a test market in a few West Coast cities, and then moved to regional markets. By 1963 the product was distributed nationally and backed by television advertising. Macleans "whiter teeth" approach with a teenage slant was researched and proven to be successful in England where Macleans had a 20 percent market share. In 1963 its U.S. television ad budget was $392,000; then $2,398,900 in 1964; and then $3,006,200 in 1965. Pepsodent, over the years, had also used a whiter teeth approach with its most famous slogan, "You'll wonder where the yellow went" used from 1955 to 1958, and revived in 1963 and 1964. Oddly enough, it was dropped during the exact three-year period during which Macleans was making inroads with its "whiter and brighter" commercials. Success of that brand caused a host of whitener toothpastes to have entered the market in the middle 1960s: Colgate's Ultra-Brite, Alberto-Culver's Mighty White and Hazel Bishop's Plus White (a premium-priced brand). Alberto-Culver introduced its brand Mighty White to compete with other whiteners, in the fall of 1965 after two years of testing.[16]

Toothpaste advertisers in the whitening competition had to be careful about their claims because trade associations like the National Association of Broadcasters agreed that advertisers could not simply claim a toothpaste made teeth white — only whiter. That was because white was a relative term with some teeth being naturally more yellow than others, and a toothpaste could at best only restore teeth to their natural color. As the fluoride decay fighters and the whiteners battled it out it left some remaining brands desperately searching for something different to market. One gimmick could be found in Colgate's Bite 'n' Brush product, then being test marketed in two cities. The idea was for children to chew the Bite 'n' Brush tablets and get ingredients lodged in areas of the back teeth that were hard to reach with a brush. Colgate had another gimmick then being test marketed in the form of a super-size Colgate Dental Cream with a roll-up key so people would not waste toothpaste.[17]

In England in 1963 Macleans lost a few percentage points in market share due to fluoride toothpaste inroads. When its ad agency studied the situation it concluded, after conducting a major consumer study, the majority of respondents were most interested in cleaner and whiter teeth. All of which underscored the feeling among Macleans marketers that toothpaste was really regarded as a cosmetic and not as a technical item. Also, Macleans learned from the study that the product was going nowhere with the teenage market in Britain. That led to Macleans launching a major ad campaign in the UK that stressed the cosmetic aspects of the product and also emphasized a youthful image. Started in July 1964 that campaign included commercials in some 1,500 cinemas (where 50 percent of the audience was in the 16 to 24 age group) and caused the brand's market share to move that year from 17.9 percent to 20.1 percent.[18]

Lever Brothers joined the whiter competition at the start of 1967 when it launched a new "bright white" formula Pepsodent with zirconium silicate. Ads stressed the new Pepsodent got even hard-to-whiten teeth whiter and depicted the "bright white" Pepsodent as the toothpaste for "socially active" young adults. Meanwhile, Colgate-Palmolive expanded distribution of Ultra-Brite toothpaste from four test markets (where the product was said to have done well) to an area containing about one-third of the nation. As well, ads continued to promise whiter, brighter teeth, fresher breath, and to hail the product as the best thing to happen to kissing since mouthwash. Not to be outdone, Bristol-Myers began to test market Vote toothpaste in three cities — it also promised whiter teeth. P&G was alone among the major makers in having no entry in the whitening derby. But it was testing a stannous fluoride version of Gleem called Super Gleem. Macleans had started the whiteness bandwagon and, as of the start of 1964, it was the fourth-ranked toothpaste with a 7 percent market share, trailing Crest at 30 percent, Colgate's 25 percent, and Gleem at 14 percent, but ahead of Pepsodent's 6 percent.[19]

Some 18 months later the toothpaste industry was worth about $300 million annually. In the whitener market Macleans had been the leader for about five years, from the time it went to national distribution in the U.S. But the arrival of Colgate-Palmolive's Ultra-Brite in the summer of 1968 changed all that. By the summer of 1968 it had 10 percent of the toothpaste market, after $8 million had been spent on ads and promotion in the introductory campaign. Colgate conducted a massive sampling and couponing effort for Ultra-Brite with a 3.25 ounce sample tube of Ultra-Brite delivered to 85 percent of American households at least once — some homes received as many as three sample tubes. That was followed by cents-off coupon mailings. As Ultra-Brite's introductory campaign started to wane Bristol-Myers launched a national effort for its whitener brand, Vote, also using sampling and couponing. Vote had $5 million spent on its debut but had a market share of just 2 to 3 percent; Plus White had 2 percent, new formula Pepsodent whitener had a 4 percent share, and Macleans had 7 percent. A submarket of the whitener area involved combination whiteners and mouthwashes, such as Close-Up (Lever) then in test markets and Plus White (Hazel Bishop) then also in test marketing. Industry observers then felt the whitener toothpaste market would level off at about 25 percent of total paste sales. Macleans and Plus White were youth-oriented whiteners; Vote was positioned as an adult whitener; Ultra-Brite emphasized that it gave the user's mouth sex appeal. Colgate then had about 35 percent of the toothpaste market (Colgate Dental Cream, 24 percent; Ultra-Brite, 10 percent; Cue, 1 percent) while Procter & Gamble had about 42 percent (Crest, 31 percent; Gleem, 11 percent), Bristol-Myers's Fact, a fluoride toothpaste introduced two years earlier, in 1966, then had only about a 1 percent share.[20]

Indirectly ADA criticized the new whiteners in late 1968 when it stated it was possible for a dentifrice to be "excessively harsh for regular use by the general public," meaning a dentifrice that contained an abrasive that could damage tooth surfaces and foster decay. Reportedly, marketers of the whiteners, Colgate's Ultra-Brite, Beecham's Macleans, Bishop Industries' Plus White and Bristol-Myers' Vote and Fact, had prepared defenses of their formulas in case a public reaction against whiteners set in as a result of the dental group's warning, or any direct attacks by the ADA. But none of the latter ever came and public defenses were not necessary.[21]

Although the ADA had little to say publicly about the whiteners many dentists found them to be too abrasive and individually, across the country, made that known to their patients who asked about that product class. It may have been one of the reasons that whiteners fell flat around the early 1970s, at least for a time.[22]

When business reporter Morton Pader wrote about trends in toothpaste in 1971 he mentioned that the fluoride pastes took about one-third of the market, leaving much of that market inaccessible to marketers trying to promote a cosmetic item; they only had about 65 percent of the market left available to them, what Pader considered to be the cosmetic segment. "Innovation was expressed in new flavors, visual stimuli, and packaging," explained Pader, then came whiteners. When Close-Up was launched nationally in 1970 it had a number of novelty features; it was a whitener; it had an unusual cinnamon-type flavor unlike that of any other dentifrice then marketed; and it was a clear paste. Pader argued it "further pointed to a growing public trend to accept, and perhaps even seek, new innovations and sensations" in toothpastes. Gleem II (reformulated as a sodium fluoride toothpaste) tried to combine both cosmetic and therapeutic themes by arguing it fought cavities while also brightening teeth. Wondering about future direction in the industry Pader speculated one area might be a dentifrice that removed dental plaque — since the elimination thereof could result in a major reduction in cavities. He would be proved right.[23]

After about a generation in the wilderness whiteners became popular again in the 1990s. EPI Products introduced EpiSmile around the nation in 1989. It was a product, said the maker, which contained the chemical whitener calcium peroxide. Originally the product was introduced in 1985 as Super-Smile but was renamed following the sale of the product to EPI Products of Beverly Hills, California, later in the 1980s. It was not a cheap product as a four-ounce pump canister cost $12, more than four times as much as most other toothpastes.[24]

EpiSmile was invented by a New York dentist named Irwin Smigel, who claimed the substance whitened teeth by gently dissolving the protein film that contained stains and plaque. There were no independent studies on the product's efficacy and safety, only the maker's "own clinical evidence."[25]

Yet in the two years from 1989 to 1991, according to *Newsweek*, dozens of teeth whitening products flooded the market, promising to brighten yellow, stained teeth for about $10. More involved this time around, the ADA worried about product safety. It warned that regular use of oxygenating agents (the principal chemicals used in most whiteners) could damage mouth tissue and tooth pulp. Said Kenneth Burrell, director of the ADA Council on Dental Therapeutics, "While [whiteners] may be safe and effective, we haven't seen enough data to recommend them for the public." The most common oxygenating agent was carbamide peroxide, which, in contact with saliva, released a highly reactive concentration of oxygen. That process was said to remove superficial stains, including those from coffee and cigarettes. Marketers claimed their products did not need FDA approval because they were marketed as cosmetics while the FDA said if those products changed the body's structure or function, they would be classified as drugs, and subject to FDA regulation.[26]

Journalist Bernice Kanner reported at the start of 1994 that whiteners had been experiencing strong growth with prices and profits that outstripped those from other pastes. Those whitening toothpastes generally then sold for $7 to $10 a tube and had profit margins of around 25 percent, more than double that of traditional toothpastes. In 1993 sales of whiteners rose 25 percent to $51 million while at the same time, sales of toothpaste overall increased just 3 percent to $1.2 billion. Goaded by dentists in 1991, the FDA, worried about the possible health effects of peroxide-based whiteners, raised the question of whether whiteners should be classified as drugs. Thus, said Kanner, many makers of traditional toothpastes were finessing their whitening claims, implying such a benefit without proclaiming it.[27]

For many mainstream marketers, continued Kanner, touting baking soda as an ingredient was a subtle way to suggest whitening. No baking soda toothpaste had ever claimed to actually whiten teeth, but Americans believed it did, she said. Baking soda toothpastes then accounted for 20 percent of the market, compared to 3 percent five years earlier, in 1989. In January 1993 Crest launched a baking soda toothpaste although P&G called it a "flavor option" and contended Crest was more concerned with cavity prevention than with aesthetics. Six months earlier Chesebrough-Pond's Close-Up brand announced a "dual whitening system." Colgate had just launched an Ultra-Brite baking soda dentifrice, promising bright, shiny teeth, but shied away from calling it a whitener. Chesebrough-Pond had also just introduced Mentadent, combining fluoride, baking soda and peroxide. Said Close-Up brand manager Helayna Minsk, "All our research indicates that whitening is a big, unmet need. The specialty brands and three-step kits have proven that. We've found that no matter how white people's teeth are, they still want them whiter, and that they haven't yet found the product that delivers enough whiteners."[28]

Kanner thought much of it had to do with an aging population less concerned about decay and with teeth more prone to yellowing and staining. Said Dr. Alan J. Goldstein, a specialist in cosmetic dentistry, "We're a culture that's increasingly concerned about our appearance and increasingly into do-it-yourself quick fixes, especially when they're hyped as dramatic and foolproof. People see these products as cheaper than having their teeth cleaned." Whitening agents had been around for decades with Sheffield Laboratories, maker of

Natural Tooth White, claiming it pioneered the field with its first bleaching toothpaste in 1912. During the 1980s, and beyond, home whitening kits (not, of course, toothpastes) caught on. For example, Natural Tooth White kits were advertised on a 30-minute infomercial; within a year consumers ordered a million of those kits at $49.95 each. Consumers could also receive a specific whitening procedure at their dentist's office. In October 1991, the FDA reclassified 10 home bleach kits as drugs, and not cosmetics. One maker sued and the FDA went into a seemingly endless period of re-evaluating its position.[29]

When *Mademoiselle* magazine profiled six whiteners in 1995 it did not say those products would whiten your teeth but it clearly left that impression, in a piece that was uncritically accepting of the whiteners. Those pricey whitening pastes were Close-Up Original Red Gel Toothpaste with dual whitening system ($2.19), Mentadent ($3.99), Rembrandt Whitening Toothpaste ($8.99), SuperSmile ($12), Pearl Drops Stain-Fighting Baking Soda Whitening Toothpaste ($3.49), and Colgate Platinum Whitening toothpaste with Fluoride ($5.99).[30]

Morton Pader's speculation that plaque-fighting toothpastes could become the next big fad in dentifrices started to come true in the mid–1980s. Writing in *Business Week* in 1985 Zachary Schiller echoed that view when he reported the next big development in the toothpaste field was to be an "all-out war on plaque, the thin bacterial film which is a major cause of the gum disease that afflicts most adult Americans." The ADA's Council on Dental Therapeutics was then in the process of attempting to adopt a set of standards for evaluating the effectiveness of anti-plaque pastes. By June 1985 the panel was expected to begin studying individual products, said council secretary Edgar W. Mitchell. All the major toothpaste manufacturers were said to be then working quietly and secretly on anti-plaque products. A few were reported to be in test marketing.[31]

Writing in *Fortune* magazine in 1985, Eleanor Johnson Tracy described plaque as a colorless film of bacteria that built up on the teeth and together with its calcified version, called tartar, was a leading cause of gum disease and tooth loss, and a source of great anxiety to aging baby boomers. Because fluoride toothpastes had drastically reduced tooth decay, she explained, gum disease had become the number one dental problem in America, affecting 75 percent of adults. At that point the toothpaste industry had sales of about $1 billion a year and more plaque-fighting products had been introduced, Dentagard from Colgate-Palmolive and Crest Tartar Control Formula from P&G. Dentagard made no claim it had a special plaque fighting chemical but Crest declared it contained the special cleansing agent sodium pyrophosphate. Other items positioned as anti-plaque brands were Check-Up and Viadent (made by the new-to-the-toothpaste market Vipont Laboratories, Colorado). Said Tracy, "The best way to prevent plaque, according to brochures accompanying some products, is to brush and floss your teeth regularly and maintain a healthy diet. If that sounds like the advice dentists have been giving for years — it is." In 1984 Check-Up (marketed in the novelty dispenser — a pump canister) took 2 percent of the overall market.[32]

Colgate spent an estimated $30 million to roll-out Dentagard in 1985 while Crest spent about $50 million to launch Crest Tartar Control Formula; Crest had 30.5 percent of the market then while Colgate had 27.8 percent, up from 18 percent five years earlier in 1980. Business reporter Kathleen Deveny observed, "But Dentagard is more a marketing innovation than a technological one. It is basically the same toothpaste Colgate has always sold. The mechanical action of brushing, not chemical ingredients, fights the plaque. And almost any toothpaste, used with enough elbow grease, removes plaque, says the ADA."[33]

In a 1985 piece in *Newsweek* Susan Katz argued there was no evidence that gum disease was increasing; it was only that baby boomers were aging, and worried. According to Katz the ADA had issued no official standards nor made any official statements on the supposed plaque-fighters and its seal of acceptance on some plaque-fighting pastes referred only to their cavity-fighting abilities and that the ability of toothbrush bristles to brush off plaque enabled any toothpaste to make anti-plaque claims. Samuel Yankell, a dental researcher at the University School of Dental Medicine, said, "I should have the same advertising claims on my fingernail." Dentagard advertised that it reduced plaque by as much as 45 percent and gingivitis by as much as 37 percent. "These results are based not on new active ingredients but on improved package instructions about proper brushing and flossing," said Yankell. Check-Up declared it contained microsil, an abrasive that enhanced the mechanical effects of brushing. "I'd say that anyone who properly brushes with an 89-cent tube of fluoride toothpaste, and flosses daily, will certainly be able to remove plaque," remarked Dr. Jean Campbell, a consumer adviser to the ADA. Crest had sidestepped the plaque controversy, continued Katz, by focusing instead on tartar, a cement-like substance formed when the dead bacteria from plaque joined up with minerals in the saliva to crystallize on the teeth. While it did not cause gum disease, tartar could build up and irritate the gums.[34]

Jane E. Brody explained in the *New York Times* in 1986 that plaque was the leading cause of tooth loss in adults; that it started forming within minutes after a person brushed his teeth and if left undisturbed for 24 hours or longer, it hardened into tartar, or calculus, which required professional dental instruments to remove. Wondering if any of those plaque-fighters, then all the rage, worked, Brody answered her question by stating, "To begin with, the bare toothbrush, used with elbow grease, is far more effective than is any toothpaste in removing plaque. Second, no toothpaste can clean where the toothbrush cannot reach, so high risk areas will not necessarily be helped by brushing. Third, just because they are advertised as plaque attackers doesn't mean they can combat plaque." First to arrive was Check-Up, followed by Crest Tartar Control Formula and Dentagard. Johnson & Johnson was then marketing Prevent. Brody concluded that Dentagard and Check-Up had no special ingredients to fight plaque, however, she noted that Check-Up contained the additional abrasive agent microsil, which its maker claimed functioned as a mechanical aid in removing plaque. Crest Tartar Control and Prevent contained chemicals called "sequestering agents," which had been shown to inhibit tartar build-up, according to *Consumer Reports*.[35]

The big three paste makers — P&G, Colgate-Palmolive, and Lever Brothers — were all fighting to gain a share in the plaque-fighter field in mid–1987. Colgate had an ad campaign underway claiming research on its newest entry, Colgate Tartar Control, showed it was better than Crest's at removing the substance. CBS-TV had just rejected P&G's objection to the ad claims that Colgate made in its recent television commercials. Lever had introduced Extra-Strength Aim and claimed superiority over both Crest and Colgate in cavity fighting. Also, Lever was launching tartar control companions to Aim and Close-Up. According to one survey, tartar control toothpastes then accounted for almost one-third of the overall market.[36]

Reportedly, the FDA was becoming more concerned about the ever-bolder therapeutic claims being made by these products regarding tartar and plaque removal when the products themselves were classified by the FDA as having cosmetic benefits only. Staff members at the FDA were said to have expressed dismay when references to tartar and plaque began appearing in ad claims, but the issue was given low priority by the agency since the claims were not considered to have caused any health damage. Paste marketers had been trying to avoid FDA scrutiny by limiting their claims to the removal or reduction of plague and tartar above the gum line, where the relationship to gum disease was not well documented.[37]

The ADA's Council on Dental Therapeutics by this time awarded two different seals, one for fluoride content and one for plaque removal (none had been yet awarded in the latter category to a toothpaste). However, there was a worry that consumers got confused and thought a seal was for plaque or tartar removal when it was for fluoride. That confusion had forced the ADA to modify the wording of the fluoride seal that was currently to be used on tartar control toothpastes. Those seals then had to carry the words "the product has been shown to reduce the formation of tartar above the gum line but has not been shown to have a therapeutic effect on periodontal disease." Still not satisfied, one major toothpaste maker had asked the ADA for written clarification on its position on tartar. ADA was also in a dispute with Lever over its newly introduced Extra-Strength Aim paste. Although the new Lever brand had received FDA approval through its new-drug approval process, the ADA had not granted its fluoride seal because the ADA did not like Lever ads that made a "50% more fluoride" claim, versus the leading brands.[38]

Journalist Bernice Kanner argued in 1988 that marketers had been trying for five years — with little success — to sell Americans on toothpastes (and mouthwashes) that supposedly dissolved plaque. Although one-third of all toothpastes sold then were billed as plaque-fighters, Maurice Kelly, vice president of marketing at Beecham Products, pointed out that not one major toothpaste was selling plaque-fighting ability as a major, exclusive benefit. "They're pitching taste, fluoride, cavity-fighting capability, and tartar control instead," he added. Crest Tartar Control, introduced in 1985, then had 17.6 percent of the total market (Crest's overall share was 37 percent) and Kanner noted that already many anti-plaque toothpastes had abandoned the field. For example, Oral-B Laboratories Zendium came on the market in 1983 and went off early in 1986. Colgate would not confirm that it was prepared to halt production of its four-year-old brand Dentagard but conceded that sales were only moderate. In Kanner's view the plaque crusade began in 1983 when Zendium toothpaste (and Viadent oral rinse — a mouthwash) hit the drugstores. Next came Check-Up toothpaste in 1984. Truman Susman, president of Pfizer's Oral Research Labs, commented that "many plaque fighters simply aren't very effective. Truth is, anti-plaque toothpastes don't do a lot, although the process of brushing does. Dentists are telling their patients that, and people can't really see or feel the difference to justify their investments" (some plaque-fighters cost quite a bit more than regular toothpastes). The shift by makers away from plaque-fighter to tartar-fighter pastes had to do with the FDA since it considered plaque — which played a part in gum disease such as gingivitis — was a medical problem and thus, products that claimed to fight plaque came under its purview. The agency considered tartar — which did not play a part in gum disease such as gingivitis — a cosmetic problem and therefore not under its purview. Lever Brothers joined the fray with Aim Anti-Tartar and Close-Up Tartar Control toothpastes in mid–1987. And Colgate, said Kanner, "has essentially abandoned plaque, preferring a tartar attack. It has dropped all reference to gingivitis from labels and ads" and had shifted its emphasis to tartar control and to children's products.[39]

At the start of 1991 both P&G and Colgate were racing along to get out the next generation of super protection pastes to market, but were having problems with the FDA. On the brink of launching Ultra Protection Crest, P&G learned the product was likely to be delayed for at least two years because the FDA had determined the paste's active ingredient — triclosan — to be a new drug. The new Crest formula was said, by the company, to fight gum disease. Because of the FDA order, an ad campaign to have cost $32 million had to be scrapped; P&G had already presented the product to the retail trade. The anti-bacterial triclosan had to undergo the FDA's new-drug application process, which could take from 24 to 36 months to complete, after supporting data was submitted. That FDA action was also a setback for Colgate, who planned on using its own new formula, Colgate Gum Protection Formula, which also contained triclosan, to capture its share of the market. Both Colgate and P&G then marketed triclosan-containing toothpastes outside the U.S. To that point Colgate had not asked the FDA for formal new-drug approval. P&G had told retailers that Ultra Protection Crest had been clinically shown to kill bacteria, a leading cause of gum disease, and the product was positioned as an "anti-plaque toothpaste," according to one retailer. Unilever's Chesebrough-Pond's unit skirted the edges of the issue with the launch of Close-Up Anti-Plaque toothpaste that was then being sold to retailers. Its active ingredient was stannous fluoride and a company spokesman claimed the brand "stops the bacterial growth and inhibits adhesion [of bacteria] on the surface of the tooth," which she classified as "a cosmetic claim that doesn't need approval." However, the FDA had traditionally viewed plaque-fighting claims as therapeutic rather than cosmetic.[40]

Celebrity dentist Jonathan Levine developed an aromatherapeutic toothpaste in 2003. GoSmile's mood fixers included a citrus-scented morning version of the paste, said to stimulate the senses, and a lavender and chamomile-spike night-time variation, meant to help calm you down. The price for the product was $30 for two tubes. Reportedly, stars such as Halle Berry, Kim Cattrall, Sarah Jessica Parker, and even Robert De Niro were fans of GoSmile toothpaste.[41]

13

Toothpaste, General, 1960–2008

The average number of [tooth] brushings per capita per day is well under one. — Morton Pader, 1971.

You can brush with plain old Acme fluoride and have gorgeous teeth. If you brush and floss, use a regular toothpaste with fluoride, and get regular dental checkups, you'll do fine. — Dr. Eric Spieler, 1998.

In the toothpaste industry in general, as this period began, Crest dominated the $235 million annual dentifrice market with a 50 percent share (Crest, 30 percent; Gleem, 20 percent) with Colgate Dental Cream with Gardol in second place with a 25 percent share of the market.[1]

When Dental Survey Publications conducted a 1964 survey they sent a questionnaire to a random sample of 5,000 dentists. Some 780 (15.6 percent) of the dentists returned the survey. One result revealed that 72.1 percent of the respondents recommended Crest toothpaste to their patients, 14.5 percent recommended Cue, and 9.7 percent picked Sensodyne. In the toothpowder category 25.3 percent recommended Caroid, 19.2 percent opted for Py-Co-Pay, and 15.1 percent picked Dr. Lyons.[2]

According to the Toilet Goods Association, Americans consumed $252.4 million worth of toothpaste in 1964, not counting toothpowders. While that market was said to be shared by no less than 100 brands only a handful of them were significant. P&G's Crest and Gleem continued to rank number one and number three in sales, respectively, while Colgate ranked second with five brands: Colgate Dental Cream with Gardol, Colgate Fluoride, Colgate Chlorophyll, Brisk-Activated, and Cue. Lever Brothers was estimated to rank third in sales with four brands: Chlorodent, Pepsodent, Pepsodent Fluoride, and Stripe. Other large-selling brands included Ipana Durenamel (Bristol-Myers), Kolynos (American Home Products), Listerine Toothpaste (Warner-Lambert Pharmaceutical) and Phillips (Sterling Drugs). Some 73 percent of industry sales were then accounted for by just three brands: Crest, 32 percent; Colgate Dental Cream with Gardol, 24 percent; Gleem, 17 percent.

Around 15 years earlier (1950) the drugstore was the principal outlet for the product, but by 1964 it was the supermarket. On average, the industry was said to spend 20 percent of its sales dollar for advertising. "Dentifrice manufacturers have long tried to enlist the aid of dentists in selling their product," commented business reporter Goody Solomon in *Barron's*. "They advertise in professional journals, send detail men to contact dentists personally, and give them displays and literature for their waiting-rooms, along with free samples to be distributed to patients."[3]

As unlikely as it seemed, industrial espionage even played a part in the dentifrice industry. Eugene Andrew Mayfield, 26, was indicted on April 1, 1965, by a federal grand jury, accused of plotting to sell a million dollar secret plan of one major company to its greatest rival. Mayfield was a junior executive at Procter & Gamble until he quit in July 1964. Five months later, according to the government, he sought to hand over to the Colgate-Palmolive Company, for $20,000, a 188-page budget supplement outlining the 1964–1965 marketing strategy of P&G for its Crest toothpaste. Colgate agreed to pay, but only after consulting the FBI, which was interested in a possible violation of interstate commerce regulations.[4]

Next, Mayfield telephoned from Chicago near his home to a Colgate man in New York to set up a meeting. The pair arranged to meet in a specified men's toilet in the Trans World Airlines terminal at Kennedy Airport on November 14, 1964. They did so and entered adjoining cubicles after which Mayfield passed over the copied document while the Colgate man passed over $20,000 in marked bills. Then Mayfield walked out and into the arms of waiting FBI agents. He was arrested and charged under Title 18, United States Code, Sec. 2314, with using the telephone to further a dishonest scheme. Assistant United States attorney Leonard J. Theberge told the court that P&G estimated the Crest budget document was worth more than $1 million to any competitor since it contained highly confidential material on the marketing strategy for the coming year. When first offered the document Colgate faced a dilemma. First, the document offered could conceivably have been a fake intended to mislead, or simply stolen by a disgruntled employee. In any case the purchaser could clearly be put at the mercy of the seller, reasoned Colgate, so the firm decided to call in the FBI. Mayfield pled guilty in federal court in August 1965 to using the telephone to further a dishonest scheme and faced a maximum penalty of 10 years in prison and a $10,000 fine. Sentencing was set for September 23.[5] When Mayfield again appeared in court, he received a suspended sentence.

By the end of 1965 the toothpaste industry was estimated to be worth $285 million annually. Colgate-Palmolive's Cue received its ADA recognition in February that year, followed by Bristol-Myers' Fact in October — to join Crest as the second and third pastes so honored by the dental group. Media reporter Ralph Tyler remarked, "The ADA endorsement is so desirable that for the first time in history an important segment of television advertising has come under the control of a body of professional men." He meant, of course, the ADA's Council on Dental Therapeutics, which required all ad copy of a brand using the ADA statement of recognition to be continuously reviewed by the council, whether the ad was destined for television, print or radio. In Tyler's opinion that review was "exacting." For example, he said, one advertiser, preparing a 30-second commercial for his ADA–recognized brand of paste was told by the council to change the words "brush, brush, brush" to "brush, brush, brush after meals." Peter Goulding, ADA director of public relations, said the entrance of the council into the field had "a profound and salutary effect on dentifrice advertising. We think it is better today than at any time in the last 20 years." In general, those ads could not place "undue emphasis" on the role of the toothpaste itself and had to point out the necessity of frequent brushings, regular dental care and cutting down on sweets. Market shares in the fall of 1965 were Crest, 34 percent; Colgate with Gardol, 25 percent; Gleem, 15 percent; Macleans, 8 percent; Pepsodent, 5 percent; Cue five percent; Hazel Bishop's Plus White, 3 percent; Stripe, 2.5 percent; Ipana, 2 percent.[6]

According to *Sponsor* magazine the toothpaste market had expanded threefold in 16 years, from $94.3 million in 1950 to almost $300 million in 1966. Aggressive television advertising was said to have always played an important role in toothpaste success stories. In 1965 the seven leading dentifrice advertisers spent over $45 million on television, with the two market leaders, P&G and Colgate, accounting for almost 80 percent of toothpaste television spending. P&G's television spending on dentifrice ads in 1964 was $21.5 million; Colgate spent $10.5 million. For the following year P&G spent $18.5 million while Colgate's expenditure was $16.5 million. Lever's brands Pepsodent and Stripe, and Beecham's Macleans, were backed almost exclusively by television. The *Sponsor* piece declared, "Industry marketing strategy has radically changed, making toothpaste readily accessible in supermarkets and promoting it heavily with point-of-purchase material, special deals and premiums." While drugstores were once the principal outlet, accounting for 45 percent of all dentifrice sales in 1950, by the mid–1960s about 75 percent of all toothpaste sales were made in supermarkets. ADA approval had done little to lift the sales of either of the fluoride brands Cue or Fact. Estimates were, 12 to 18 months after ADA recognition of those two, that each had a 1 percent to 2 percent share of the total market. One ad executive thought the reasons for that failure had to do with "no freedom for original context in commercials and no new story-line advantage over Crest." All the toothpastes with ADA recognition found it to be a mixed blessing precisely because of that. Fluoride toothpastes had gone from zero percent to 40 percent of the market in 10 years. Colgate's sodium fluoride entry Brisk had been dropped by this time. Toothpowders had not been an important part of the dentifrice market for years but were still used by some dedicated consumers. Remaining brands, as of late 1966, included Dr. Lyons Tooth Power, Dr. Lyons Ammoniated Tooth Powder, Amm-i-dent the Ammoniated Tooth Power; Pepsodent Tooth Powder, and Pepsodent Ammoniated Tooth Powder.[7]

The U.S. toothpaste market (at retail, all outlets, in millions of dollars) was as follows: 1956, $178.3 (86.9 percent regular paste, 13.1 percent whiteners); 1957, $202.3 (79.8 percent, 10 percent fluorides, 10.2 percent whiteners); 1958, $222.8 (80.3, 8.6, 11.1); 1959, $227.8 (79.3, 9.8,10.9); 1960, $234.8 (74.9, 14.5 — year of Crest recognition —10.6); 1961, $243.7 (60.4, 31.3, 8.3); 1962, $236.9 (54.8, 37.4, 7.8); 1963, $244.9 (52.6, 39.5, 7.9); 1964, $260.2 (52.3, 36.6, 11.1); 1965, $281.6 (44.2, 33.3, 18.5, 4.0 — combination of whitener and fluoride).[8]

For the first time the American Dental Association conduced a study, in 1970, that rated commercial toothpastes according to their abrasiveness. The reason for the study was to aid dentists in giving advice to patients concerning dentifrices. The report was compiled by the ADA's Council on Dental Therapeutics with another reason for the study being the group's concern about the degree of abrasiveness of dentifrices (whitening pastes were then quite popular). The ADA worried that too much abrasiveness might damage teeth. However, the report concluded that it was likely that significant amounts of enamel would not be lost by the judicious use of most of the dentifrices then being marketed. "It should be noted, however, that the compulsive brusher may wear away significant amounts of dental enamel, especially with the more abrasive formulations," added the report.[9]

Business reporter Morton Pader estimated dentifrice sales to be around $325 million in 1970 and observed that no one brand ever expanded the total dentifrice market to an extent substantially beyond its normal growth rate. That is, when Crest surged upwards it did so by taking share from other brands, not by increasing the toothpaste market overall. Based on an annual toothpaste consumption in America of perhaps 150 million pounds to 200 million pounds per year Pader made a "very crude" estimate that "the average number of brushings per capita per day is well under one."[10]

Consumers Union selected a broad array of dentifrices — 32 pastes and one powder — for evaluation in April 1972 and had a team of dental experts at a leading university test them for the consumer group. Consumers Union's selection included 12 fluoride-bearing pastes and a number of products that promised brighter and whiter results. A key finding by Consumers Union was that people under 25 should stick with the decay-fighting ability of ADA–recognized products while older people with sound gums should please themselves, cautioned only to avoid relatively abrasive products. Pointed out was that while fluoride did inhibit decay, especially in children's teeth, not all fluoridated dentifrices delivered the benefits of fluoride to the teeth. Not only did the fluoride have to be in a suitable form to enter tooth enamel but also had to unite with the enamel to produce a uniformly distributed, acid-resistant result; other ingredients of a paste could modify or even negate the fluoride's action in reducing cavities. For Consumers Union, that was all the more reason to pick a brand with ADA recognition, showing the therapeutic usefulness of the brand had been validated. At that time the only ADA accepted fluoride pastes were Crest Regular, Crest Mint, and Colgate MFP.[11]

Dr. Lyons Tooth Powder was the only powder tested and was included by Consumers Union only as a representative toothpowder and not even listed in the ratings, further evidence of the decline of powders almost to the point of non-existence. It was found to be among the more efficient cleaners and polishers in the study but was also two to seven times more abrasive than any other product in the study and was dismissed by Consumers Union as "too abrasive for regular use, but okay for occasional application to remove stains." Consumers Union added that none of the tested dentifrices contained whitening ingredients (ads proclaiming such for Close-Up, Vote, Pearl Drops, and Macleans notwithstanding), bleaches or anything else that could in any way alter the natural color of a person's teeth. All the more effective polishers among the test products were among the more abrasive. Items tested by Consumers Union came in a total of 14 sizes ranging from two ounces to 7.25 ounces and included such oddities as 3.1, 6.2, and 6.35 ounces, making comparison shopping difficult. The U.S. Department of Commerce, acting under the Fair Packaging and Labeling Act, published a standard, effective April 1, 1971, that limited toothpaste to five sizes (1.5, 3.0, 5.0, 7.0, 9.0 ounces, by weight). But compliance with that standard was voluntary, not mandatory. Complicating the situation further, toothpastes differed markedly in specific gravity — that is, they were not all equally thick or thin. A thick paste could weigh more than an equal measure of a thin one without providing any bonus in the number of brushings a person could squeeze out of a tube. The Commerce Department's standard tried to get around the problem by allowing relatively thin or thick pastes the option of packaging "on a comparable volume basis in tubes of approximately the same dimensions" as more typical products.[12]

The toothpaste market reached an estimated value of $425 million annually in 1977, spent on at least 22 brands, not counting house brands or expensive imports. ADA recognition remained limited to three pastes: Crest (with stannous fluoride). Colgate MFP (sodium fluoride) and Macleans (sodium fluoride).[13]

American Druggist estimated 1978 retail sales of toothpaste to be $600 million (with 21.5 percent, $129 million, being sales at drugstores) with 60 percent of all toothpaste sales being made at supermarkets. Retail sales of toothbrushes were estimated at $120 million (with 54.2 percent, $65 million, at drugstores).[14]

For its 1984 evaluation *Consumer Reports* tested 27 brands, 16 of them containing fluoride. "Through the adolescent years, children certainly should use an ADA–accepted fluoridated product, and it's possible that adults can benefit as well from fluoridated toothpaste," concluded *Consumer Reports*. "Adults with receding gums should use the least abrasive product they can find. For both groups then, the clear first choice is Colgate Regular. We've check-rated that brand because it's fluoridated and bears the ADA seal, and because it's low in abrasion. What's more, its cost per month is low." That marked the first time *Consumer Reports* had specifically named a brand as its favorite toothpaste. Also noted by *Consumer Reports* was a rise in the popularity of sodium bicarbonate, plain baking soda, as a dentifrice, something *Consumer Reports* had itself recommended back in 1936. Cited as a modern example was Colgate-Palmolive's Peak, a brand the consumer group felt to be extremely expensive for baking soda and pretty dear for toothpaste, also. Peak cost *Consumer Reports* about 35 cents an ounce, compared to two cents an ounce for Arm & Hammer Baking Soda. At this time there were 11 toothpastes with the ADA approval (three Crest versions, two Colgate, two Aim, two Macleans, one Aqua-Fresh, and one Gleem). Although approved, Gleem chose not to use the ADA recognition statement in its ad copy. Looking at brands on a cost per month basis (assuming twice daily use with roughly ½ inch of product per use) Pepsodent was the cheapest at 48 cents per month (tied with Colgate Gel) while Peak at 78 cents per month was the most expensive (Macleans Peppermint was next at 71 cents). Crest Regular cost 64 cents per month.[15]

In 1986 *Consumer Reports* returned to toothpastes to note that when Crest Tartar Control Formula was launched free samples were sent to an "astounding" 70 percent of America's households, and that 98 percent of all Americans brushed their teeth. Chemical agents to fight plaque did exist, said

Consumer Reports, but in all the brands it tested (claiming to be plaque-fighters) it found none of those ingredients. However, *Consumer Reports* did admit that Crest Tartar Control Formula and the brand Prevent both contained chemicals clinically proven to stop tartar from accumulating. That was less than impressive as they did nothing to dissolve existing tartar, only the build-up of new stuff. To protect oneself against tooth decay and gum dis-

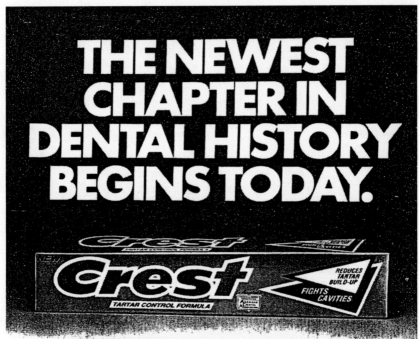

Crest came out with another new and improved product, 1985.

ease *Consumer Reports* recommended brushing and flossing regularly and thoroughly. With respect to what a person put on the brush *Consumer Reports* recommended using a fluoride, regardless of age, and the least abrasive paste that got the teeth clean. Other factors included taste (a personal preference) and cost while "factors not to consider include anti-plaque and anti-tartar claims. Every toothpaste removes plaque whenever you brush; dentifrices that position themselves as 'plaque attackers' are only telling half-truths. And most readers probably do not need a special tartar-inhibiting toothpaste." *Consumer Reports* was annoyed with the confusion it felt then existed in the public mind over ADA seals for fluoride then on some brands that positioned themselves as anti-plaque pastes (such as Aim, Aqua-Fresh, and Dentagard) even though the seal was for fluoride and cavity prevention. *Consumer Reports* thought the public could be confused and think the seal applied to plaque. Concluded *Consumer Reports*, "The ADA, by allowing such gratuitous claims on toothpastes bearings its name, has cheapened an otherwise worthy public service it provides."[16]

In the matter of trivia, Bernice Kanner reported in 1988 that women bought two-thirds of all toothpaste while in the following year the *New York Times* observed the cost of a 6.4 ounce tube of toothpaste in various nations, in U.S. dollars for 1988, was as follows: Athens, 1.48; Buenos Aires, 0.73; Cairo, 1.47; Hong Kong, 1.35; Jakarta, Indonesia, 3.66; London, 1.70; Mexico City, 1.30; Milan, Italy, 2.96; Munich, West Germany, 2.82; Nairobi, Kenya, 1.29; New York City, 2.36; Paris, 2.37; Stockholm, 3.00; Sydney, Australia, 2.01; Tokyo, 2.52.[17]

Writing in 1990, journalist Anthony Ramirez remarked that the costs involved in a tube of toothpaste selling in America for $1.99 were: raw materials and labor, 99 cents; selling, general, and administrative expenses, 37 cents; manufacturer's profit, 34 cents; retailer's mark-up, 29 cents. He added that most toothpastes in the marketplace were similar in formula and price. Each had a mild abrasive like the watery sand known as hydrated silica; sodium lauryl sulfate to dispense the abrasive, and glycerin, a moistening agent to keep the material gooey. Other ingredients included carrageenan, a thickener, plus an artificial sweetener like saccharin, for flavor, or a form of sugar like sorbitol, which did not promote tooth decay. According to Ramirez, market shares were as follows: P&G, 37.6 percent (Crest, 36.4 percent; Gleem, 1.2 percent); Colgate, 29.6 percent (Colgate, 26.9 percent; Viadent, 1.0 percent; Ultra-Brite, 1.7 percent); Unilever, 11.0 percent (Close-Up, 5.3 percent; Aim, 4.9 percent; Pepsodent, 0.8 percent); SmithKline Beecham, 11.9 percent (Aqua Fresh, 11.9 percent); all others, 9.9 percent (including Sensodyne from Dentco at 1.9 percent, Pearl Drops from Carter Wallace at 1.5 percent,

Topol from Topol at 1.3 percent; Arm & Hammer from Church & Dwight at 0.8 percent; Check-Up from S. C. Johnson at 0.5 percent; and Tom's of Maine at 0.3 percent. At one extreme P&G had toothpaste sales that exceeded $500 million annually while Tom's of Maine posted yearly sales of $10.5 million.[18]

When *Consumer Reports* tested toothpastes once again, in 1992, it evaluated some four dozen brands, spread across no fewer than 10 subcategories. Regular paste (1) contained fluoride to fight decay, abrasives to combat stain, and detergents to help suds away plaque. An example was Colgate Regular at 30 cents an ounce. Extra-strength paste (2) could help people especially prone to cavities, and older people with receding gums. An example was Aim Extra Strength, which contained about 50 percent more fluoride than most, costing 27 cents an ounce. Anti-plaque paste (3) claimed to curb plaque-making bacteria, although *Consumer Reports* argued that all toothpastes helped strip away plaque. Viadent Anti-Plaque at 67 cents an ounce was an example. Anti-tartar paste (4) contained chemicals to slow the build-up of tartar. While those products might help prevent tartar they could not remove any already on the teeth. A brand in this category was Crest Tartar Control Original at 31 cents an ounce. Soda paste (5) had baking soda added to a paste as an abrasive. It was a mild abrasive and only a mild cleaner. *Consumer Reports* thought perhaps the public was buying such products in the mistaken belief that baking soda prevented gum disease. Arm & Hammer Dental Care at 46 cents an ounce was an example in this category.[19]

Kiddie paste (6) came in flashy colors and unusual flavors like tutti-frutti and was designed to appeal to those with new teeth and sweet teeth. One example was Oral-B Muppets at 45 cents an ounce. Desensitizing paste (7) was for people with receding gums with exposed softer tissue that could make teeth sensitive to heat, cold, or pressure. These toothpastes could dull such pain by sealing tiny tubules in teeth or disrupting nerve impulses. An example was Sensodyne at 97 cents an ounce. Smokers paste (8) was often more abrasive than regular toothpaste in order to scrub off tobacco, coffee, tea and other stubborn stains. In this category was Topol Spearmint, costing 80 cents an ounce. Natural paste (9) boasted natural ingredients and flavors but contained no saccharin, artificial color or preservatives. However, they did have a detergent that was common to many other toothpaste. Tom's of Maine Cinnamint, at 55 cents an ounce, was in that category. Whitening paste (10) contained special ingredients that were supposed to make teeth look whiter. Some brands in this category contained peroxide bleach. One example was Rembrandt at $3.39 an ounce, which contained a papaya enzyme.[20]

Consumer Reports's recommendations were that everyone should brush at least twice a day with a fluoride toothpaste. In this evaluation *Consumer Reports* check-rated Colgate-Palmolive's Ultra-Brite Original, a brand that hadn't been advertised for a decade but which *Consumer Reports* found to be superior in its cleaning test, contained adequate fluoride and was not overly abrasive. At $1.50 for a six-ounce tube, it was also a relatively inexpensive paste. The organization concluded that in general the ADA seal was a reliable endorsement of a product's performance and the accuracy of its claims: "The ADA seal is a consistent indicator of a product's effectiveness."[21]

As the number of subcategories within the toothpaste industry continued to grow, more and more articles appeared in the media offering buying advice for the product. A piece by Katja Shaye in *Good Housekeeping* in February 1996 reviewed the various types such as plaque-attackers, tartar fighters, natural pastes, whiteners, and new gum-care products concluding, for example, that whiteners mostly did not work and had not yet been endorsed by the ADA but were "dazzlingly expensive."[22]

Another such article appeared in *Better Homes and Gardens* in May 1998, written by Patricia Hittner. By then there were seven kinds of Crest toothpaste, which were further divided into gels and pastes. Colgate-Palmolive made more than a dozen kinds of toothpaste while at least eight other major makers offered multiple formulations. Said Dr. Eric Spieler, a Philadelphia dentist who also lectured at the University of Pennsylvania School of Dental Medicine, "You can brush with plain old Acme fluoride toothpaste and have gorgeous teeth. If your brush and floss, use a regular toothpaste with fluoride, and get regular dental checkups, you'll do fine." Dr. William van Dyk, a dentist in San Pablo, California, and adjunct professor at the University of the Pacific in San Francisco, thought one difference in recent times was in advertising. In the past, he said, makers emphasized various product attributes such as spearmint taste, or a clean fresh feeling while recent ad copy carried specific recommendations for conditions, such as gum disease or halitosis. "A lot of manufacturers are taking their claims to the public, instead of trying just to convince the dentist or hygienist," he explained. "They are trying to go around the usual experts."[23]

According to Hittner, about 60 percent of the dental products initially submitted met ADA standards and received a seal. Manufacturers had to reapply for the seal every three years, or any time after they altered a product's chemical composition. Many dentists recommended only toothpastes with the ADA seal. Slightly more than half the adults polled by the ADA said the seal influenced which brand they bought. After 20 years of selling toothpaste, Tom's of Maine (established in 1970) natural toothpaste received its first ADA Seal of Acceptance in 1995 for three of its fluoride pastes — spearmint, cinnamon, and fennel. The company decided to apply for the seal after receiving inquiries from customers asking why its pastes did not carry it. Dentists then declared that everyone — not just children — benefited from using toothpastes with fluoride. No over-the-counter whitening pastes then had an ADA seal because while the products may have lightened superficial stains caused by coffee or tobacco, said van Dyk, they did not actually whiten teeth.[24]

In an August 1998 evaluation of toothpastes, *Consumer Reports* also mentioned the bewildering array of choices then available. Crest and Colgate alone accounted for more than 110 pastes and gels in various formulas, flavors, packages, and sizes. The biggest recent toothpaste launch — introduced in 1997 — was Colgate-Palmolive's Colgate Total, positioned as a do-everything product to prevent cavities and gingivitis, control tartar, and clear away plaque. One of its principal ingredients was an antibacterial chemical called triclosan. Total became the top-selling toothpaste in America in only four months.[25]

In that evaluation *Consumer Reports* tested 39 different toothpastes, 13 of which has whitening as part of their name or claimed to whiten teeth. Neither the FDA nor the FTC nor the ADA had defined what a whitening toothpaste was, what ingredients it should contain, or what exactly it was supposed to do. That left makers free to claim whatever they wanted. Crest Extra Whitening, for example, promised to help "the natural whiteness of your teeth come through." Aquafresh Whitening pledged to "weaken and remove ... stains [so] teeth can return to their natural whiteness." More explicit in claiming to actually lighten the color of the tooth enamel was Rembrandt toothpaste with ad copy on the box declaring, "When used twice a day, every day, Rembrandt can whiten even clean teeth by up to two shades." That was a reference to the Vita shade guide, which dentists used to match crowns and bridges to natural teeth. After testing Rembrandt, and the other supposed whiteners, *Consumer Reports* concluded "Rembrandt can cite its own clinical tests that say they show how well the products whiten. But our test didn't produce any whitening of the tooth enamel with any product." Professional bleaching (done by a dentist at a cost of $300 to $600) could make teeth up to seven or eight shades whiter, with the results lasting 1.5 to three years.[26]

Colgate Total's huge success caused Crest to lose its long-held number one ranking in the toothpaste field. With a 5.6 percent increase in market share in 1998 Colgate ended the year at 29.6 percent with P&G's Crest in second place with a 25.6 percent market share.[27]

U.S. retail sales of oral care products, including dental products, gum, mouthwash, breath fresheners, and implements and appliances, amounted to $7.2 billion in 2004. That same year tooth cleaners (paste, gel, powder, and so on) were used by 196,760,000 American adults (93.3 percent of the population); manual toothbrushes were used by 184,377,000 adults (87.5 percent); and powered brushes were used by 61,977,000 adults (29.4 percent)[28]

Also for 2004 the global oral hygiene market sizes were as follows, in millions of U.S. dollars: oral hygiene (total), 21,480.4; toothpaste, 12,492.2; manual toothbrushes, 4,485.7; mouthwashes and dental rinses, 2,081.1; denture care, 1,335.0; mouth fresheners, 534.4; dental floss, 552.0; sales of power brushes (total), 4,108.6, which broke down to 2,342.4 for battery brushes and 1,766.3 for electric toothbrushes. By region the oral hygiene market was as follows: Western Europe, 6,313.5; Eastern Europe, 1,339.3; North America, 4,676.7; Latin America, 2,392.6; Asia Pacific, 5,498.2; Australasia, 354.2; Africa and the Middle East, 905.9. Company share of the global oral care market was, in 2003: Colgate-Palmolive, 22.5 percent; Glaxosmithkline, 11.5 percent; Unilever Group, 9.2 percent; Procter and Gamble, 8.3 percent; Gillette, 4.8 percent; Pfizer, 4.7 percent; Lion Corp., 3.4 percent; Johnson and Johnson, 2.7 percent; Sunstar, 2.0 percent; Henkel, 1.5 percent; private label, 3.9 percent; and others, at 25.5 percent, brought the total to 100 percent. Global brand share of oral care products was, for 2003: Colgate, 12.7 percent; Signal (Unilever), 6.6 percent; Oral-B (Gillette), 4.5 percent; Crest (Procter and Gamble), 4.2 percent; Aquafresh (Glaxo), 4.0 percent; Listerine (Pfizer), 2.9 percent; Close-Up (Unilever), 2.0 percent; Reach (Johnson and Johnson), 2.0 percent; Sensodyne (Glaxo), 1.9 percent; private label, 3.9 percent; others, 52.8 percent. Sales of manual toothbrushes grew 10.06 percent from 1997 to 2004, and 7.07 percent from 2003 to 2004. The sales increases of battery brushes for those two periods were, respectively, 39.51 percent and 4.68 percent, while the increases for electric toothbrushes were 41.38 percent and 7.45 percent.[29]

For the 52 weeks ending September 9, 2007, the dollar volume of sales of oral care products in U.S. drugstores was as follows: toothpaste, $331,921,000; mouthwash and dental rinse, $231,882,000; manual toothbrushes, $165,166,000; dental accessories and tools, $157,482,000; oral pain relief, $107,827,000; tooth whitening, $105,958,000; power toothbrushes, $72,303,000; dental floss, $49,855,000; breath freshener sprays and drops, $12,418,000; portable oral care, $6,464,000.[30]

Advertising of toothpaste in the modern era remained almost as outrageous as in earlier times despite a more activist approach by the ADA. Makers had less trouble from federal government regulators but that had more to do with a decline in the power of the regulating agencies than with the toothpaste ad copy.

14

Toothpaste, Advertising and Marketing, 1960–2008

Don't you think that Bristol-Myers or the agency could sell this item on its own merits by simply following good, ethical and basic advertising principles?—William V. Humphrey, 1967.

Enough free toothpaste samples were distributed to cover the entire nation's toothbrushing needs for a full week.—Lever Brothers, 1972.

The great toothpaste wars have been won and lost in kids' mouths. Their vote decides the brand for the family. And they vote sweet.—Hercules Segalas, 1982.

Colgate Junior is a gel with sparkles and a fruity bubble-gum-like taste. It is squeezed from its dispenser in star-shaped strips.—Richard Stevenson, 1988.

A long standing irritation for dentists (and physicians with regard to other products) had been the use by manufacturers of actors in ads who gave the impression they were dentists (or other medical personnel) through clothing, props, and so on, while not actually saying the model was a dentist. Supposedly such a strategy lent an ad credibility by giving what could be construed as a medical endorsement. To control that situation the so-called man-in-white rule went into effect July 1, 1963, and eliminated the appearance of doctors, dentists, nurses, and related health professionals — and actors depicting them — in the television advertising of health products. Also eliminated by the rule were hospitals, medical offices, prescription pads and similar professional settings and props. It was part of the television advertising code of the National Association of Broadcasters and was put in place to help counter creating the impression in commercials that products or services enjoyed widespread medical endorsement when such was not the case. After 18 months the code had its language tightened a bit to stop those who had tried to create that impression with some vague language. Under the clarified section the code's unacceptable phrase list then included "two out of three doctors recommend," "many doctors prefer," or "your dentist will tell you," for example.[1]

When Macleans toothpaste achieved success in the US in the early 1960s it was the result of careful market research, said David C. Stewart, president and CEO of the brand's ad agency Kenyon & Eckhardt. "While many people look to a toothpaste to prevent tooth decay, a very large number are primarily interested in getting teeth white. Crest, Colgate and other brands were hammering on the decay-prevention story," he explained, of his firm's research results. Also determined was that Macleans had greater appeal for adults than kids so its ad campaigns stressed whiteness and were aimed at adults.[2]

For 1964 the six leading dentifrice advertisers spent more than $40 million on television to hype their toothpastes; television got 91 percent of the total ad budgets. Account executive Albin Nelson pointed out that most dentifrice advertisers employed dental health themes in their advertising and selected television because of its ability to reach "the most people of all ages on a frequent basis." He believed advertising had not only increased the annual sales volume but had also "given stability to the market by urging the good habit." During that year Procter & Gamble had spent $23,134,700 on measured media ads for Crest and Gleem brands ($21,508,200 on television — 93 percent of the total, $1,136,000 on magazines, $290,500 on newspapers); Colgate-Palmolive spent $12,070,100 for Colgate Dental Cream, Cue, and Target ($10,104,400 — 84 percent, $1,949,000, $16,700); Lever Brothers spent $4,657,700 on Pepsodent and Stripe ($4,621,400 — 99 percent, $30,300, $6,000); Beecham Products spent $2,398,900 for Macleans (100 percent on television); Bristol-Myers spent $2,087,800 on Ipana and Ipana Durenamel ($1,803,600 — 86 percent, $284,200): Alberto-Culver spent $253,100 for Mighty White (100 percent on television).[3]

Despite protests from the candy industry, Bristol-Myers said, at the start of 1967, that it planned to continue its Fact toothpaste ads that advised the public to avoid sweets. Bristol-Myers declared its stand was endorsed by the ADA and that it intended to stand on that endorsement. Copy for the Fact ads asserted, "Sweets. Every day your child eats every sweet thing he can get his teeth into. He should avoid sweets. They are bad for teeth. And brush with Fact toothpaste. That's good for teeth. Fact has doubled its available fluoride. Fact works harder to prevent cavities sweets can start, because fluoride is sugar's enemy. If you eat too many sweets, no toothpaste, not even Fact, can completely stop cavities. Avoid sweets. See your dentist regularly and brush with Fact. Fact works hard to prevent cavities." The official ADA position on which the commercials were based was stated in an ADA *Journal* editorial in January 1967: "There is indeed a causal relationship between sugar and dental decay." That ADA editorial recommended that the National Confectioners Association "take its head out of the sand, get out of the business of writing fairy tales, and adopt a positive program designed to reduce a well-known health hazard."[4]

William V. Humphrey, public relations director for the National Confectioners Association, wondered, "Don't you think that Bristol-Myers or the agency could sell this item on its own merits by simply following good, ethical and basic advertising principles?" Humphrey decried the Fact ads in which a product "is being offered to the public at the expense of another product." Howard J. Klein, director of advertising for candy importer Murray-Allen Imports, remarked, "At most, the anti-sweet copy is arguable, its ethics are questionable; and at least, it indicates a creative bankruptcy at the agency." He charged that Bristol-Myers' use of commercial time for the ostensible purpose of teaching good dental health was "beyond the ethical prerogative and good taste of a major American corporation." Armin Schaper, ad manager of Delson Candy and president of the Association of Manufacturers of Confectionary & Chocolate, said he was "aroused and up in arms" and had protested to Bristol-Myers. "Our policy is that there are few more egregious tactics than for one industry to attack another to support a product and that such an attack is in violation of the National Association of Broadcasters' code." New York confectionary firm Chunky Corporation felt the ADA had not established a case indicating confections or any other sugar products were any more cavity causing than other foods. "But if they feel that sugared products are so bad, why doesn't Bristol-Myers have the nerve to go after companies that produce sugar-coated cereals, such as General Foods?" added a Chunky spokesperson. "They wouldn't dare, because they know that companies like that have the advertising dollars to fire back at them and the new toothpaste they are trying to establish."[5]

As of November 1968 Ipana was officially a dead toothpaste brand. In the opinion of Bristol-Myers marketing executives its life might have been extended a bit longer if it had come up with an early answer to fluoride, or an advertising slogan to match the effectiveness of some of its earlier ones. As of the fall of 1967 Ipana's advertising was cut off, followed by the stoppage in production a little over a year later. Death of the brand was blamed on "a long period of attrition" dating back to the entry of strong new competition in the early 1950s. Prior to that, Ipana had been a regular in the top three toothpaste brands. Then came the 1950s and the arrival of P&G's Gleem, for example, and things were never quite the same for Ipana. Following that came years of gradual erosion in which Ipana, said reporter John Revett, "never really came up with a way to weather the market." At least one strong attempt to regain market share was made, however, with the introduction in 1964 of Ipana Durenamel, launched after Crest opened up the fluoride market in

1960, but the brand did not catch on. In May 1966 a final effort to revive the brand was made, and boost its share that had slipped to 2 percent, when Bristol-Myers got a new ad agency for the account. But after a few unsuccessful radio and television ads Ipana closed out its advertising career.[6]

Not quite a year later in September 1969, two entrepreneurs picked up the name Ipana, after it was abandoned by Bristol-Myers, with the intention of reviving the brand. Elliott Royce was president and John Howe was board chairman of the newly formed Ipana Inc., with offices in Hopkins, Minnesota. Royce said he expected sales of at least one million tubes of the paste (reformulated to include stannous fluoride) over the first 12 months. The toothpaste was being manufactured and packed for Ipana Inc. by Watkins Products of Winona, Minnesota, a door-to-door merchandising company. With blue and white tubes and cartons the new Ipana closely resembled the old Ipana last produced by Bristol-Myers. Royce explained he picked up the name because he was convinced it was still familiar enough to sell a lot of toothpaste. Initially he relied on word-of-mouth publicity and news stories to spread the news about the rebirth of Ipana although he conceded Ipana would have to be advertised in order to hold a place on store shelves. Having no illusions about Ipana becoming a major player in the toothpaste market again, Royce concluded, "We'll be satisfied with 1% or even half of that."[7]

When Colgate launched Colgate Dental Cream with MFP in November 1968 it announced it expected its $16 million campaign for the new brand would take it to number one in the market. That launch was the culmination of several years of work with the additive MFP and meant that Colgate's previous wonder additive, Gardol, was finished. As Gardol faded from the promotional stage Colgate with MFP was positioning itself as the new general cavity fighter, "superior to the best known stannous fluoride"— meaning, of course, Crest. Said Bob Castle, senior vice president at the ad agency Ted Bates & Company and account director on Colgate, "We have $16,000,000 to spend, and we'll drive our story home and drive it home hard." Some 14 years earlier Colgate had 37 percent of the market, P&G's Gleem was second at 12 percent and Crest was third with 10 percent. Then stannous fluoride and ADA recognition moved Crest to number one and Colgate plunged to 20 percent. Since then Colgate had gone as high as 27 percent but mostly was in the low 20s range and "the cost to maintain a share in the low 20s we felt too heavy to sustain without a dramatic change in the product's presentation," commented Castle. Outlining Colgate's years of frustration as it sought the right combination to battle Crest he said, "We studied the Crest user and learned that she's sold on the product, really locked in. She believed the ADA seal, the authority of the dentists, that nothing else can prevent cavities." Then Colgate came up with clinical tests saying it had the advanced fluoride and decided after all those years they could finally make a dent. "[W]e had to decide to drop the word 'Gardol' and concentrate on MFP, with no slice-of-life, no gimmicks, just testimonials from MFP users and the offer of the clinicals."[8]

Part of the campaign for MFP involved 20 million free samples of the new brand. Colgate believed that campaign had to differentiate the brand from all others. Industry observers felt one reason that Colgate's Cue paste had failed was that its ads told the same story as did Crest advertising. George H. Lesch, president and CEO of New York's Colgate-Palmolive Corporation, admitted, "Let's face it, we fell flat on our faces with Cue and we dropped a hell of a lot of money [$12 million]."[9]

At a 1969 workshop on new product introduction sponsored by the Association of National Advertisers one talk was given by John E. Grimm, a Colgate-Palmolive vice president, who observed that Colgate invested $700,000 and three years of preparation "to get the most successful new toilet article product introduced by anyone ... ever." Starting in 1963 Colgate–Palmolive conducted field tests that showed consumers were interested in a toothpaste that "brightens your teeth and freshens your breath," favored one particular flavor, and liked the name Ultra-Brite. In 1966 the company tested advertising and the product itself (by way of free sample) in Spokane, Washington, and Kansas City, Missouri, at first and later that year expanded its test marketing sites to Denver and Fort Wayne, Indiana. Grimm told his audience that by the beginning of 1967 Colgate-Palmolive had learned from its test marketing that Ultra-Brite was exceeding the market share objective it had set, its sampling was most effective, and it had created some advertising awareness although the executive admitted it "was only average." Before launching a national advertising campaign on television and in newspapers for Ultra-Brite in 1967, added Grimm, several commercials were tested and one selected. (For all new products in whatever field conventional wisdom had it that it was necessary to have alternative commercials ready to go at a moment's notice, just in case the chosen one fell flat, or proved to be unexpectedly controversial, and so forth.) When Grimm gave his talk in 1969 Ultra-Brite had about 11 percent of the market, which translated to around $30 million in yearly sales.[10]

Journalist Craig Whitney wrote a piece in 1969 about how a confusing number of sizes for many products (including toothpaste) made it harder for consumers to comparison shop. A new regulation in New York City (effective on November 20, 1969) from the city's Department of Consumer Affairs, required that labels include the price per pound, quart, or other unit to sim-

Independent Research Verifies Effectiveness of World's Largest-selling Toothpaste:

Newest Clinical Test Confirms

Colgate a Leader in Reducing New Cavities!

Read what happened when Colgate with Gardol was clinically tested against the most widely accepted fluoride dentifrice

**▶ COLGATE'S ROLE
IN NEW TEST FOR CAVITY REDUCTION**

In October, 1960, a group of independent dental investigators set out to determine the value of Colgate's Gardol formula in reducing new cavities in the 7 to 17 year age group—the age when teeth are most vulnerable to decay. To make the test the most critical possible, the researchers chose to measure Colgate with its ingredient, *Sodium N-Lauroyl Sarcosinate* (Gardol), against the leading stannous fluoride toothpaste, which had previously shown effectiveness in cavity reduction. Hundreds of dental patients in the most cavity-prone age group were selected from the student body of a large school in the Southeastern United States. These students were then divided into two groups and instructed to use exactly the same dentist-recommended brushing method. For the next two years, one group was to brush only with Colgate's exclusive Gardol formula. Another group only with the leading stannous fluoride toothpaste.

**▶ COLGATE'S CLINICAL ACHIEVEMENT
IN CAVITY REDUCTION**

At the end of two years—over half a million brushings later—supervising dentists carefully checked results, group-for-group. Colgate's Gardol formula against the stannous fluoride formula. So there would be no chance of human error, these dental records were then analyzed and compared by the most advanced electronic computing machines. Statistically, it was discovered that in this test* Colgate with Gardol had achieved the same low incidence of new cavities as the stannous

*Journal of Dentistry for Children, First Quarter, 1963.

fluoride formula. When you consider that the study was conducted among the most cavity-prone of all age groups, results achieved by the group brushing with Colgate are even more significant. This study —one of many planned to acquaint you and your dentist with the Colgate-Palmolive Company's continuing interest in dental hygiene— shows what today's Colgate Dental Cream can do in reducing tooth decay. Its results are wonderful assurance that even the youngest family member can brush with Colgate . . . in the complete program of oral hygiene dentists recommend.

**▶ YOUR DENTIST'S ROLE
IN CAVITY REDUCTION**

In announcing the results of this study, the makers of Colgate Dental Cream emphasize their agreement with leading dental authorities that no toothpaste—fluoride or non-fluoride—can substitute for care and treatment of teeth by your family dentist. Seeing your dentist regularly is *the most important part* of any dental-health program. Important, too, is his advice on diet, as well as *how* to brush, *when* to brush, and *how often* to brush.

Now you can be a "one-toothpaste family" again with best-tasting Colgate...confident Colgate's Gardol formula is clinically tested!

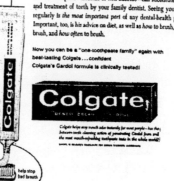

Colgate helps any mouth odor instantly for most people—has that between-teeth cleaning action of penetrating Gardol foam and the most mouth-refreshing toothpaste taste in the whole world!

Brush with Colgate...reduce new cavities...help stop bad breath

Colgate explained the situation, 1963.

plify the shopper's task but did not cover toothpaste. At the start that regulation applied to all meats, fish, bread, cereals, cooking oils, carbonated soft
drinks, beer, napkins, facial tissues, and toilet tissues. Most toothpaste makers packaged their products in five tube sizes, ranging from 1.75 ounces to
8.75 ounces. They also used different names for similar sizes. Colgate in the
1.75 ounce tube was described as a personal size while the same tube was
medium for Gleem users. Pepsodent referred to its 3.25 ounce size as giant;
Colgate called theirs medium while Gleem labeled that size as large. When
Whitney asked makers to explain their package sizes and descriptions he found
"they were generally reluctant or unwilling to explain them." James C.
Macuithey, Bristol-Myers public relations officer, consulted with other executives for a few days before he called Whitney back to declare, "We don't want
to say anything about our methods of packaging at this time." Lee Bloom, a
lawyer at Lever Brothers, remarked, "This is a very competitive business and
we don't like to give out too much information on how we make our decisions."[11]

A top level scientific panel evaluated toothpastes for the Food and Drug
Administration (FDA) and when that agency released the results in 1970 it
said eight of the 10 brands studied did not live up to their advertisements as
cavity preventers. The FDA announced it would begin action to rescind marketing approval for the eight brands as currently advertised. The findings
came from a study conducted by a panel from the National Academy of Sci-
ences and the National Research Council. One toothpaste studied, Crest, was
found effective in the prevention of tooth decay while another, NDK Dentifrice, was found possibly effective. Judged ineffective in the prevention of
tooth decay were Brisk Activated Tooth Paste, Colgate Chlorophyl Tooth
Paste with Gardol, Colgate Dental Cream with Gardol, Antizyme Tooth Paste,
Kolynos Fluoride Tooth Paste, Super Amm-i-dent, Amm-i-dent Tooth Paste,
and Amm-i-dent Toothpowder.[12]

That scientific panel was charged with reviewing drugs placed on the
market before 1963 when the Kefauver-Harris law took effect providing for
pre-clearance of effectiveness claims for drugs and related products. Various
panels of experts recruited at the FDA's request reviewed claims for nearly
3,000 drugs introduced between 1938 and 1962, including several hundred
over-the-counter drugs and dentifrices. Those eight deemed to be ineffective
were given 30 days to submit additional data to the FDA, to show effectiveness, before steps were taken to remove them from the market. Although
some of those eight had been heavily advertised in the past, most had been
discontinued or were little promoted in 1970. Colgate's Brisk Activated had
been discontinued in 1966; Colgate with Gardol had been replaced by Col-

gate with MFP some two years earlier and Colgate Chlorophyl was then manufactured only "in very limited supply to satisfy a few customers." A Block Drug spokesman said none of the Amm-i-dent items had been promoted in almost 15 years and while they were all still manufactured the spokesman said sales "are very minimal" and "it's a dead issue as far as we are concerned."[13]

Among the claims for those eight rejected brands which the FDA contended could not be substantiated were: "stays active against tooth decay all day," "helps harden and strengthen the structure of tooth enamel on contact and helps prevent decay," "destroys bad breath originating in the mouth," and "cleans your breath while it cleans around each and every tooth."[14]

. Consumer advocate Ralph Nader charged in July 1971 that toothpastes containing stannous fluoride stained teeth. He asked the government to require warning labels on the toothpaste tubes. As well, he asked the FTC to require a halt to ad claims that Colgate with MFP was a "tooth toughener," arguing that the FDA had recently reported those claims were completely unsupported by scientific evidence.[15]

Replying to Nader's charges that stannous fluoride in a toothpaste left a brown stain on teeth rather than cleaning them, the ADA said the consumer advocate was "misleading the public and persuading people not to use effective dentifrices. Mr. Nader's people are not only wrong [in their charges], but they also show a very shallow knowledge of the structure of tooth enamel." According to the ADA Nader's Center for Corporate Responsibility wrote the dental organization two weeks earlier for comment on the charges before they were released publicly but "apparently they didn't wait for our answer ... before releasing their charges."[16]

Also annoyed with toothpastes, but for different reasons, was U.S. Senator Claiborne Pell (Dem., Rhode Island) who disclosed in 1971 results from a U.S. Army study that indicated some brands of toothpaste caused painful gum inflammation. Pell said the Army Institute of Dental Research had tested 10 brands of popular toothpastes and that one survey was said to have found the following levels of stomatitis (gum inflammation) among users: Crest, 3.8 percent; Colgate, 16.3 percent; Vote, 21.9 percent; Plus White, 25 percent; Ultra-Brite, 31.3 percent; Macleans, 37.5 percent. Results from a second survey were Crest, 8.0 percent; Colgate, 12 percent; Gleem, 30 percent; Ultra-Brite, 37 percent; Macleans, 57 percent. According to Pell the first survey had included 929 users while the second one covered 128 people. In Chicago the ADA said it and the National Institute of Dental Research had evaluated the Army project and had "uniformly condemned the study as fundamentally unsound." Said the ADA in a statement, "Senator Pell was informed in detail of the study's serious deficiencies. His decision to release the study may well cause more people, including children, to stop using dentifrices that curb dental decay. This would be a serious disservice to public health.[17]

Doctor Sheva Rapoport, vice president of the American Association of Women Dentists, observed, also in 1971, that many of the fluoride toothpastes failed to get ADA recognition because they did not work, mostly because they contained an unstable form of sodium fluoride that was ineffective when mixed with the saliva. She noted another popular claim for toothpaste was its ability to kill germs that caused decay and bad breath and concluded, "This is certainly one of the most far-fetched ads." At best, she continued, a toothpaste could alleviate the condition of bad breath only for a matter of minutes. Dentifrice formulations then typically contained 20 percent to 40 percent abrasive, 10 percent to 30 percent moistening agent, 20 percent to 30 percent water, 1 percent to 5 percent thickening agent, plus a foaming agent and flavoring mixture. With respect to the ad claims of whiteners Rapoport said, "Actually, the color of the tooth is predetermined and the external application of toothpaste cannot change it. It is comparable to a claim of a soap to change a skin color and effect a lightening or brightening of one's complexion. Such claims are simply not justified." She concluded, "Many people could effectively brush their teeth clean without toothpaste, using a toothbrush and water only. It would require instruction and practice, but it could be done. However, toothpaste does aid the brush and does make the job somewhat easier and more pleasant." She did accept that ADA recognized fluoride pastes were effective and important for children, but did not mention such products for adults.[18]

The advertising claims of eight leading brands of toothpaste and three denture cleaners were called into question in December 1971 by the FTC with the agency ordering the eight makers to furnish documentation within 60 days to support selected "concrete" claims for their products such as "fights cavities better," "has the lowest abrasion level," and "removes stubborn stains between teeth in minutes." Those manufacturers were Beecham (Macleans), P&G (Crest and Gleem II), Colgate-Palmolive (Colgate and Ultra-Brite), Lever Brothers (Pepsodent and Close-Up), and Carter-Wallace (Pearl Drops Tooth Polish). They accounted for 92 percent of the industry's $325 million business in 1970, with toothpaste advertising costs in the same period amounting to $56 million. Gerald J. Thain, FTC assistant director for advertising, explained the commission's action should not suggest the FTC "believes the claims are false or subject to challenge — but the public is entitled to know what substantiation exists." The toothpaste industry was the fifth one requested to supply materials substantiating advertising in a program the commission began in July 1971. Material had already been submitted from manufacturers involved in the following industries: automobiles, televisions, electric shavers, and air conditioners.[19]

Business writer Fred Danzig argued in 1972 that the mass-marketing approach for a toothpaste invariably called for three things: sampling, cents-off offers (either through print ads or mailings), and close attention to the dental profession. Another approach he mentioned was counterpositioning whereby, rather than challenging Crest head-on, for example, the campaign targeted those who cared more about breath freshness or whiteners, or both, but avoided the cavity-fighting story. That approach had been taken by Beecham for its Macleans, Colgate with Ultra-Brite, Lever with Close-Up, and Carter-Wallace with Pearl Drops. In 1968 the eight major brands then on the market spent a total of $41.5 million in measured media ads while for 1971 the major dentifrice marketers spent $58 million to promote nine brands.[20]

Although Danzig said that heavy ad spending did not necessarily assure lasting success for a brand he added, "But there are some recent efforts that, within limits, support the premise that massive ad spending, couponing and sampling will get the brand off the ground, establish it at a significant share level, and then place it at the mercy of the next new brand's introductory push." Ultra-Brite received about $8 million in promotional support when it went national in 1967 and achieved nearly $30 million in sales. Much of Ultra-Brite's budget went for a massive sampling and couponing effort with more than 40 million U.S. households receiving at least one 3.25 ounce tube. A cents-off coupon mailing followed. In 1969, so much free toothpaste was delivered to households by Lever (for Close-Up) and Colgate (for another Ultra-Brite campaign) that, as Lever stated in its annual report, "Enough free toothpaste samples were distributed to cover the entire nation's toothbrushing needs for a full week."[21]

In 1975 Crest remained number one in the market with 40 percent followed by Colgate Dental Cream at 19 percent, Aim at 12 percent, Close-Up at 10 percent, Ultra-Brite at 5 percent and Gleem at 5 percent.[22]

Rolled out in 1954 Gleem was P&G's first national dentifrice brand and by 1960 Gleem, with a 20 percent market share, trailed only Colgate Dental Cream at 35 percent. One month after Crest received ADA approval in 1960 a study showed Crest unit purchases had risen 39 percent and that 34 percent of the purchasers were brand switchers—13 percent from Gleem, 6 percent and less from each of several other brands. Two years later Crest had a 27 percent share, Colgate had 24 percent, and Gleem was at 18 percent. By 1968 Gleem had fallen to 8 percent. With the addition of fluoride and a campaign positioning it as "really two toothpastes in one," Gleem II — as it became known — moved up to around 10 percent. But then along came Close-Up as a whitener and Aim (both from Lever), its companion fluoride gel, and Gleem lost more ground finishing up at about a 5 percent share at the end of 1975.[23]

Toothpaste sales totaled $521 million in 1976, up $41 million over 1975. Three companies dominated that market, claiming a 95 percent share together and spending most of the advertising dollars. P&G (42.5 percent of the market: 36.5 percent from Crest and 6 percent from Gleem), Colgate-Palmolive (27.5 percent: 20.5 percent from Colgate Dental Cream and 5.4 percent from Ultra-Brite), and Lever Brothers (25 percent of the market from Aim, Close-Up, and Pepsodent) spent a total of $80 million on toothpaste advertising in 1976. Of that total, $49 million was spent on national television, $25 million on spot television, $4.1 million on magazines, $973,000 on newspapers, $412,000 on spot radio, $139,000 on network radio, and $446,000 on ads in newspaper supplements.[24]

By 1980 the toothpaste market was worth $659 million annually with ad spending at an all-time high of $111 million. P&G remained number one with a 35 percent share while Colgate continued at number two with a 25 percent share. It had produced a new campaign for Ultra-Brite that promised "a smile so white it gets you noticed." Surprisingly in third spot was Beecham's Aqua-Fresh at 15 percent, after $19 million was spent promoting it in its first year, allowing it to move to that 15 percent point within one year of its introduction to American retailers. Aqua-Fresh's success caused the sales of its stablemate, Macleans, to suffer.[25]

The first gel toothpaste was Close-Up (Lever, 1970), a product that appealed to the young who were concerned about their breath and the whiteness of their teeth. Then Lever brought out Aim (1974), a gel that also contained fluoride, which broadened the market by getting parents to buy it for younger children who enjoyed the consistency and flavor. Then Beecham brought out Aqua-Fresh (1979) and the three gel brands grew to 32 percent of the total market in 1980 from 8 percent in 1970. P&G was then, in 1981, testing Crest Gel in a few spots with ad themes that included, "A new Crest flavor children will love" and "The only gel with fluoristat," while Colgate–Palmolive was launching Colgate Winterfresh Gel into national distribution.[26]

Journalist Bernice Kanner reported Americans spent about $1 billion in 1981 on two billion ounces of toothpaste, 9.1 ounces per person. With respect to the gel craze Kanner remarked, "To the casual toothbrusher this may seem to be a lot of sound and fury signifying nothing. After all, gels don't do anything better than old-fashioned toothpaste. They don't fight cavities, freshen breath, or whiten teeth any better than the old, opaque, white standby." She felt the big selling point was taste. Said Jack Salzman, analyst at Smith Barney, Harris Upham & Company, "Historically, taste wasn't considered a big factor in attracting and keeping a large market share. It's obviously a major preference now." Tooth decay had become less of an issue, thought Kanner, because of the success of water fluoridation that led to fewer and fewer new cavities appearing in teeth. Most people were said to choose a toothpaste for its flavor with spearmint the most popular taste, followed by peppermint, cinnamon, and wintergreen. Hercules Segalas, an analyst at the brokerage house Drexel Burnham Lambert observed that flavor was the most expensive ingredient in toothpaste; the second costliest element was the tube; the third was the active ingredient. Three of the top flavors were very sweet, and that was because of children. "The great toothpaste wars have been won and lost in kids' mouths," explained Segalas. "Their vote decides the brand for the family. And they vote sweet."[27]

For all the money spent on advertising dentifrices, said Kanner, "toothpaste advertising is appallingly bad. It is also appallingly similar. The commercials are almost invariably the slice-of-life kind, except that these slices are from lives no one really lives." Ads for example, where two young boys knowledgably discussed toothpaste as no boys really would, or families that fought over toothpaste selection. Kanner blamed some of the poor quality ad work on the ADA Council on Dental Therapeutics and its less than effective oversight. In Germany, toothpaste then was available in aerosol cans and pump canisters. "Imagine a nice tutti-frutti, rich-colored gel in an aerosol container," said Segalas. "That's tomorrow." He also predicted a future in which there would be fewer brands of toothpaste.[28]

As of 1982 the ADA recommended only five accepted brands of toothpaste: Crest, Colgate with MFP, Aim, Aqua-Fresh, and Macleans with Fluoride. "The American Dental Association feels very strongly that the five accepted dentifrices are the ones that should be used by children, young adults and adults because of the demonstrated benefits from fluoride," said Dr. Edgar W. Mitchell, secretary of the ADA Council on Dental Therapeutics. Standards of performance for toothpastes were first established in the 1930s when the ADA's Council began rating products as "accepted," "unaccepted," or "provisionally accepted."[29]

As a $1 billion a year industry in 1982 the toothpaste market was dominated by four makers — P&G, Colgate, Lever, and Beecham — who accounted for about 93 percent of the total market sales. Morton Pader of Lever Brothers reported that toothpaste production in the U.S. ranged between 200 million and 250 million pounds annually, about one pound per person per year. Approximately 80 percent of all toothpaste brands sold contained fluoride (the therapeutic brands). Despite that, a trade publication account felt marketing ploys were more along the flavor and form lines because "public saturation with the message about cavity prevention for fluorides probably accounts for the fact that ads in print and commercials put so much stress on flavor, breath-sweetening qualities, and the spiral design of the gel-spiked toothpaste." The *Los Angeles Times* reported in 1981 that all types of promotion and advertising that year for toothpaste (including sampling, couponing, special-price promotions, and retail trade deals) reached $305 million. Market share in 1982 was as follows: Crest, 35 percent; Colgate, 22 percent; Aqua-Fresh, 11 percent; Aim, 7 percent; Ultra-Brite, 3 percent; Gleem, 3 percent; Pepsodent, 2 percent.[30]

Pump dispensers for toothpaste became a fad in 1984 when Colgate announced a national distribution of its flagship brand Colgate in a pump dispenser. That move came on the heels of Minnetonka Incorporated's national distribution of its Check-Up, a pump-dispensed toothpaste, backed by a $20 million ad campaign. Colgate was expected to spend $30 million on its launch. Grant Wood, vice president of marketing at Minnetonka, said he believed his company's roll-out of Check-Up "was a factor in the haste" with which Colgate moved to debut its pump-dispensed product. "It could be argued," said Wood, "that a dispenser system being introduced by such a company as Colgate will generate more awareness [for the category]. It could help more than hurt." Colgate's campaign involved a heavy couponing component, including face values up to 75 cents and the mailing of samples to 95 percent of all U.S. dentists.[31]

By the end of 1984 Lever and P&G had versions of Aim and Crest in pump dispensers in separate test markets. Beecham was to join the group early in 1985 with a version of Aqua-Fresh in a pump. Minnetonka then announced it would be the first to introduce toothpaste in flip-top containers, in test markets, under its Check-Up brand. To keep pace Colgate-Palmolive was then testing its own flip-top toothpaste tube in a test market under the Dentagard brand name. At the end of 1984 pump-dispensed brands were said to have achieved a 15 percent market share in cities where they were sold having captured the public's imagination, especially in households with young children.[32]

The Germans invented a version of the pump 10 years earlier, around 1975. Since March 1984 when Check-Up was first introduced (until January 1985) 20 million 6.5 inch, 4.1 ounce stand-up pump containers of the mint-flavored paste had been sold at $2.39 (compared with $1.40 or so for a similar amount of toothpaste in a standard tube). When Colgate introduced its own pump later in 1984 it had a suggested retail price of $1.69 for 4.5 ounces.[33]

U.S. church groups associated with the National Council of Churches asked Colgate-Palmolive in 1986 to withdraw the brand name "Darkie" used on a toothpaste marketed exclusively by the firm in the Far East because the term was offensive and racist. Darkie was then a 60-year-old product sold widely in Hong Kong, Malaysia, Taiwan, and other Far East countries. Colgate insisted the term Darkie was not derogatory in the countries where the toothpaste was sold and that the firm had no plans to market the product in the U.S. or any Western English–speaking nation. Also, said Colgate, it had no plans to remove the product or change the brand name.[34]

Over two years later, in 1988, reporter Mark Fortune complained, "A top-hatted, bright-eyed minstrel — a grinning simpleton. This is the racist characterization of blacks presented to Asian consumers of Colgate-Palmolive Co.'s best-selling 'Darkie' brand toothpaste." Fourteen months after it was confronted with a shareholder resolution calling for a change in the product's name and imagery, the company still had not removed the racist trademark from the toothpaste's package. It became part of Coglate's product line in 1985 when Colgate acquired a 50 percent interest in the Hong Kong–based Hawley & Hazel Chemical Company, which manufactured Darkie toothpaste. The push to abolish the logo began in October 1985 when the New York–based Interfaith Center on Corporate Responsibility (ICCR), a nationwide coalition of religious institutional investors, received a Darkie toothpaste package from a disgruntled American living in Thailand. Since then the ICCR had organized a strong and growing protest campaign that included organizations such as the NAACP and the National Urban League. "The use of the term 'darkie' has always been a pejorative one," said Dara Demmings, an ICCR director. "The graphic, which ostensibly is Al Jolson in blackface, is a caricature that could be construed as being a black person. It is stereotypical and offensive."[35]

At first Colgate balked at making any changes, maintaining the term was not derogatory in the countries where the product was sold. However, after the shareholder reaction and a series of meetings with the ICCR in January 1987 Colgate said it would begin to test market name and logo alternatives for the paste. As time passed it insisted it was not dragging its feet. However, speculation was that the firm was loathe to tamper with a product that had held a 40 percent share of the Far East market for 60 years. One test market of a brand named Dakkie reportedly carried the same insulting logo. And in April 1988 Hawley & Hazel launched a new toothpaste in Japan called Mouth Jazz that carried a logo similar to that on the Darkie package — a minstrel in silhouette. Colgate spokesman Gavin Anderson said, of that logo, "I don't think it's indicative of a minstrel at all. It's a black-faced person wearing a top-hat."[36]

After more than three years of pressure from shareholders and religious groups, Colgate-Palmolive said in January 1989 it would rename Darkie and redesign its logotype, a minstrel in blackface. Reuben Mark, chairman and CEO of Colgate-Palmolive, said, of the product's name and logotype, "It's just plain wrong. It's just offensive. The morally right thing dictated that we must change. What we have to do is find a way to change that is least damaging to the economic interests of our partners." The name was to be changed to Darlie and the new logotype was to be a portrait of a man of ambiguous race wearing a silk top hat, tuxedo and bow-tie. Reporter Douglas McGill felt that logo was almost identical to the old one, except for the complexion. To reduce confusion and to avoid lost sales Colgate said it would change the name in stages over the coming year with the logotype to be replaced the following year. Annual sales of Hawley & Hazel (almost all from Darkie) amounted to less than 3 percent of Colgate-Palmolive's worldwide total sales. When he made his announcement Mark insisted Colgate had been negotiating with Hawley & Hazel to change the name and logo ever since "the day after" Colgate bought its 50 percent share. Originally the name and logotype had been conceived in the 1920s when Hawley & Hazel's CEO visited the U.S. and saw Al Jolson. That executive thought Jolson's wide smile and bright teeth would make an excellent toothpaste logo. As it sought a new name for the paste one of the steps Colgate-Palmolive took was to run a computer program that listed all possible one-letter changes in the word Darkie. From that list, and from names suggested by several professional marketing firms, came a list of around 20 names, from which Darlie was chosen.[37]

Full page ads on April 17, 1989, in Singapore in the *Straits Times* announced that Darkie was changing its name to Darlie. The ad carried the same blackface logo as in the past.[38]

Comparative ads for Lever Brothers' Extra Strength Aim toothpaste came under fire in 1987 first from P&G and Colgate-Palmolive and then from the National Advertising Division of the Council of Better Business Bureaus. Claims made in those Lever advertisements included, "No matter how hard you try, you just can't squeeze as much cavity-fighting fluoride out of Crest as you can out of this" and "Sorry Colgate. Looks like your 20 years of maximum fluoride protection have gone right down the tubes." Spots also claimed the Lever brand had proven superior cavity-fighting ability. However, the trouble with that claim was that it was based on tests against regular Aim, although a reader could easily assume it meant Crest or Colgate. In its monthly report for June, the National Advertising Division questioned whether industrywide comparative claims could be based on comparisons against Lever's own brands.[39]

The never-ending quest for something new led the industry, at the end of the 1980s, to launch toothpaste for children. Colgate-Palmolive introduced Colgate Junior, backed by a $9 million national ad campaign. Beecham had been the first in the children's market, bringing out a bubble-gum flavored version of its Aquafresh in 1985 while in 1987 P&G introduced Crest for Kids and the Gillette Company's Oral-B Laboratories rolled out a Muppets brand. According to reporter Richard Stevenson, "Colgate Junior is a gel with sparkles and a fruity, bubble-gum-like taste. It is squeezed from its dispenser in star-shaped strips."[40]

Late in 1988 the FDA asked six toothpaste and mouthwash makers to remove from their labels statements that the products prevented gum disease and plaque build-up. In those warning letters the FDA asked the makers to remove such claims from their labels or submit evidence and petitions requesting approval of the label wording. Michael Shaffer, FDA spokesman, stressed it was a labeling issue and not a serious health hazard. The companies involved were Beecham (Aqua-Fresh), Colgate-Palmolive (Colgate toothpaste and mouthwashes), Rydelle-Lion (Check-Up toothpaste), Vipont (Viadent toothpaste and oral rinse), Warner Lambert (Listerine mouthwash), and Oral Research Laboratories (Plax dental rinse).[41]

Another subcategory that developed within the industry was the natural toothpaste. Thomas Chappell and wife Kate moved to Kennebunk, Maine, in the 1970s where they began to develop a line that included toothpastes and deodorants made from all-natural ingredients. By 1982 Tom's of Maine was a success with annual sales of $1.5 million, nearly all of which came from health food stores. Chappell knew if he wanted to expand he would have to get his items into the big chains but he did not want his products to be stuck in the health product section. He wanted his toothpaste on the shelf next to Crest and Colgate competing as a natural alternative. So he hired several people as vice presidents who knew marketing and who managed to place Tom's of Maine toothpaste in major retail outlets in the manner that Chappell had hoped. By 1989 sales stood at $8 million a year. More expensive than regular toothpaste, a 3-ounce tube of Tom's all-natural toothpaste retailed for $2.39, compared to about $1.65 for a 4.6-ounce tube of Colgate or Crest.[42]

Dentifrice sales moved from $1.4 billion in 1990 to $1.6 billion in 1994, according to business reporter Bette Popovich. There were approximately 188 million adult Americans in 1994, 93 percent used toothpaste while 63 percent used mouthwash. New products continued to flood the toothpaste market with Naples, New York–based marketing Intelligence Service noting that 43 new dentifrice formulations went on the shelf in 1994, with a total of 55 stock keeping units. From January to February 1995, three new dentifrices with nine stock keeping units were brought to market. Popovich said the hot trend then were pastes that combined baking soda and peroxide in one brand. P&G had 32 percent of the market in 1994, with Colgate-Palmolive second at 22 percent. One of the new items launched in 1995 was Colgate Baking Soda & Peroxide with Tartar Control Toothpaste (backed by a $35 million promotional campaign). Some six months earlier Colgate rolled out Colgate Platinum Whitening Toothpaste with Fluoride, developed, reportedly, for use as a maintenance paste by patients who underwent professional tooth-whitening or as a daily dentifrice. P&G was then debuting Crest Gum Care Toothpaste. Formulated with an ingredient called TheraMint, it was described as a "unique stannous fluoride formulation ... clinically proven to reduce gingivitis associated with plaque."[43]

Commenting on the toothpaste wars in 1995, reporter Zachary Schiller remarked, "More than anything, the toothpaste wars demonstrate the power of advertising and image. After all, many dentists say that brushing with any good paste and flossing are the main keys to dental health." Dr. Max List-garden, professor of periodontics at the University of Pennsylvania, advised people, with respect as to what toothpaste to buy, to get one with fluoride and one that was on sale: "That's how I shop for toothpaste."[44]

Colgate-Palmolive cleared the last regulatory hurdle in America in 1997 for selling its newest brand, Colgate Total toothpaste, the first paste approved for marketing as effective in simultaneously fighting gingivitis, plaque and cavities. Negotiations between the maker and the FDA over product labeling had bogged down but had then been resolved with the agency's approval given for marketing. Total was then marketed everywhere around the world by Colgate with great success. Within a few months of its national distribution in the U.S. in 1998 its American success moved Colgate back to the number one spot in sales among toothpaste makers—a spot it had not held since 1960 when its decades-long hold on top spot was broken by the ADA recognized Crest.[45]

According to market researcher Information Resources Inc., as of early in 2004, there were 160 brands of toothpaste on the market. They were filled with ingredients said to fight cavities, control tartar, attack bacteria, whiten teeth, and freshen breath. One could find herbal and natural products, along with those for sensitive teeth, for smokers, and even for women only. A new brand hitting the market at that time was said to contain liquid calcium that "fills in crevices in your tooth's enamel," according to the product's manu-facturer. But, said journalist Robert Davis, "In truth, experts say that a basic paste with fluoride is all that most of us really need."[46]

Datamonitor Product-scan was an online database that monitored the introduction of products. It found that 112 new toothpastes were sold in 2004.

Figures from Intelligent Resources Inc. showed that Americans spent $1 billion on toothpaste over a 52-week period ending in the summer of 2005, as well as $439.7 million on manual toothbrushes and $194.6 million on powered brushes.[47]

For the 52 weeks ending November 4, 2007, sales of toothpaste through mass market outlets (drugstores, supermarkets, and discount stores — except Wal-Mart Stores) totaled $1,259,296,000 from 477,906,600 units. Sales in drug stores totaled $334,613,200 from 120,148,700 units. Top three selling brands (drug stores) were Colgate Total, $30,654,380 (9.16 percent), Crest Whitening Plus Scope, $30,543,040 (9.13 percent), and Crest, $25,279,360 (7.55 percent).[48]

Even as mundane a product as toothpaste was not safe from counterfeiting. Two individuals and two companies pled guilty in August 2008 in Brooklyn, New York, to charges of trafficking in counterfeit Colgate toothpaste. Saifoulaye Diallo, 51, from the Bronx, and Habib Bah, 47, from Queens, New York, and two New York firms, Mabass Inc. and Vidtape Inc., admitted during the plea hearings to having trafficked in a combined total of 518,028 tubes of counterfeit toothpaste with an estimated retail value of $730,419. Lab tests conducted on a sample of the counterfeit product by the Food and Drug Administration and Colgate-Palmolive revealed it lacked fluoride as well as containing some micro-organisms that could have been a health risk to users. Information revealed the packaging on the counterfeit toothpaste was substantially indistinguishable from the legitimate product except that it contained spelling and grammar errors.[49]

15

Conclusion

The search for cleaner and whiter teeth has apparently been ongoing for many centuries. Items such as twigs, fiber pencils, toothpicks and the human forefinger have been used in the past as toothbrushes, sometimes with something added to them as a dentifrice; sometimes they were used alone. Although the ancestor of the modern brush may have arrived in the 1700s, it was not until the late 1800s that the modern era of the toothbrush truly started.

As the prominence of the brush grew and as the use of it spread not everyone was enthusiastic. From the late 1800s until the mid to late 1920s many professionals in the health field saw the toothbrush as a menace, as a spreader of disease. Partly there was justification in that idea due to some poor usage practices of the time: brushes were not allowed to dry completely between uses, all family implements were stored in the same glass, unhygienic retail counter displays were common, and the habit of each family member to rub the brush over the surface of the toothpowder container. In response to those criticisms came changes in hygiene practices, such as toothbrushes being retailed in individual cartons and the slow acceptance of the toothbrush by health professionals, and laypeople, alike, of the toothbrush as being useful in oral hygiene.

Virtually all the early brushes were made of hogs' hair natural bristles but at the end of the 1930s the natural bristle gave way to the synthetic-bristled brush (nylon), which soon came to dominate. By the early 1940s a large number of brush makers were in the field and consumer magazines started to publish buying advice articles on them, a sign of their by then almost universal acceptance and usage in America.

Over time, with the exception of the coming of synthetic bristles there was no technological change made in the brush. After World War II, to convince people the toothbrush was really evolving, manufacturers began to vary the form of the brush: the shape of the head, the shape of the handle, the angle of the head and/or handle, the number or configuration of the tufts of bristles, and so on. The toothbrush industry was unanimous in complaining Americans used their brushes far too long and did not replace them often enough. Given the low-tech nature of the brush, its relatively cheap cost, and low profits, the industry worked off and on to convince the public that what it really needed was the electric toothbrush. It was the 1960s before the powered implement arrived to stay but despite the industry's best efforts to have the electric brush take control of the field it was largely unsuccessful. Most people continued to use, to this day, manual brushes, even those who happened to own electric ones. It was one of the few examples where a low-tech, simple, and inexpensive method of performing a task managed to hold its own, and even prevail, over a high-tech, complex, and expensive way of doing the same job.

While a wide variety of ingredients had been used to make dentifrices in the past it was also the latter half of the 1800s when the modern era for toothpaste arrived, especially after the 1890s when the collapsible metal tube became available for paste. The first nationally known dentifrice was a red liquid, Sozodont, which came on the market in 1859, but was only a quack patent preparation consisting mainly of alcohol, as did so many quack medicines of that era. It disappeared within a few decades but Dr. Lyon's Tooth Powder (introduced in 1874) lasted for a very long time. By about 1900 most Americans, if they used a dentifrice at all, utilized a homemade preparation. Those who chose to use a commercially prepared product overwhelmingly chose powder.

The years 1900 to 1945, roughly, were boom years for dentifrices as most of the brands that dominated the industry for decades arrived, or came to prominence, in the first couple of decades of that period, such as Colgate, Pepsodent, and Ipana. Slowly powder yielded to paste and by 1945 only a small proportion of dentifrice users opted for powder, although experts agreed there was no inherent reason to choose paste, and powder was usually cheaper. With the spread of the use of commercially prepared dentifrices the American Dental Association (ADA) got involved in a formal way in 1932 when it established a Council on Dental Therapeutics to examine the composition of products and claims of dental usefulness. Even when consumer publications evaluated dentifrices, as they started to do in the late 1930s and continuing into the 1940s, they all agreed that brushing was important but it was the brush itself that was important and not what was put on it. Dentifrices were viewed by most professionals as next to useless.

Despite that consensus Americans were turned into a nation wherein almost everybody used a dentifrice, and a commercially prepared one, even though all the experts felt they were of little or no use, except as an aid to the brush as a cleanser. And despite the fact that organizations such as the ADA and Consumers Union urged people to use the simple-to-make homemade preparations. Americans became dentifrice users through the power of advertising. Starting in 1900 with simple ads those claims were increasingly embellished as mass advertising came to dominate, especially after World War I as each manufacturer tried to outdo his rivals with more and more outrageously exaggerated claims. False claims abounded in this period but did succeed in creating a nation of commercially prepared toothpaste users.

So blatantly false were so many of the advertising claims that both the ADA and the federal government stepped in to complain and, in some cases, to take action. Such wars between dentists and the federal government against toothpaste makers would come and go over time and remained a feature of the scene up until the present. Dentists were especially incensed over ads that featured models made up to look like dentists — supposedly producing more credibility for their ads — and eventually the so-called men-in-white ads were abolished. During the late 1930s and early 1940s the Federal Trade Commission (FTC) issued a flurry of cease and desist orders against various toothpaste manufacturers over various advertising claims.

The period roughly from 1946 to 1960 came to be cynically described for the toothpaste industry as the era of the additive. One after another new wonder ingredients were added to toothpaste, to allow it to perform even greater miracles; such as, for example, ammoniated, chlorophyll, anti-enzyme, surface-active detergents, and fluoride. Partly that strategy was based on a belief that something new had to happen in an industry every so often, that the public would tire of the same old ads for the same old ingredients; and partly it was due to so many makers in the field each trying to capture more market share. It was accepted in the industry that the overall market for paste was saturated, that the market could not be expanded beyond normal growth expectations and a maker could only increase his share by taking market share from one or more of his rivals. When Consumers Union tested dentifrices in 1949 — at a time when it still regarded them as cosmetics only, with no therapeutic value — it reported on a bewildering array of 93 leading brands.

Ad claims of makers remained as controversial in this era as in the past with the makers continuing to insist, in their ad copy, that their products had widespread therapeutic value. As late as 1959 an official position of the ADA was that it recognized dentifrices solely as helpful adjuncts in cleaning the teeth. While the government, through the FTC, still sometimes challenged maker ad claims it did so less often and with less success as its limited resources worked against the agency. For the agency had to work from the disadvantage that when a toothpaste maker made an outrageously false claim the FTC had to prove the claim was false rather than, as should have been the case, have the maker prove the claim to be true.

Procter & Gamble had introduced Crest with fluoride in 1955 but the item had got off to a relatively slow start. All that changed in August 1960 when the ADA gave official recognition to Crest as an effective decay fighting toothpaste. For the first time the ADA had recognized a dentifrice as having therapeutic value. It changed forever the relationship between dentists and the toothpaste industry. After recognition was extended to Crest a controversy erupted within the ADA over whether or not the organization should be involved in granting recognition to specific brands, given the public was sure to see recognition as endorsement. For several years other makers attacked ADA for its Crest recognition, even to the point of trying to get individual dentists to sponsor bills at ADA conventions designed to rescind endorsement. Crest, of course, rocketed to number one as the top-selling toothpaste.

Other makers quickly followed Crest by introducing a fluoride paste of their own. In the period from around 1960 to the present new and more wonder additives marched to the forefront, to reinforce the idea that something different had to happen, or seem to have happened. After fluoride came improved fluoride formulations, baking soda paste (a return to the homemade preparations of the very early 1900s), whiteners (also a return to the past), plaque fighters, and tartar control pastes. Most in the field argued those toothpastes were not therapeutic with respect to plaque and tartar (a bare brush and elbow grease produced equal results) but ads made openly therapeutic claims. ADA liked to think its entry into the field, by giving its seal of approval to certain products, led to a lessening of egregious toothpaste ad claims but that was likely only wishful thinking.

More niche products surfaced with desensitizing pastes, smokers toothpaste, natural pastes, and brands aimed specifically at children. Pump canisters were marketed; gels began to compete with paste. Evidence of that proliferation could be seen in 1998 when Crest and Colgate alone accounted for over 110 pastes and gels in various formulas, flavors, packages, and sizes. Ad claims in this period were almost as outrageous as in earlier periods but there was less government interference and involvement as a weakened regulatory system had neither the time nor the resources to respond in any adequate fashion.

The history of the toothpaste industry in 20th-century America has been a testament to the power of the advertising industry to sell a product for which there was little need (homemade cleansers were easily and cheaply produced) despite the fact that all responsible experts pointed out the product was of little value. It was a history of false ad claims, some more outrageous than others, a trend that has continued to the present, with the deck stacked against the FTC whenever that agency did try to regulate the field.

And then came fluoride toothpaste, the one wonder ingredient that really was a wonder ingredient. When it first appeared in a toothpaste in 1955 the few articles that mentioned it attacked it cynically as they pointed out fluoride came on the heels of so many other miracle items — ammoniated, chlorophyll, detergents, and so forth — that had all fallen flat. The arrival of fluoride pastes did not alter the trend to introduce new wonder ingredients though; the only difference was that since fluoride worked it remained part of most toothpastes, whereas most wonder ingredients disappeared after a few years or perhaps a decade.

Prior to fluoride the best professional advice about toothpaste, despite all the gimmicks in the field, was to use no paste at all (or to use a home-made powder as a cleanser if so desired), brush regularly and floss regularly. And that was it. Today, the best professional advice about toothpaste, despite all the gimmicks in the field, is to buy any good fluoride paste, brush regularly and floss regularly. And that is it.

Chapter Notes

Chapter 1

1. David W. McLean. "The art of the tooth-brush." *Hygeia* 13 (September, 1935): 824.
2. Ibid., pp. 824–825.
3. Martha Hill Hommel. "Tongue scrapers and toothbrushes." *Hobbies* 546 (July, 1951): 58.
4. Ibid.
5. Lon W. Morrey. "One good word for toothpaste ads." *Today's Health* 32 (October, 1954): 13.
6. Morton Pader. "Dentifrices: problems of growth, pt. 1." *Drug & Cosmetic Industry* 108 (June, 1971): 37.
7. Patrick Ryan. "So keep on smilin'—even if you are radioactive." *Smithsonian* 7 (December, 1976): 144.
8. Ren Glasser. "Ask the dentist." *Family Health* 10 (July, 1978): 14.
9. Deborah Blumenthal. "Taking a pasting." *New York Times Magazine*, June 20, 1982, p. 68.
10. "Toothpastes." *Consumer Reports* 57 (September, 1992): 605; "Which toothpaste is right for you?" *Consumer Reports* 63 (August, 1998): 14.
11. "The evolution of the tooth-brush." *Literary Digest* 89 (June 12, 1926): 22.
12. "Curiosities of the tooth brush." *Scientific American* 75 (September 19, 1896): 233.
13. Anthony Ramirez. "Growth is glacial, but the market is big, and so is the gross." *New York Times*, May 13, 1990, sec 3, p. 11.
14. Goody Solomon. "Look ma, no cavities." *Barron's* 45 (January 4, 1965): 4; Esther M. McCabe. "The toothbrush and family oral hygiene." *Parents' Magazine* 38 (May, 1963): 14.
15. Don Wharton. "Why we brush our teeth." *Reader's Digest* 53 (July, 1948): 140.
16. Peter C. Goulding. "Miracles in toothpaste?" *Today's Health* 35 (February, 1957): 34.
17. Don Wharton, op. cit., pp. 139–140.
18. Ibid.

Chapter 2

1. Annie E. Lane. "Toothpowder or gunpowder." *Fortnightly Review* 83 (April, 1905): 729–731.
2. "Condemns the toothbrush." *New York Times*, March 2, 1912, p. 12.
3. "Her young audience get tooth brushes." *New York Times*, September 28, 1912, p. 6.
4. "The tooth-brush indicted." *Literary Digest* 50 (May 22, 1915): 1211.
5. "In defense of the toothbrush." *Literary Digest* 51 (December 4, 1915): 1283.
6. "How to sterilize a tooth-brush." *Literary Digest* 52 (April 29, 1916): 1217.
7. "Toothbrush drills today." *New York Times*, May 19, 1917, p. 13.
8. "Police get book on teeth." *New York Times*, April 29, 1922, p. 8.
9. W. F. G. Thacher. "Economic determinism and the tooth-brush." *Printers' Ink* 128 (August 7, 1924): 78, 70.
10. Esther M. McCabe. "The toothbrush and family oral hygiene." *Parents' Magazine* 38 (May, 1963): 14.
11. August Belden. "How Rubberset cleared the way for Albright tooth brushes." *Printers' Ink* 126 (February 28, 1924): 25.
12. Ibid., pp. 25–26.
13. Ibid., pp. 26, 28.
14. Oliver T. Osborne. "The toothbrush." *Good Housekeeping* 81 (November, 1925): 218–219.
15. "15% use tooth brushes." *New York Times*, October 9, 1927, sec 2, p. 6.
16. William M. Gardner. "The toothbrush; is it a menace?" *Hygeia* 6 (May, 1928): 249–250.
17. "The tested toothbrush." *Hygeia* 7 (March, 1929): 254–255.
18. "The evolution of the tooth-brush." *Literary Digest* 89 (June 12, 1926): 22.
19. George H. Wandel. "Selecting a toothbrush." *Hygeia* 10 (June, 1932): 500.
20. Ad. *Saturday Evening Post*, March 15, 1930, p. 161.
21. "Color to the rescue." *Printers' Ink* 172 (July 4, 1935): 58, 60.
22. "Toothbrush trade-in." *Business Week*, May 3, 1933, p. 11.
23. "Trade-ins for toothbrushes." *Printers' Ink* 163 (May 11, 1933): 52.
24. "Comes double action." *Printers' Ink* 167 (April 5, 1934): 64.

25. "Three-way contest." *Printers' Ink* 168 (September 6, 1934): 20.

26. David W. McLean. "The art of the toothbrush." *Hygeia* 13 (September, 1935): 825–827.

27. "Synthetic bristles." *Business Week*, July 16, 1938, p. 34.

28. "Waterproof brush." *Business Week*, July 30, 1938, p. 19.

29. Andrew M. Howe. "Inter-line teamwork." *Printers' Ink* 184 (July 21, 1938): 13–15.

30. "Miracle-Tuft clicks." *Business Week*, October 14, 1939, pp. 40–41.

31. "Toothbrush troubles." *Business Week*, June 29, 1940, pp. 30, 32.

32. "Nylon toothbrush, 25 cents." *Business Week*, September 21, 1940, p. 30.

33. "Bristling rivalry." *Business Week*, December 14, 1940, p. 40.

34. Andrew M. Howe. "Fibrex vs. Exton." *Printers' Ink* 193 (December 27, 1940): 21–22.

35. "Toothbrushes." *Consumers' Research Bulletin* 10 (June, 1941): 11–13.

36. "Toothbrushes and tooth care." *Consumers' Research Bulletin* 12 (September, 1943): 5–7.

37. "It's the toothpaste." *Consumers' Research Bulletin* 15 (June, 1945): 7–8.

Chapter 3

1. "Faith in tooth powder prepares way for new product." *Printers' Ink* 162 (March 2, 1933): 10, 12.

2. John Allen Murphy. "How Kolynos sells in 88 countries." *American Business* 8 (January, 1938): 22.

3. Ibid., pp. 23–24, 57.

4. "Kolynos dental cream." *Sales Management* 100 (January 1, 1968): 31.

5. Bernice Kanner. "The gelling of America." *New York* 15 (March 29, 1982): 12.

6. "Forhan's for the gums." *Sales Management* 96 (April 1, 1966): 35.

7. John Revett. "Ipana dies as B-M shifts ad stress to Vote." *Advertising Age* 39 (November 11, 1968): 10.

8. Fred Danzig. "Magic of ADA seal keeps Crest No. 1 toothpaste titan." *Advertising Age* 43 (1972): 66–67.

9. W. A. Dawson. "Tooth powders." *Scientific American Supplement* 49 (April 7, 1900): 20301.

10. "Dentifrices." *Hygeia* 10 (February, 1932): 175.

11. "Tooth paste." *Hygeia* 10 (July, 1932): 662.

12. Charles H. Dickson. "Grocery trade-mark helps new drug product." *Printers' Ink* 161 (December 22, 1932): 38.

13. Ibid., pp. 38–39.

14. "Discriminating buyers." *Printers' Ink* 172 (July 11, 1935): 76, 78.

15. "Powder and paste." *Business Week*, August 17, 1935, p. 26.

16. "50 years ago." *Consumer Reports* 51 (March, 1986): 145.

17. Ibid.

18. "Studies of germ-killing power of toothpastes." *Science News Letter* 34 (August 27, 1938): 141.

19. "Dentifrices battle on." *Business Week*, October 14, 1939, p. 40.

20. Albert G. Ingallis. "Is your pet dentifrice safe?" *Scientific American* 163 (August, 1940): 82.

21. "Brushing your teeth with powder." *Consumers' Research Bulletin* 13 (January, 1944): 13

22. Ibid., pp. 13–15.

Chapter 4

1. Peter C. Goulding. "Miracles in toothpaste?" *Today's Health* 35 (February, 1957): 34, 44.

2. Don Wharton. "Why we brush our teeth." *Reader's Digest* 53 (July, 1948): 141.

3. Ibid.

4. Ad. *Saturday Evening Post* 176 (September 5, 1903): 14.

5. "90 per cent of Pepsodent's sales cost is advertising." *Printers' Ink* 139 (June 16, 1927): 164.

6. Ibid., pp. 164, 167–168.

7. Fred Danzig. "Magic of ADA seal keeps Crest No. 1 toothpaste titan." *Advertising Age* 43 (February 20, 1972): 67.

8. Ibid.

9. Ibid., pp. 67, 77.

10. "The layman does what the professional does not." *Printers' Ink* 133 (December 3, 1925): 166.

11. Ibid., pp. 166, 168.

12. Marshall Beuick. "How Lehn & Fink is cutting waste in sampling dentists." *Printers' Ink* 17 (October 14, 1931): 40.

13. "Finds selling force in fear appeal." *Printers' Ink* 158 (March 10, 1932): 47.

14. Ibid., p. 48.

15. Edward Plaut. "Faith with action." *Printers' Ink* 162 (March 16, 1933): 17–18.

16. H. A. Weissman. "Advertising success story: Dr. Lyon's." *Printers' Ink* 167 (April 26, 1934): 7, 10.

17. Ibid., pp. 12, 108–109.

18. "Pepsodent consignment." *Printers' Ink* 175 (May 28, 1936): 20.

19. Stuart Sherman. "2,253,125 in this contest." *Printers' Ink* 178 (February 25, 1937): 6–8, 113.

20. Malcolm Hart. "Loss leader is touted by

Pepsodent as greatest advertising drive opens."
Printers' Ink 182 (January 27, 1938): 12.
21. Charles Luckman. "Pepsodent's 7 points."
Printers' Ink 186 (March 9, 1939): 15.
22. Ibid., pp. 15–16.
23. Ibid., pp. 16–17.
24. Ad. *Saturday Evening Post*, February 17,
1940, p. 103.
25. "Pepsodent turns publisher." *Printers' Ink*
197 (October 3, 1941): 15–16.

Chapter 5

1. Catherine Hackett. "The dentifrice
racket." *New Republic* 61 (January 15, 1930): 216.
2. Ibid.
3. Ibid., pp. 217–218.
4. Ibid., p. 218.
5. "Dentists willing to endorse ethical dentifrice advertisers." *Printers' Ink* 150 (February 13,
1930): 161–162.
6. H. H. Bunzell. "Truth versus advertising."
Science 73 (March 13, 1931): 286.
7. "Toothpaste has value only as cleanser."
Hygeia 9 (July, 1931): 683.
8. "Toothpaste facts and fancies." *Scientific
American* 148 (January, 1933): 39.
9. McCready Sykes. "The obverse side."
Commerce and Finance 22 (August 23, 1933): 735.
10. Jerome W. Ephraim. "The truth about
dentifrices." *American Mercury* 33 (September,
1934): 77–78.
11. Ibid., p. 78.
12. Ibid., pp. 78–79.
13. C. B. Larrabee. "Dentists and advertising." *Printers' Ink* 172 (July 25, 1935): 65, 68–70.
14. "Kolynos ad claims barred." *New York
Times*, June 10, 1937, p. 41.
15. "New dental anesthetic paste prevents pain
in many cases." *Science News Letter* 32 (July 24,
1935): 51–52.
16. Samuel M. Gordon and Eleanore B. Du-
four. "Doctor, what dentifrice shall I use?" *Hygeia*
15 (August, 1937): 714.
17. Ibid., pp. 714, 716, 762.
18. Ibid., pp. 762–763.
19. Ibid., pp. 716, 763.
20. Blake Clark. "Taking dentifrice ads to the
cleaners." *Reader's Digest* 43 (August, 1943): 19.
21. Ibid., pp. 19–20.
22. Ibid., p. 20.
23. Ibid., pp. 20–21.
24. Ibid., pp. 21–22.
25. Ibid., p. 25.
26. Ibid., pp. 22–23.
27. R. M. Cunningham, Jr. "Toothpaste ads v.
the truth." *New Republic* 114 (March 4, 1946): 313.
28. Ibid., pp. 313–314.

29. Ibid., p. 314.
30. Ibid., p. 315.

Chapter 6

1. "Preventive toothpowder." *Newsweek* 33
(February 14, 1949): 44.
2. "Comes the revolution." *Newsweek* 33
(April 11, 1949): 66.
3. George J. Abrams. "The marketing program behind Amm-i-dent's spectacular rise."
Printers' Ink 227 (April 22, 1949): 25–27.
4. Ibid., pp. 27, 48.
5. "Standards set up on dentifrice ads." *New
York Times*, May 26, 1949, p. 45.
6. "The teeth of the battle." *Time* 53 (May
23, 1949): 90.
7. Bernard Tolk. "New ammoniated dentifrices flood the market; established brands split
on launching line." *Printers' Ink* 227 (May 6,
1949): 102, 107.
8. "Dentists warned on decay curbs." *New
York Times*, June 5, 1949, p. 77.
9. Harold Aaron. "What about ammoniated
dentifrices?" *Consumer Reports* 14 (June, 1949):
273.
10. Ibid., pp. 273–274.
11. Ibid., p. 275.
12. "Wafers and cure-alls." *Consumer Reports*
14 (September, 1949): 405.
13. "Value of ammoniated powders questioned." *Science News Letter* 57 (May 20, 1950):
313.
14. "Ammoniated dentifrices." *Science Digest*
28 (July, 1950): 55.
15. "Tooth paste and tooth powder." *Consumer Reports* 14 (August, 1949): 346.
16. Ibid., pp. 346–348.
17. Ibid., p. 349.
18. Henry C. Link. "What is happening in
the dentifrice field?" *Advertising Agency and Advertising and Selling* 42 (September, 1949): 48, 128.
19. "Chlorophyll tooth paste." *Science Digest*
26 (September, 1949): 51.
20. "Pepsodent is green." *Newsweek* 38 (October 8, 1951): 77–78.
21. "Green gold." *Time* 59 (April 14, 1952):
102.
22. "Green grow the brushes." *Newsweek* 39
(June 23, 1952): 73.
23. "Dentocillan." *Time* 56 (September 4,
1950): 41.
24. "Taste governs dentifrice choice." *Science
News Letter* 64 (November 14, 1953): 310.
25. Albert Q. Maisel. "What's all this about
anti-enzyme toothpastes?" *Reader's Digest* 63 (December, 1953): 10.
26. Ibid., pp. 11–13.

27. "New tooth data called anti-enzyme set-back." *New York Times*, January 24, 1954, p. 31.
28. "Battle of the toothpaste additives." *Business Week*, May 22, 1954, p. 41.
29. Ibid.
30. Ibid., pp. 41–42.
31. Walter Goodman. "The toothpaste tournament." *New Republic* 135 (July 30, 1956): 15–17.
32. "Tooth pastes." *Consumer Reports* 19 (April, 1954): 164–166.
33. Ibid., pp. 164–165.
34. "Tooth paste and tooth powder." *Consumer Reports* 14 (August, 1949): 351; "Wafers and cure-alls." *Consumer Reports* 14 (September, 1949): 405.
35. "Fluoride tooth paste." *Science News Letter* 67 (February 12, 1955): 100.
36. "Fluoride toothpaste." *New York Times*, February 17, 1955, p. 33.
37. "Toothy." *Newsweek* 46 (November 14, 1955): 88, 90.
38. Bruce Bliven, Jr. "Next: fluoride toothpaste." *Colliers* 137 (January 6, 1956): 32–34.
39. Walter Goodman, op. cit., p. 17.
40. Peter C. Goulding. "Miracles in toothpaste?" *Today's Health* 35 (February, 1957): 44.

Chapter 7

1. Carroll J. Swan. "National distribution for new product achieved almost overnight." *Printers' Ink* 221 (October 17, 1947): 35–37.
2. D. H. Williams. "Ten commandments for launching a new product." *Advertising & Selling* 40 (November, 1947): 33–34+.
3. Don Wharton. "Why we brush our teeth." *Reader's Digest* 53 (July, 1948): 142.
4. "Cash and caries; the dentists look at dentifrices." *Consumer Reports* 15 (March, 1950): 126.
5. "Many dentifrices seen as deceptive." *New York Times*, December 7, 1951, p. 21.
6. "Dental association hits toothpaste claims." *Science News Letter* 64 (July 11, 1953): 21.
7. "Toothpaste ads scored." *New York Times*, September 30, 1953, p. 32.
8. "Peril to health seen in bogus dental ads." *New York Times*, October 2, 1953, p. 14.
9. Howard A. Rusk. "Success of tooth paste ads stirs dentists into attack." *New York Times*, October 4, 1953, p. 83.
10. "ADA urges dentifrice advertisers to curb misleading claims." *Printers' Ink* 245 (October 9, 1953): 53.
11. James J. Nagle. "News of the advertising and marketing fields." *New York Times*, December 20, 1953, sec 3, p. 9.
12. Robert J. Flood. "They're feudin', fightin'

and sellin'." *Printers' Ink* 247 (May 14, 1954): 45–46, 48.
13. "Ads for miracle toothpastes decried by head of dental unit." *New York Times*, December 8, 1955, p. 39.
14. Philip Schuyler. "Pulitzer Prize winner writes toothpaste ads." *Editor & Publisher* 90 (August 10, 1957): 15.
15. Carl Spievogel. "Advertising: Shhh!— Bottled toothpaste." *New York Times*, October 6, 1957, sec 3, p. 10.
16. Carl Spievogel. "Advertising: and now, striped toothpaste." *New York Times*, January 15, 1958, p. 40.
17. "Kolynos *Coronet* ad reprints going to 75,000 dentists." *Advertising Age* 30 (May 18, 1959): 12.
18. "Kolynos, ADA face brushoff in backing miracle claims." *Printers' Ink* 267 (May 29, 1959): 12.
19. "TV toothpaste ads rigged, expert says." *New York Times*, November 12, 1959, p. 25.

Chapter 8

1. "U.S. seizes toothpaste." *New York Times*, May 22, 1949, sec 3, p. 5.
2. "F.T.C. cracks down on Bristol-Myers." *New York Times*, November 30, 1949, p. 41.
3. "Dentists assail some ads on toothpaste; urge Congress force proof of claims." *New York Times*, July 18, 1958, p. 11.
4. "U.S. aide disputes cigarette claims." *New York Times*, July 19, 1958, p. 17.
5. "Dentists ask law putting burden of proof on toothpaste advertisers." *Advertising Age* 29 (July 21, 1958): 1, 75.
6. "Inquiry rebukes F.T.C. on false ads." *New York Times*, August 18, 1958, p. 15.
7. "Toothpaste ads criticized by dentists." *Science Digest* 44 (November, 1958): 72.
8. "U.S. curbs sought on dentifrice ads." *New York Times*, November 4, 1959, p. 71.
9. "Flemming in warning." *New York Times*, November 10, 1959, p. 48.
10. "U.S. asked to curb toothpaste ads." *New York Times*, December 8, 1959, p. 51.
11. Bess Furman. "F.T.C. wants data on dentifrice ads." *New York Times*, December 9, 1959, p. 52.
12. "Dentists ask law on toothpaste ads, urge advertiser bear burden of proof." *Advertising Age* 30 (December 14, 1959): 4.
13. "FTC hits Colgate for Gardol shield claims." *Advertising Age* 30 (November 23, 1959): 1, 129.
14. "Colgate fights charge." *New York Times*, January 29, 1960, p. 12.

15. "Colgate defends Gardol ads, hits FTC bad faith." *Advertising Age* 31 (February 1, 1960): 1–2.

16. Robert Alden. "Advertising: Colgate and F.T.C. in dispute." *New York Times*, August 5, 1960, p. 33.

17. Alvin Shuster. "F.T.C. charges 4 TV ads use false props to support claims." *New York Times*, January 15, 1960, pp. 1, 58.

18. "TV ad is defended." *New York Times*, January 16, 1960, p. 43.

19. "Any toothpaste can clean smoke stains, Lever lawyers say." *Advertising Age* 32 (July 10, 1961): 22.

20. "Pepsodent TV ads could have made it clear they referred to fresh stains, FTC told." *Advertising Age* 33 (September 24, 1962): 4.

21. "FTC finds ads for Pepsodent not deceptive." *Advertising Age* 33 (October 22, 1962): 1, 113.

Chapter 9

1. "Majority of toothbrushes found defective by survey." *Science News Letter* 54 (September 11, 1948): 168.

2. "Many old toothbrushes still being used." *Science News Letter* 74 (August 16, 1958): 104.

3. "Tests of toothbrushes." *Consumer Bulletin* 42 (March, 1959): 29–30.

4. "Will new toothbrushes spur static field?" *Printers' Ink* 276 (September 8, 1961): 11–13.

5. "Pycopay TV ads boost new shape." *Advertising Age* 33 (May 21, 1962): 114.

6. "How Du Pont uses the new to update the old." *Printers' Ink* 288 (July 17, 1964): 15.

7. "Dental publications survey tells brands dentists suggest." *Advertising Age* 35 (September 14, 1964): 71.

8. "Manual toothbrushes hold line against automatics, admen report." *Advertising Age* 36 (February 1, 1965): 10.

9. Kristian S. Palda and Carry M. Blair. "A moving cross-section analysis of demand for toothpaste." *Journal of Marketing Research* 7 (November, 1970): 448.

10. "Toothbrushes." *Changing Times* 25 (May, 1971): 13–14.

11. Morton Pader. "Dentifrices: problems of growth, pt. 1." *Drug & Cosmetic Industry* 108 (June, 1971): 38.

12. "FTC eases up in Dr. West's pact." *Advertising Age* 42 (May 3, 1971): 2.

13. "The toothbrush." *American Druggist* 171 (May 1, 1975): 31–33.

14. Jennifer Alter. "Toothbrush makers' lament: who notices." *Advertising Age* 53 (October 4, 1982): 66.

15. Ibid.

16. "Is your toothbrush making you sick?" *Parents' Magazine* 62 (March, 1987): 17.

17. David O. Born. "Baffled by brushes." *Saturday Evening Post* 259 (May/June, 1987): 18–19.

18. "New ways to save your teeth." *Consumer Reports* 54 (August, 1989): 506; "Electric toothbrushes." *Consumer Reports* 57 (September, 1992): 613.

19. Dawn Margolis. "Toothbrush trivia." *American Health* 11 (December, 1992): 15.

20. Pat Sloan. "Dep joins toothbrush rush with grip that changes color." *Advertising Age* 64 (June 7, 1993): 6.

21. Trish Hall. "Brush-a, brush-a, brush-a, just isn't enough anymore." *New York Times*, June 16, 1993, p. C8.

22. Maryanne Thumser. "Brush away the toothbrush dilemma." *Good Housekeeping* 221 (August, 1995): 153.

23. "Brushing up on toothbrushes." *McCall's* 122 (June, 1995): 44.

24. Pat Sloan. "Colgate, J&J to pour $30 mil into toothbrush extensions." *Advertising Age* 67 (February 26, 1996): 3, 45.

25. George F. Will. "The perils of brushing." *Newsweek* 133 (May 10, 1999): 92; "What's in a claim?" *www.smile-on.com/news*, July 26, 2000.

26. Greg Winter. "No ads, but strong sales for electric toothbrushes." *New York Times*, December 13, 2000, p. C2.

27. "Toothbrush is king of inventions." *Weekly Reader-Edition 4* 84 (March 7, 2003): 4.

28. "Brushing teeth for all round health." *British Dental Journal* 198 (March 12, 2005): 257.

29. "Survey reveals dentists ditch manual toothbrushes." *US Newswire*, February 23, 2006.

30. Cory Servaas. "Taking care of your toothbrushes." *Medical Update* 28 (Issue 7, 2007): 2.

31. Brendan I. Koerner. "Zapping that icky toothbrush." *New York Times*, January 16, 2005, sec 3, p. 2.

32. Robert Davis. "Killing toothbrush bacteria." *Wall Street Journal*, March 15, 2005, p. D4.

33. "New niche creates opportunities." *Chain Drug Review*, February 4, 2008, p. 20.

34. Eddy Ramirez. "Get a new toothbrush." *U.S. News & World Report* 145 (December 29, 2008): 49.

35. Joseph Pereira. "Got a song stuck in your head? Try brushing." *Wall Street Journal*, February 25, 2005, pp. B1, B3.

36. Arianne Cohen. "Toothbrush that sings." *New York Times Magazine*, December 11, 2005, p. 98.

37. Warren Buckleitner. "That tune in your head could be your toothbrush." *New York Times*, March 1, 2007, p. C10(L).

38. Martha Schindler Connors. "This is a

toothbrush or a drill sergeant." *New York Times,* December 20, 2007, p. G3(L).

39. "O-T-C best sellers." *Chain Drug Review,* January 7, 2008, p. 62.

Chapter 10

1. "An electrical tooth-brush." *Scientific American* 125 (September 24, 1921): 226.
2. "Electric tooth brush out." *New York Times,* October 9, 1937, p. 30.
3. "Fleapower motors." *Business Week,* March 15, 1941, pp. 68–69.
4. "Will new toothbrushes spur static field?" *Printers' Ink* 276 (September 18, 1961): 11.
5. "A safety report on electric toothbrushes." *Consumer Reports* 27 (May, 1962): 255.
6. "How GE put a charge in (and under) a toothbrush." *Printers' Ink* 280 (July 20, 1962): 44–45.
7. "Electric toothbrushes." *Consumer Reports* 27 (August, 1962): 376.
8. Ibid., pp. 376–378.
9. "3 added starters set for full power toothbrush race." *Advertising Age* 33 (August 6, 1962): 2.
10. Goody Solomon. "The electric toothbrush." *Barron's* 42 (October 1, 1962): 11, 20.
11. "Summing up on electric toothbrushes." *Consumer Reports* 28 (April, 1963): 186–187.
12. "Power toothbrush: worth the money?" *Changing Times* 17 (November, 1963): 38.
13. "Electric toothbrushes." *Consumer Bulletin* 47 (March, 1964): 22, 26.
14. Lydia Wallack. "What a really new product can do." *Printers' Ink* 287 (April 17, 1964): 39–40.
15. Ibid., pp. 40–41.
16. John Avery Snyder. "Stop the brush, I want to get off." *Atlantic Monthly* 213 (May, 1964): 119.
17. "GE and Squibb toothbrushes get dental group nod." *Advertising Age* 35 (August 31, 1964): 215.
18. "Dental publications survey tells brands dentists suggest." *Advertising Age* 35 (September 14, 1964): 71.
19. "Electric toothbrushes." *Consumer Reports* 31 (August, 1966): 402–403.
20. "Electric toothbrushes." *Consumer Reports* 34 (March, 1969): 138–141.
21. Jane E. Brody. "Personal health." *New York Times,* April 2, 1986, p. C6.
22. Robb Deigh. "Arming yourself to the teeth." *U.S. News & World Report* 104 (June 27, 1988): 62.
23. "Electric toothbrushes." *Consumer Reports* 57 (September, 1992): 611–613.

24. "Consumer brush-off." *Stores* 77 (January, 1995): 60, 62.
25. Mary Lord. "Oral power tools." *U.S. News & World Report* 124 (April 20, 1998): 64–65.
26. "Brushing under power." *Consumer Reports* 63 (August, 1998): 15–16.
27. Robert Berner. "Why P&G's smile is so bright." *Business Week,* August 12, 2002, pp. 58, 60.
28. Mary Carmichael. "Less power to you." *Newsweek* 141 (January 27, 2003): 73.
29. Jack Neff. "Power brushes a hit at every level." *Advertising Age* 74 (May 26, 2003): 10.
30. Rebecca Harris. "A brush with brains." *Marketing Magazine* 110 (September 26, 2005): 5.
31. Samuel Solley. "Oral-B battery powered brush rapped by greens." *Marketing* (UK), March 8, 2006, p. 6.
32. "Power toothbrushes." *Chain Drug Review,* February 4, 2008, p. 20.

Chapter 11

1. "Dentists okay of Crest as bar to decay elates P&G." *Advertising Age* 31 (August 1, 1960): 1, 101.
2. Ibid., p. 101.
3. "Dentifrice found to prevent decay." *New York Times,* August 2, 1960, p. 26.
4. "Can P&G's Crest take — and hold — lead in the $235-million dentifrice field?" *Printers' Ink* 272 (August 5, 1960): 12–13.
5. Ibid., p. 13.
6. "Toothpaste ad battle looms." *Business Week,* August 6, 1960, p. 28.
7. "P&G's Crest sprints after ADA boost." *Printers' Ink* 272 (August 26, 1960): 11.
8. "P&G makes capital of ADA O.K. in Crest ads." *Advertising Age* 31 (August 29, 1960): 2, 178.
9. Lawrence Bernard and John Crichton. "Dentists tag along with ADA on Crest." *Advertising Age* 31 (September 5, 1960): 1.
10. "Sindlinger, BofA find Crest gains in sales, impact." *Advertising Age* 31 (September 26, 1960): 2.
11. "How good is Crest toothpaste?" *Consumer Reports* 25 (October, 1960): 513.
12. "ADA head insists Crest endorsement will spur truth in all toothpaste ads." *Advertising Age* 31 (October 24, 1960): 1, 110.
13. "Tell public, too, that Crest is approved, not endorsed, toothpaste rivals urge ADA." *Advertising Age* 32 (January 23, 1961): 54.
14. Ibid.
15. "Ex-ADA head hits dental group approval of Crest." *Advertising Age* 32 (June 19, 1961): 4.

16. "Dentists battle over toothpaste ad policies." *Advertising Age* 32 (October 23, 1961): 1, 12.
17. Ibid., p. 12.
18. "Science and the news" *Science* 134 (October 27, 1961): 1349.
19. "Flack ack-ack." *Newsweek* 58 (October 30, 1961): 62–63.
20. Bruce Bliven, Jr. "And now a word from our sponsor." *New Yorker* 39 (March 23, 1963): 83, 130.
21. Peter C. Riesz and Abe Shuchman. "Responses to the ADA Crest endorsement." *Journal of Advertising Research* 14 (February, 1974): 21–23.
22. "All over their faces." *The Economist* 257 (October 4, 1975): 83.
23. Carolyn Allmon. "Advertising and sales relationships for toothpaste: another look." *Business Economics* 17 (September, 1982): 58; Roger D. Carlson. "Advertising and sales relationships for toothpaste." *Business Economics* 16 (September, 1981): 37–38.
24. Richard W. Stevenson. "Crest stages a turnaround." *New York Times*, April 24, 1986, pp. D1, D6.
25. Dana Canedy. "P&G seeks to stem loss of smile share." *New York Times*, June 20, 1997, pp. D1, D4.
26. "P&G back to basics with Crest." *Advertising Age* 77 (July 3, 2006): 12.

Chapter 12

1. "Colgate's fluoride, Cue, enters dentifrice derby." *Advertising Age* 32 (August 14, 1961): 1, 86.
2. "Colgate's 3-month $3,751,000 campaign hikes share 1.5%." *Advertising Age* 34 (August 26, 1963): 249.
3. "Advertising." *Time* 84 (August 7, 1964): 82.
4. "Cue, too." *Newsweek* 64 (August 10, 1964): 59.
5. Fred Danzig. "Colgate's Cue gets recognition by ADA." *Advertising Age* 35 (August 3, 1964): 1, 73.
6. "Super Stripe gets dental group okay; ads to aim at kids." *Advertising Age* 37 (June 6, 1966): 2.
7. "Dentifrice market is becoming 2-front war." *Advertising Age* 39 (October 7, 1968): 3, 99.
8. "And now, the brush-in." *Time* 92 (November 15, 1968): 62, 64.
9. "Dentists endorse Colgate formula." *Business Week*, October 11, 1969, p. 46.
10. Sandra Salmans. "Fighting decay, and each other." *New York Times*, April 6, 1981, p. D1.
11. Ibid., p. D4.
12. Ibid.

13. "ADA head insists Crest endorsement will spur truth in all toothpaste ads." *Advertising Age* 31 (October 24, 1960): 110.
14. Cathy Sears. "Baking soda toothpastes." *American Health* 13 (April, 1994): 19.
15. "Toothpaste ads vie for favor on flavor." *Advertising Age* 37 (August 1, 1966): 2.
16. "Toothpaste squeeze is TV bonanza." *Sponsor* 20 (October 31, 1966): 35–36.
17. Ibid., pp. 36, 38.
18. Ibid., p. 33.
19. "Lever to put heaviest ad push behind bright white Pepsodent." *Advertising Age* 38 (January 30, 1967): 1, 119.
20. Fred Danzig. "New formulas jumble dentifrice marketing." *Advertising Age* 39 (July 8, 1968): 1, 38.
21. "Dentifrice market is becoming 2-front war." *Advertising Age* 39 (October 7, 1968): 99.
22. "Dentists endorse Colgate formula." *Business Week*, October 11, 1969, p. 46.
23. Morton Pader. "Dentifrices: problems of growth, pt. 2." *Drug & Cosmetic Industry* 109 (July, 1971): 36, 38, 40.
24. Deborah Blumenthal. "A promise of brighter smiles." *New York Times*, May 20, 1989, p. 54.
25. Anthony Ramirez. "Growth is glacial, but the market is big, and so is the gross." *New York Times*, May 13, 1990, sec 3, p. 11.
26. "Whiter smiles have dentists frowning." *Newsweek* 117 (January 14, 1991): 45.
27. Bernice Kanner. "The white brigade." *New York* 27 (January 17, 1994): 11.
28. Ibid.
29. Ibid., pp. 11–12.
30. "Whiten up." *Mademoiselle* 101 (March, 1995): 68.
31. Zachary Schiller. "Look Ma, no plaque: the next dental frontier." *Business Week*, March 4, 1985, p. 36.
32. Eleanor Johnson Tracy. "Plaque attackers." *Fortune* 111 (May 13, 1985): 73–74.
33. Kathleen Deveny. "Colgate puts the squeeze on Crest." *Business Week*, August 19, 1985, pp. 40–41.
34. Susan Katz. "The great plaque-off." *Newsweek* 106 (October 28, 1985): 76.
35. Jane E. Brody. "Personal health." *New York Times*, April 2, 1986, p. C6.
36. Laurie Freeman and Nancy Giges. "FDA may take nip at toothpaste claims." *Advertising Age* 58 (May 25, 1987): 50.
37. Ibid.
38. Ibid., p. 69.
39. Bernice Kanner. "Tartar time." *New York* 21 (October 31, 1988): 16, 20.
40. Jennifer Lawrence and Judann Dagnoli. "FDA order halts P&G, Colgate toothpaste intros." *Advertising Age* 62 (February 11, 1991): 1, 44.

41. Steven Cojocaru. "Behind the scans." *People* 60 (September 15, 2003): 142.

Chapter 13

1. "What's ahead for soaps?" *Sponsor* 15 (November 20, 1981): 27.
2. "Dental publications survey tells brands dentists suggest." *Advertising Age* 35 (September 14, 1964): 71.
3. Goody Solomon. "Look ma, no cavities." *Barron's* 45 (January 4, 1965): 4.
4. David Anderson. "Executive seized as a business spy." *New York Times*, April 2, 1965, p. 1.
5. Ibid., p. 25; "A toothpaste spy admits plot to sell Crest's campaign." *New York Times*, August 6, 1965, p. 29.
6. Ralph Tyler. "The squeeze is on in toothpastes." *Television Magazine* 22 (December, 1965): 37–38.
7. "Toothpaste squeeze is TV bonanza." *Sponsor* 20 (October 31, 1966): 27–30+.
8. Ibid., p. 29.
9. "Dentifrice abrasivity rated by ADA group." *American Druggist* 162 (November 30, 1970): 36.
10. Morton Pader. "Dentifrices: problems of growth, pt. 1." *Drug & Cosmetic Industry* 108 (June, 1971): 38.
11. "Toothpaste." *Consumer Reports* 37 (April, 1972): 251.
12. Ibid., pp. 253, 255.
13. "All about: selecting a toothpaste." *New York Times*, March 16, 1977, p. C11.
14. "Getting a bigger share of the dental products market." *American Druggist* 179 (June, 1979): 55–56.
15. "Toothpastes." *Consumer Reports* 49 (March, 1984): 138–140.
16. "Toothpastes." *Consumer Reports* 51 (March, 1986): 144–149.
17. Bernice Kanner. "Picks and plans." *New York* 21 (October 17, 1988): 29–30; "Toothpastes around the world." *New York Times*, January 15, 1989, sec 5, p. 3.
18. Anthony Ramirez. "Growth is glacial, but the market is big, and so is the gross." *New York Times*, May 13, 1990, sec 3, p. 11.
19. "Toothpastes." *Consumer Reports* 57 (September, 1992): 602–603.
20. Ibid., p. 603.
21. Ibid., p. 606.
22. Katja Shaye. "The last word on … toothpaste." *Good Housekeeping* 222 (February, 1996): 127.
23. Patricia Hittner. "Putting the squeeze on toothpaste." *Better Homes & Gardens* 76 (May, 1998): 120.

24. Ibid., pp. 122, 126.
25. "Which toothpaste is right for you?" *Consumer Reports* 63 (August, 1998): 11.
26. Ibid., p. 13.
27. Robert Berner. "Why P&G's smile is so bright." *Business Week*, August 12, 2002, p. 60.
28. Joseph Tarnowski. "Word of mouth." *Progressive Grocer* 84 (January 1, 2005): 66–68.
29. Claire Briney. "Oral hygiene becomes oral vanity." *Global Cosmetic Industry* 173 (April, 2005): 48–50.
30. "Oral care sales in chain drug stores." *Chain Drug Review*, November 5, 2007, p. 37.

Chapter 14

1. "Medical-dental taboos stronger." *Broadcasting* 68 (January 18, 1965): 46, 48.
2. "Stewart tells how research boosted Macleans toothpaste." *Advertising Age* 36 (January 18, 1965): 74.
3. "$40 million of dentifrice ad budgets go to TV." *Sponsor* 19 (August 9, 1965): 53.
4. "Fact's anti-sweets ad theme is big toothache for candy industry." *Advertising Age* 38 (January 16, 1967): 2.
5. Ibid., p. 84.
6. John Revett. "Ipana dies as B-M shifts ad stress to Vote." *Advertising Age* 39 (November 11, 1968): 10.
7. "Ipana returns to fray." *Advertising Age* 40 (September 15, 1969): 2, 105.
8. Fred Danzig. "Colgate sees itself ousting Crest as no. 1." *Advertising Age* 40 (January 13, 1969): 8.
9. "More for Lesch?" *Forbes* 103 (March 1, 1969): 30–31.
10. "How to make new brands sell." *Broadcasting* 76 (May 26, 1969): 32.
11. Craig Whitney. "What's the price? It's hard to tell." *New York Times*, September 28, 1969, p. 48.
12. "8 top toothpastes criticized by F.D.A." *New York Times*, July 21, 1970, p. 70.
13. "FDA report gives nod to therapeutic claims for Crest, Colgate with MFP." *Advertising Age* 41 (July 27, 1970): 6.
14. "FDA okays claims for some toothpastes, but questions 8 leaders." *American Druggist* 162 (August 10, 1970): 30.
15. "Nader lays staining to some toothpastes." *New York Times*, July 9, 1971, p. 36.
16. "ADA says Nader is misleading public." *Advertising Age* 42 (July 12, 1971): 1, 63.
17. "Toothpaste study released by Pell." *New York Times*, August 6, 1971, p. 32.
18. Sheva Rapaport. "Toothpaste." *Consumer Bulletin* 54 (August, 1971): 7–9.

19. "Trade commission questions toothpaste ad claims." *New York Times*, December 23, 1971, p. 13.

20. Fred Danzig. "Magic of ADA seal keeps Crest no. 1 toothpaste titan." *Advertising Age* 43 (February 20, 1972): 64, 66.

21. Ibid., p. 66.

22. Nancy Giges. "P&G's Crest efforts taking aim against Lever share." *Advertising Age* 47 (January 26, 1976): 2.

23. Nancy Giges. "WRG lose Gleem to Leo Burnett." *Advertising Age* 47 (April 19, 1976): 2.

24. "Toothpaste & mouthwash." *Media Decisions* 13 (April, 1978): 148, 150.

25. "The big squeeze in toothpaste." *New York Times*, September 21, 1980, p. 21.

26. Philip H. Dougherty. "Toothpaste faces gel challenge." *New York Times*, October 22, 1981, p. D16.

27. Bernice Kanner. "The gelling of America." *New York* 15 (March 29, 1982): 12.

28. Ibid., pp. 16, 18.

29. Deborah Blumenthal. "Taking a pasting." *New York Times Magazine*, June 20, 1982, pp. 68–69.

30. "Dentifrices: a state of the industry report." *Drug & Cosmetic Industry* 132 (April, 1983): 28–29.

31. Nancy Giges and Gay Jervey. "Colgate joins shift to pump for dentifrice." *Advertising Age* 55 (May 28, 1984): 1, 64.

32. "Pump paste brushes off skeptics." *Advertising Age* 55 (December 31, 1984): 3, 13.

33. "Bob Taylor's toothpaste pump puts the squeeze on all those messy tubes." *People Weekly* 23 (January 14, 1985): 76.

34. "Church groups want racist toothpaste off shelves." *Jet* 70 (April 14, 1986): 32.

35. Mark Fortune. "Colgate's racist log leaves bad taste." *Black Enterprise* 18 (July, 1988): 21.

36. Ibid.

37. Douglas C. McGill. "Colgate to rename a toothpaste." *New York Times*, January 27, 1989, pp. D1, D4.

38. "A new name for toothpaste." *New York Times*, April 18, 1989, p. D25.

39. "NAD report takes aim at Aim." *Advertising Age* 58 (July 20, 1987): 51.

40. Richard W. Stevenson. "Advertising." *New York Times*, October 7, 1988, p. D15.

41. "U.S. challenges claims on toothpaste and mouthwash labels." *New York Times*, October 9, 1988, p. 31.

42. Laura Jereski. "Hearts, minds and market share." *Forbes* 143 (April 3, 1989): 80, 82.

43. Bette Popovich. "Year of the toothpaste." *Chemical Marketing Reporter* 247 (May 8, 1995): SR16.

44. Zachary Schiller. "The sound and the fluoride." *Business Week*, August 14, 1995, p. 48.

45. "New toothpaste from Colgate set." *New York Times*, July 15, 1997, p. D5.

46. Robert J. Davis. "Brushing up on toothpastes." *Wall Street Journal*, March 9, 2004, p. D3.

47. Alina Tugend. "Smile, you're in the dental care aisle." *New York Times*, August 6, 2005, p. C6.

48. "O-T-C best sellers." *Chain Drug Review*, January 7, 2008, p. 62.

49. "Two individuals plead guilty to trafficking in more than half a million tubes of counterfeit toothpaste." *US Newswire*, August 21, 2008.

Bibliography

Aaron, Harold. "What about ammoniated dentifrices?" *Consumer Reports* 14 (June, 1949): 273–275.

Abrams, George J. "The marketing program behind Amm-i-dent's spectacular rise." *Printers' Ink* 227 (April 22, 1949): 25–27+.

Ad. *Saturday Evening Post* 176 (September 5, 1903): 14.

_____. *Saturday Evening Post*, March 15, 1930, p. 161.

_____. *Saturday Evening Post*, February 17, 1940, p. 103.

"ADA head insists Crest endorsement will spur truth in all toothpaste ads." *Advertising Age* 31 (October 24, 1960): 1, 110.

"ADA says Nader is misleading public." *Advertising Age* 42 (July 12, 1971): 1, 63.

"ADA urges dentifrice advertisers to curb misleading claims." *Printers' Ink* 245 (October 9, 1953): 53.

"Ads for miracle toothpastes decried by head of dental unit." *New York Times*, December 8, 1955, p. 39.

"Advertising." *Time* 84 (August 7, 1964): 82.

Alden, Robert. "Advertising: Colgate and F.T.C. in dispute." *New York Times*, August 5, 1960, p. 33.

"All about: selecting a toothpaste." *New York Times*, March 16, 1977, p. C11.

"All over their faces." *The Economist* 257 (October 4, 1975): 83.

Allmon, Carolyn. "Advertising and sales relationships for toothpaste: another look." *Business Economics* 17 (September, 1982): 55–61.

Alter, Jennifer. "Toothbrush makers' lament: who notices." *Advertising Age* 53 (October 4, 1982): 66.

"Ammoniated dentifrices." *Science Digest* 28 (July, 1950): 55.

"And now, the brush-in." *Time* 92 (November 15, 1968): 62, 64.

Anderson, David. "Executive seized as business spy." *New York Times*, April 2, 1965, pp. 1, 25.

"Any toothpaste can clean smoke stains, Lever lawyers say." *Advertising Age* 32 (July 10, 1961): 22.

"Battle of the toothpaste additives." *Business Week*, May 22, 1954, pp. 41–42.

Belden, August. "How Rubberset cleared the way for Albright tooth brushes." *Printers' Ink* 126 (February 28, 1924): 25–26, 28.

Bernard, Lawrence, and John Crichton. "Dentists tag along with ADA on Crest." *Advertising Age* 31 (September 5, 1960): 1, 87.

Berner, Robert. "Why P&G's smile is so bright." *Business Week*, August 12, 2002, pp. 58–60.

Beuick, Marshall. "How Lehn & Fink is cutting waste in sampling dentists." *Printers' Ink* 17 (October 14, 1931): 40.

"The big squeeze in toothpaste." *New York Times*, September 21, 1980, p. 21.

Bliven, Bruce, Jr. "And now a word from our sponsor." *New Yorker* 39 (March 23, 1963): 83–84+.

_____. "Next: fluoride toothpaste." *Colliers* 137 (January 6, 1956): 32–34.

Blumenthal, Deborah. "A promise of brighter smiles." *New York Times*, May 20, 1989, p. 54.

_____. "Taking a pasting." *New York Times Magazine*, June 20, 1982, pp. 68–69.

"Bob Taylor's toothpaste pump puts the squeeze on all those messy tubes." *People Weekly* 23 (January 14, 1985): 76.

Born, David O. "Baffled by brushes." *Saturday Evening Post* 259 (May–June, 1987): 18–19, 92.

Briney, Claire. "Oral hygiene becomes oral vanity." *Global Cosmetic Industry* 173 (April, 2005): 48–50.

"Bristling rivalry." *Business Week*, December 14, 1940, p. 40.

Brody, Jane E. "Personal health." *New York Times*, April 2, 1986, p. C6.

"Brushing teeth for all round health." *British Dental Journal* 198 (March 12, 2005): 257.

"Brushing under power." *Consumer Reports* 63 (August, 1998): 15–16.

"Brushing up on toothbrushes." *McCall's* 122 (June, 1995): 44.

"Brushing your teeth with powder." *Consumers' Research Bulletin* 13 (January, 1944): 13–15.

Buckleitner, Warren. "That tune in your head could be your toothbrush." *New York Times*, March 1, 2007, p. C10(L).

Bunzell, H. H. "Truth versus advertising." *Science* 73 (March 13, 1931): 286.

"Can P&G's Crest take — and hold — lead in the $235-million dentifrice field?" *Printers' Ink* 272 (August 5, 1960): 12–13.

Canedy, Dana. "P&G seeks to stem loss of smile share." *New York Times*, June 20, 1997, pp. D1, D4.

Carlson, Roger D. "Advertising and sales relationships for toothpaste." *Business Economics* 16 (September, 1981): 36–39.

Carmichael, Mary. "Less power to you." *Newsweek* 141 (January 27, 2003): 73.

"Cash and caries; the dentists look at dentifrices." *Consumer Reports* 15 (March, 1950): 126.

"Chlorophyll tooth paste." *Science Digest* 26 (September, 1949): 51.

"Church groups want racist toothpaste off shelves." *Jet* 70 (April 14, 1986): 32.

Clark, Blake. "Taking dentifrice ads to the cleaners." *Reader's Digest* 43 (August, 1943): 19–23.

Cohen, Arianne. "Toothbrush that sings." *New York Times Magazine*, December 11, 2005, p. 98.

Cojocaru, Steven. "Behind the scans." *People* 60 (September 15, 2003): 142.

"Colgate defends Gardol ads, hits FTC bad faith." *Advertising Age* 31 (February 1, 1960): 1–2.

"Colgate fights charge." *New York Times*, January 29, 1960, p. 12.

"Colgate's 3-month, $3,751,000 campaign hikes share 1.5%." *Advertising Age* 34 (August 26, 1963): 249.

"Colgate's fluoride, Cue, enters dentifrice derby." *Advertising Age* 32 (August 14, 1961): 1, 86.

"Color to the rescue." *Printers' Ink* 172 (July 4, 1935): 58, 60.

"Comes double action." *Printers' Ink* 167 (April 5, 1934): 64.

"Comes the revolution." *Newsweek* 33 (April 11, 1949): 66.

"Condemns the toothbrush." *New York Times*, March 2, 1912, p. 12.

Connors, Martha Schindler. "This is a toothbrush or a drill sergeant." *New York Times*, December 20, 2007, p. G3(L).

"Consumer brush-off." *Stores* 77 (January, 1995): 60, 62.

"Cue, too." *Newsweek* 64 (August 10, 1964): 59.

Cunningham, R. M., Jr. "Toothpaste ads v. the truth." *New Republic* 114 (March 4, 1946): 313–315.

"Curiosities of the tooth brush." *Scientific American* 75 (September 19, 1896): 233.

Danzig, Fred. "Colgate sees itself ousting Crest as no. 1." *Advertising Age* 40 (January 13, 1969): 8.

_____. "Colgate's Cue gets recognition by ADA." *Advertising Age* 35 (August 3, 1964): 1, 73.

_____. "Magic of ADA seal keeps Crest no. 1 toothpaste titan." *Advertising Age* 43 (February 20, 1972): 25+.

_____. "New formulas jumble dentifrice marketing." *Advertising Age* 39 (July 8, 1968): 1, 38.

Davis, Robert. "Killing toothbrush bacteria." *Wall Street Journal*, March 15, 2005, p. D4.

Davis, Robert J. "Brushing up on toothpastes." *Wall Street Journal*, March 9, 2004, p. D3.

Dawson, W. A. "Tooth powders." *Scientific American Supplement* 49 (April 7, 1900): 20301–20302.

Deigh, Robb. "Arming yourself to the teeth." *U.S. News & World Report* 104 (June 27, 1988): 62.

"Dental association hits toothpaste ad claims." *Science News Letter* 64 (July 11, 1953): 21.

"Dental publications survey tells brands dentists suggest." *Advertising Age* 35 (September 14, 1964): 71.

"Dentifrice abrasivity rated by ADA group." *American Druggist* 162 (November 30, 1970): 36.

"Dentifrice battle on." *Business Week*, October 14, 1939, p. 40.

"Dentifrice found to prevent decay." *New York Times*, August 2, 1960, p. 26.

"Dentifrice market is becoming 2-front war." *Advertising Age* 39 (October 7, 1968): 3, 99.

"Dentifrices." *Hygeia* 10 (February, 1932): 175.

"Dentifrices: a state of the industry report."

Drug & Cosmetic Industry 132 (April, 1983): 28–29+.

"Dentists ask law on toothpaste ads, urge advertisers bear burden of proof." *Advertising Age* 30 (December 14, 1959): 4.

"Dentists ask law putting burden of proof on toothpaste advertisers." *Advertising Age* 29 (July 21, 1958): 1, 75.

"Dentists assail some ads on toothpaste; urge Congress force proof of claims." *New York Times*, July 18, 1958, p. 11.

"Dentists battle over toothpaste ad policies." *Advertising Age* 32 (October 23, 1961): 1, 12.

"Dentists endorse Colgate formula." *Business Week*, October 11, 1969, pp. 46–47.

"Dentists okay of Crest as bar to decay elates P&G." *Advertising Age* 31 (August 1, 1960): 1, 101.

"Dentists warned on decay curbs." *New York Times*, June 5, 1949, p. 77.

"Dentists willing to endorse ethical dentifrice advertisers." *Printers' Ink* 150 (February 13, 1930): 161–162.

"Dentocillin." *Time* 56 (September 4, 1950): 41.

Deveny, Kathleen. "Colgate puts the squeeze on Crest." *Business Week*, August 19, 1985, pp. 40–41.

Dickson, Charles H. "Grocery trade-mark helps new drug product." *Printers' Ink* 161 (December 22, 1932): 38–39.

"Discriminating buyers." *Printers' Ink* 172 (July 11, 1935): 76, 78.

Dougherty, Philip H. "Toothpaste faces gel challenge." *New York Times*, October 22, 1981, p. D16.

"8 top toothpastes criticized by F.D.A." *New York Times*, July 21, 1970, p. 70.

"An electrical tooth-brush." *Scientific American* 125 (September 24, 1921): 226.

"Electric tooth brush out." *New York Times*, October 9, 1937, p. 30.

"Electric toothbrushes." *Consumer Reports* 27 (August, 1962): 376–378.

"Electric toothbrushes." *Consumer Reports* 47 (March, 1964): 22–27.

"Electric toothbrushes." *Consumer Reports* 31 (August, 1966): 402–406.

"Electric toothbrushes." *Consumer Reports* 34 (March, 1969): 138–142.

"Electric toothbrushes." *Consumer Reports* 57 (September, 1992): 611–614.

Ephraim, Jerome W. "The truth about dentifrices." *American Mercury* 33 (September, 1934): 77–81.

"The evolution of the tooth-brush." *Literary Digest* 89 (June 12, 1926): 22.

"Ex–ADA head hits dental groups approval of Crest." *Advertising Age* 32 (June 19, 1961): 4.

"Fact's anti-sweets ad theme is big toothache for candy industry." *Advertising Age* 38 (January 16, 1967): 2, 84.

"Faith in tooth powder prepares way for new product." *Printers' Ink* 162 (March 2, 1933): 10, 12.

"FDA okays claims for some toothpastes, but questions 8 leaders." *American Druggist* 162 (August 10, 1970): 30.

"FDA report gives nod to therapeutic claims for Crest, Colgate with MFP." *Advertising Age* 41 (July 27, 1970): 6.

"15% use tooth brushes." *New York Times*, October 9, 1927, sec 2, p. 6.

"50 years ago." *Consumer Reports* 51 (March, 1986): 145.

"Finds selling force in fear appeal." *Printers' Ink* 158 (March 10, 1932): 47–48.

"Flack ack-ack." *Newsweek* 58 (October 30, 1961): 62–63.

"Fleapower motors." *Business Week*, March 15 1941, pp. 68–69.

"Flemming in warning." *New York Times*, November 10, 1959, p. 48.

Flood, Robert J. "They're feudin', fightin' and sellin'." *Printers' Ink* 247 (May 14, 1954): 45–48.

"Fluoride tooth paste." *Science News Letter* 67 (February 12, 1955): 100.

"Fluoride toothpaste." *New York Times*, February 17 1955, p. 33.

"Forhan's for the gums." *Sales Management* 96 (April 1, 1966): 35.

Fortune, Mark. "Colgate's racist logo leaves bad taste." *Black Enterprise* 18 (July, 1988): 21.

"$40 million of dentifrice ad budgets go to TV." *Sponsor* 19 (August 19, 1965): 53.

Freeman, Laurie, and Nancy Giges. "FDA may take nip at toothpaste claims." *Advertising Age* 58 (May 25, 1987): 50, 69.

"F.T.C. cracks down on Bristol-Myers." *New York Times*, November 30, 1949, p. 41.

"FTC eases up in Dr. West's pact." *Advertising Age* 42 (May 3, 1971): 2.

"FTC finds ads for Pepsodent not deceptive." *Advertising Age* 33 (October 22, 1962): 1, 113.

"FTC hits Colgate for Gardol shield claims." *Advertising Age* 30 (November 23, 1959): 1, 129.

Furman, Bess. "F.T.C. wants data on dentifrice ads." *New York Times*, December 9,
1959, p. 52.

Gardner, William M. "The toothbrush; is it
a menace?" *Hygeia* 6 (May, 1928): 249–
250.

"GE and Squibb toothbrushes get dental
group nod." *Advertising Age* 35 (August 31,
1964): 35, 215.

"Getting a bigger share of the dental products
market." *American Druggist* 179 (June,
1979): 55–56+.

Giges, Nancy. "P&G's Crest efforts taking
aim against growing Lever share." *Advertising Age* 47 (January 26, 1976): 2, 74.

_____. "WRG loses Gleem to Leo Burnett."
Advertising Age 47 (April 19, 1976): 2, 145.

_____, and Gay Jervey. "Colgate joins shift to
pump for dentifrice." *Advertising Age* 55
(May 28, 1984): 1, 64.

Glasser, Ren. "Ask the dentist." *Family Health*
10 (July, 1978): 14.

Goodman, Walter. "The toothpaste tournament." *New Republic* 135 (July 30, 1956):
15–17.

Gordon, Samuel M., and Eleanore B. Du-
four. "Doctor, what dentifrice shall I use?"
Hygeia 15 (August, 1937): 714–716+.

Goulding, Peter C. "Miracles in toothpaste?"
Today's Health 35 (February, 1957): 34–
35+.

"Green gold." *Time* 59 (April 14, 1952): 102.

"Green grow the brushes." *Newsweek* 39
(June 23, 1952): 70, 73.

Hackett, Catherine. "The dentifrice racket."
The New Republic 61 (January 15, 1930):
216–218.

Hall, Trish. "Brush-a, brush-a, brush-a, just
isn't enough anymore." *New York Times*,
June 16, 1993, p. C8.

Harris, Rebecca. "A brush with brains." *Marketing Magazine* 110 (September 26, 2005):
5.

Hart, Malcolm. "Loss leader is touted by Pepsodent as greatest advertising drive opens."
Printers' Ink 182 (January 27, 1938): 11–13+.

"Her young audience get tooth brushes." *New
York Times*, September 28, 1912, p. 6.

Hittner, Patricia. "Putting the squeeze on
toothpaste." *Better Homes and Gardens* 76
(May, 1998): 120+.

Hommel, Martha Hill. "Tongue scrapers and
toothbrushes." *Hobbies* 56 (July, 1951): 58–
59.

"How Du Pont uses the new to update the
old." *Printers' Ink* 288 (July 17, 1964): 15.

"How GE put a charge in (& under) a toothbrush." *Printers' Ink* 280 (July 20, 1962):
44–45.

"How good is Crest toothpaste?" *Consumer
Reports* 25 (October, 1960): 512–514.

"How to make new brands sell." *Broadcasting* 76 (May 26, 1969): 32.

"How to sterilize a tooth-brush." *Literary Digest* 52 (April 29, 1916): 1217.

Howe, Andrew M. "Fibrex vs Extron." *Printers' Ink* 193 (December 27, 1940): 21–22.

_____. "Inter-line teamwork." *Printers' Ink*
184 (July 21, 1938): 13–15.

"In defense of the toothbrush." *Literary Digest* 51 (December 4, 1915): 1283.

Ingallis, Albert G. "Is your pet dentifrice
safe?" *Scientific American* 163 (August,
1940): 82.

"Inquiry rebukes F.T.C. on false ads." *New
York Times*, August 18, 1958, p. 15.

"Ipana returns to fray." *Advertising Age* 40
(September 15, 1969): 2, 105.

"Is your toothbrush making you sick?" *Parents' Magazine* 62 (March, 1987): 17.

"It's the toothpaste." *Consumers' Research Bulletin* 15 (June, 1945): 5–8.

Jerski, Laura. "Hearts, minds and market
share." *Forbes* 143 (April 13, 1989): 80, 82.

Kanner, Bernice. "Picks and plans." *New York*
21 (October 17, 1988): 29–30.

_____. "Tartar time." *New York* 21 (October
31, 1988): 16, 20.

_____. "The gelling of America." *New York*
15 (March 29, 1982): 12, 16, 18.

_____. "The white brigade." *New York* 27
(January 17, 1994): 11–12.

Koerner, Brendan I. "Zapping that icky
toothbrush." *New York Times*, January 16,
2005, sec 3, p. 2.

"Kolynos ad claims barred." *New York Times*,
June 10, 1937, p. 41.

"Kolynos, ADA face brushoff in backing miracle claims." *Printers' Ink* 267 (May 29,
1959): 12.

"Kolynos *Coronet* ad reprints going to 75,000
dentists." *Advertising Age* 30 (May 18,
1959): 8.

"Kolynos dental cream." *Sales Management*
100 (January 1, 1968): 31.

Katz, Susan. "The great plaque-off."
Newsweek 106 (October 28, 1985): 76.

Lane, Annie E. "Toothpowder or gunpowder." *Fortnightly Review* 83 (April, 1905):
726–731.

Larrabee, C. B. "Dentists and advertising."
Printers' Ink (July 25, 1935): 65, 68–70.

Lawrence, Jennifer, and Judann Dagnoli. "FDA order halts P&G, Colgate toothpaste intros." *Advertising Age* 62 (February 11, 1991): 1, 44

"The layman does what the professional does not." *Printers' Ink* 133 (December 3, 1925): 166, 168.

"Lever to put heaviest ad push behind bright white Pepsodent." *Advertising Age* 38 (January 30, 1967): 1, 119.

Link, Henry C. "What is happening in the dentifrice field?" *Advertising Agency and Advertising & Selling* 42 (September, 1949): 48–49+.

Lord, Mary. "Oral power tools." *U.S. News & World Report* 124 (April 20, 1998): 64–65.

Luckman, Charles. "Pepsodent's 7 points." *Printers' Ink* 186 (March 9, 1939): 15–18.

Maisel, Albert Q. "What's all this about anti-enzyme toothpastes?" *Reader's Digest* 63 (December, 1953): 10–13.

"Majority of toothbrushes found defective by survey." *Science News Letter* 54 (September 11, 1948): 168.

"Many dentifrices seen as deceptive." *New York Times*, December 7, 1951, p. 21.

"Many old toothbrushes still being used." *Science News Letter* 74 (August 16, 1958): 104.

"Manual toothbrushes hold line against automatics, admen report." *Advertising Age* 36 (February 1, 1965): 10.

Margolis, Dawn. "Toothbrush trivia." *American Health* 11 (December, 1992): 15.

McCabe, Esther M. "The toothbrush and family oral hygiene." *Parents' Magazine* 38 (May, 1963): 14, 37.

McGill, Douglas C. "Colgate to rename a toothpaste." *New York Times*, January 27, 1989, pp. D1, D4.

McLean, David W. "The art of the toothbrush." *Hygeia* 13 (September, 1935): 824–828.

"Medical-dental taboos stronger." *Broadcasting* 68 (January 18, 1965): 46, 48.

"Miracle-Tuft clicks." *Business Week*, October 14, 1939, pp. 40–41.

"More for Lesch?" *Forbes* 103 (March 1, 1969): 30–31.

Morrey, Lon W. "One good word for tooth paste ads." *Today's Health* 32 (October, 1954): 13.

Murphy, John Allen. "How Kolynos sells in 88 countries." *American Business* 8 (January, 1938): 22–24+.

"NAD report takes aim at Aim." *Advertising Age* 58 (July 20, 1987): 51, 53.

"Nader lays staining to some toothpastes." *New York Times*, July 9, 1971, p. 36.

Nagle, James J. "News of the advertising and marketing fields." *New York Times*, December 20, 1953, sec 3, p. 9.

Neff, Jack. "Power brushes a hit at every level." *Advertising Age* 74 (May 26, 2003): 10.

"New dental anesthetic paste prevents pain in many cases." *Science News Letter* 32 (July 24, 1937): 51–52.

"A new name for toothpaste." *New York Times*, April 18, 1989, p. D25.

"New niche creates opportunities." *Chain Drug Review*, February 4, 2008, p. 20.

"New tooth data called anti-enzyme setback." *New York Times*, January 24, 1954, p. 31.

"New toothpaste from Colgate set." *New York Times*, July 15, 1997, p. D5.

"New ways to save your teeth." *Consumer Reports* 54 (August, 1989): 504–509.

"90 per cent of Pepsodent's sales cost is advertising." *Printers' Ink* 139 (June 16, 1927): 164, 167–8.

"Nylon toothbrush, 25 cents." *Business Week*, September 21, 1940, p. 30.

"Oral care sales in chain drug stores." *Chain Drug Review*, November 5, 2007, p. 37.

Osborne, Oliver T. "The toothbrush." *Good Housekeeping* 81 (November, 1925): 218–219.

"O-T-C best sellers." *Chain Drug Review*, January 7, 2008, p. 62.

Pader, Morton. "Dentifrices: problems of growth, pt. 1." *Drug & Cosmetic Industry* 108 (June, 1971): 36–39+.

_____. "Dentifrices: problems of growth, pt. 2." *Drug & Cosmetic Industry* 109 (July, 1971): 36+.

Palda, Kristian S., and Larry M. Blair. "A moving cross-section analysis of demand for toothpaste." *Journal of Marketing Research* 7 (November, 1970): 439–449.

"Pepsodent is green." *Newsweek* 38 (October 8, 1951): 77–78.

"Pepsodent on consignment." *Printers' Ink* 175 (May 28, 1936): 20.

"Pepsodent stain commercials not deceptive: FTC." *Advertising Age* 33 (February 26, 1962): 1–1A.

"Pepsodent turns publisher." *Printers' Ink* 197 (October 3, 1941): 15–16.

"Pepsodent TV ads could have made it clear they referred to fresh stains, FTC told." *Advertising Age* 33 (September 24, 1962): 4.

Pereira, Joseph. "Got a song stuck in your

head? Try brushing." *Wall Street Journal,* February 25, 2005, pp. B1, B3.

"Peril to health seen in bogus dental ads." *New York Times,* October 2, 1953, p. 14.

"P&G back to basics with Crest." *Advertising Age* 77 (July 3, 2006): 12.

"P&G's Crest sprints after ADA boost." *Printers' Ink* 272 (August 26, 1960): 11–12.

"P&G makes capital of ADA O.K. in Crest ads." *Advertising Age* 31 (August 29, 1960): 2, 178.

Plaut, Edward. "Faith with action." *Printers' Ink* 162 (March 16, 1933): 17–18.

"Police get book on teeth." *New York Times,* April 29, 1922, p. 8.

Popovich, Bette. "Year of the toothpaste." *Chemical Marketing Reporter* 247 (May 8, 1995): SR16, SR18.

"Powder and paste." *Business Week,* August 17, 1935, p. 26.

"Power toothbrush: worth the money?" *Changing Times* 17 (November, 1963): 37–38.

"Power toothbrushes." *Chain Drug Review,* February 4, 2008, p. 20.

"Preventive toothpowder." *Newsweek* 33 (February 14, 1949): 44.

"Pump paste brushes off skeptics." *Advertising Age* 55 (December 31, 1984): 3, 13.

"Pycopay TV ads boost new shape." *Advertising Age* 33 (May 21, 1962): 114.

Ramirez, Anthony. "Growth is glacial, but the market is big, and so is the gross." *New York Times,* May 13, 1990, sec 3, p. 11.

Ramirez, Eddy. "Get a new toothbrush." *U.S. News & World Report* 145 (December 29, 2008): 49.

Rapoport, Sheva. "Toothpaste." *Consumer Bulletin* 54 (August, 1971): 7–9.

Revett, John. "Ipana dies as B–M shifts ad stress to Vote." *Advertising Age* 39 (November 11, 1968): 10.

Riesz, Peter C., and Abe Shuchman. "Responses to the ADA Crest endorsement." *Journal of Advertising Research* 14 (February, 1974): 21–25.

Rusk, Howard A. "Success of tooth paste ads stirs dentists into attack." *New York Times,* October 4, 1953, p. 83.

Ryan, Patrick. "So keep on smilin'—even if you are radioactive." *Smithsonian* 7 (December, 1976): 144.

"A safety report on electric toothbrushes." *Consumer Reports* 27 (May, 1962): 255.

Salmans, Sandra. "Fighting decay, and each other." *New York Times,* April 6, 1981, pp. D1, D4.

Schiller, Zachary. "Look ma, no plaque: the next dental frontier." *Business Week,* March 4, 1985, pp. 36, 38.

_____. "The sound and the fluoride." *Business Week,* August 14, 1995, p. 48.

Schuyler, Philip. "Pulitzer Prize winner writes toothpaste ads." *Editor & Publisher* 90 (August 10, 1957): 15.

"Science and the news." *Science* 134 (October 27, 1961): 1349.

Sears, Cathy. "Baking soda toothpastes." *American Health* 13 (April, 1994): 19.

Servaas, Cory. "Taking care of your toothbrushes." *Medical Update* 28 (Issue 7, 2007): 2.

Shaye, Katja. "The last word on ... toothpaste." *Good Housekeeping* 222 (February, 1996): 127.

Sherman, Stuart. "2,253,125 in this contest." *Printers' Ink* 178 (February 25, 1937): 6–8+.

Shuster, Alvin. "F.T.C. charges 4 TV ads were false props to support claims." *New York Times,* January 15, 1960, pp. 1, 58.

"Sindlinger, BofA find Crest gains in sales, impact." *Advertising Age* 31 (September 26, 1960): 2.

Sloan, Pat. "Colgate, J&J to pour $30 mil into toothbrush extensions." *Advertising Age* 67 (February 26, 1996): 3, 45.

_____. "Dep joins toothbrush rush with grip that changes color." *Advertising Age* 64 (June 7, 1993): 6.

Snyder, John Avery. "Stop the brush, I want to get off." *Atlantic Monthly* 213 (May, 1964): 119–120.

Solley, Samuel. "Oral-B battery powered brush rapped by greens." *Marketing* (UK), March 8, 2006, p. 6.

Solomon, Goody. "Look ma, no cavities." *Barron's* 45 (January 4, 1965): 4.

_____. "The electric toothbrush." *Barron's* 42 (October 1, 1962): 11, 20.

Spielvogel, Carol. "Advertising: and now, striped toothpaste." *New York Times,* January 15, 1958, p. 40.

Spielvogel, Carl. "Advertising: Shhh!—bottled toothpaste." *New York Times,* October 6, 1957, sec 3, p. 10.

"Standards set up on dentifrice ads." *New York Times,* May 26, 1949, p. 45.

"Stevenson, Richard W. "Advertising." *New York Times,* October 7, 1988, p. D15.

_____. "Crest stages a turnaround." *New York Times,* April 24, 1986, pp. D1, D6.

"Stewart tells how research boosted Macleans

toothpaste." *Advertising Age* 36 (January 18, 1965): 74.

"Studies of germ-killing power of toothpastes." *Science News Letter* 34 (August 27, 1938): 141.

"Summing up on electric toothbrushes." *Consumer Reports* 28 (April, 1963): 186–187.

"Super Stripe gets dental group okay; ads to aim at kids." *Advertising Age* 37 (June 6, 1966): 2.

"Survey reveals dentists ditch manual toothbrushes." *US Newswire*, February 23, 2006.

Swan, Carroll J. "National distribution for new product achieved almost overnight." *Printers' Ink* 221 (October 17, 1947): 35–37.

Sykes, McCready. "The observe side." *Commerce and Finance* 22 (August 23, 1933): 735–736.

"Synthetic bristles." *Business Week*, July 16, 1938, p. 34.

Tarnowski, Joseph. "Word of mouth." *Progressive Grocer* 84 (January 1, 2005): 66–68.

"Taste governs dentifrice choice." *Science News Letter* 64 (November 14, 1953): 310.

"The teeth of battle." *Time* 53 (May 23, 1949): 90.

"Tell public, too, that Crest is approved, not endorsed, toothpaste rivals urge ADA." *Advertising Age* 32 (January 23, 1961): 54.

"The tested toothbrush." *Hygeia* 7 (March, 1929): 254–255.

"Tests of toothbrushes." *Consumer Bulletin* 42 (March, 1959): 29–30.

Thacher, W. F. G. "Economic determinism and the tooth-brush." *Printers' Ink* 128 (August 7, 1924): 77–78, 80, 84.

"3 added starters set for fall power toothbrush race." *Advertising Age* 33 (August 6, 1962): 2.

"Three-way contest." *Printers' Ink* 168 (September 6, 1934): 20.

Thumser, Maryanne. "Brush away the toothbrush dilemma." *Good Housekeeping* 221 (August, 1995): 153.

Tolk, Bernard. "New ammoniated dentifrices flood the market; established brands split on launching line." *Printers' Ink* 227 (May 6, 1949): 102, 107.

"Toothbrush is king of inventions." *Weekly Reader-Edition 4* 84 (March 7, 2003): 4.

"Tooth paste." *Hygeia* 10 (July, 1932): 662.

"Tooth paste and tooth powder." *Consumer Reports* 14 (August, 1949): 346–351.

"Tooth pastes." *Consumer Reports* 19 (April, 1954): 164–167.

"The toothbrush." *American Druggist* 171 (May 1, 1975): 31–33.

"Toothbrush drills today." *New York Times*, May 19, 1917, p. 13.

"Toothbrush trade-in." *Business Week*, May 3, 1933, p. 11.

"Toothbrush troubles." *Business Week*, June 29, 1940, pp. 30, 32.

"Toothbrushes." *Consumers' Research Bulletin* 10 (June, 1941): 11–13.

"Toothbrushes." *Changing Times* 25 (May, 1971): 13–14.

"Toothbrushes and tooth care." *Consumers' Research Bulletin* 12 (September, 1943): 5–8.

"Toothpaste." *Consumer Reports* 37 (April, 1972): 251–255.

"Toothpaste ad battle looms." *Business Week*, August 6, 1969, p. 28.

"Toothpaste ads criticized by dentists." *Science Digest* 44 (November, 1958): 72.

"Toothpaste ads scored." *New York Times*, September 30, 1953, p. 32.

"Toothpaste ads vie for favor on flavor." *Advertising Age* 37 (August 1, 1966): 2.

"Toothpaste & mouthwash." *Media Decisions* 13 (April, 1978): 141+.

"Toothpaste facts and fancies." *Scientific American* 148 (January, 1933): 39.

"Toothpaste has value only as cleanser." *Hygeia* 9 (July, 1931): 683.

"Toothpaste squeeze is TV bonanza." *Sponsor* 20 (October 31, 1966): 27–38.

"A toothpaste spy admits plot to sell Crest's campaign." *New York Times*, August 6, 1965, p. 29.

"Toothpaste study released by Pell." *New York Times*, August 6, 1971, p. 32.

"Toothpastes." *Consumer Reports* 49 (March, 1984): 138–143.

"Toothpastes." *Consumer Reports* 51 (March, 1986): 144–149.

"Toothpastes." *Consumer Reports* 57 (September, 1992): 602–606.

"Toothpastes around the world." *New York Times*, January 15, 1989, sec 5, p. 3.

"Toothy." *Newsweek* 46 (November 14, 1955): 88, 90.

Tracy, Eleanor Johnson. "Plaque attackers." *Fortune* 111 (May 13, 1985): 73–74.

"Trade commission questions toothpaste ad claims." *New York Times*, December 23, 1971, p. 13.

"Trade-ins for toothbrushes." *Printers' Ink* 163 (May 11, 1933): 52.

Tugend, Alina. "Smile, you're in the dental care aisle." *New York Times*, August 6, 2005, p. C6.

"TV ad is defended." *New York Times*, January 16, 1960, p. 43.

"TV toothpaste ads rigged, expert says." *New York Times*, November 12, 1959, p. 25.

"Two individuals plead guilty to trafficking in more than half a million tubes of counterfeit toothpaste." *US Newswire*, August 21, 2008.

Tyler, Ralph. "The squeeze is on in toothpastes." *Television Magazine* 22 (December, 1965): 36–39+.

"U.S. aide disputes cigarette claims." *New York Times*, July 19, 1958, p. 17.

"U.S. asked to curb toothpaste ads." *New York Times*, December 8, 1959, p. 51.

"U.S. challenges claims on toothpaste and mouthwash labels." *New York Times*, October 9, 1988, p. 31.

"U.S. curbs sought on dentifrice ads." *New York Times*, November 4, 1959, p. 71.

"U.S. seizes toothpaste." *New York Times*, May 22, 1949, sec 3, p. 5.

"Value of ammoniated powders questioned." *Science News Letter* 57 (May 20, 1950): 313.

"Wafers and cure-alls." *Consumer Reports* 14 (September, 1949): 405.

Wallack, Lydia. "What a really new product can do." *Printers' Ink* 287 (April 17, 1964): 39–41.

Wandel, George H. "Selecting a toothbrush." *Hygeia* 10 (June, 1932): 500.

"Waterproof brush." *Business Week*, July 30, 1938, p. 19.

Weissman, H. A. "Advertising success story: Dr. Lyon's." *Printers' Ink* 167 (April 26, 1934): 7+.

Wharton, Don. "Why we brush our teeth." *Reader's Digest* 53 (July, 1948): 139–142.

"What's ahead for soaps?" *Sponsor* 15 (November 20, 1961): 25–28+.

"What's in a claim." www.smile-on.com/news, July 26, 2000.

"Which toothpaste is right for you?" *Consumer Reports* 63 (August, 1998): 11–14.

"Whiten up." *Mademoiselle* 101 (March, 1995): 68

"Whiter smiles have dentists frowning." *Newsweek* 117 (January 14, 1991): 45.

Whitney, Craig. "What's the price? It's hard to tell." *New York Times*, September 28, 1969, p. 48.

Will, George. "The perils of brushing." *Newsweek* 133 (May 10, 1999): 92.

"Will new toothbrushes spur static field?" *Printers' Ink* 276 (September 8, 1961): 11–13.

Williams, D. H. "Ten commandments for launching a new product." *Advertising & Selling* 40 (November, 1947): 33–34+.

Winter, Greg. "No ads, but strong sales for electric toothbrushes." *New York Times*, December 13, 2000, p. C2.

Index

Aaron, Harold 84–85
Abrams, George 81
abrasiveness 8, 39, 45, 71, 129, 164, 175; scale of 45
acid mouth 52, 63, 73
acids 8, 42, 48, 73
ADA Abrasiveness Study 175
ADA acceptances 62, 69, 73, 195; desirability of 174; power brushes 140
ADA Council on Dental Therapeutics 40, 68–69, 71, 73–77, 86–88, 139, 140
ADA surveys 93
ADA v. Ralph Nader 191
Addis, William 10
additives, dentifrices 95–96, 104–105, 159, 187
advertising: as aid to oral hygiene 54; benefits of dentifrices 106; brushes, incentives 20–21; brushes (1940) 30–31; challenged by FTC 71, 75–78; challenged by government 109–116; claims 64; cosmetic types 162; criticized by ADA 63–64; criticized by AMA 63–64; criticized by dentists 66; criticized by government 66–68; criticized by journalists 63–64, 68–70, 77–78; dentifrices 48–63, 101–108; dentifrices, campaigns 101–102; dentifrices challenged 63–79; dentifrices, comparative claims 198; dentifrices criticized by dentists 102–104; dentifrices, enjoined 71; dentifrices, exaggerated 102–104, 110–115; dentifrices, expenditures (1957) 111; dentifrices, launch 96; dentifrices, main themes 111; Dr. Lyon's 34–35; efficacy of 51; evaluation of 175–176; exaggerated 49; false claims 36; false dentifrices 110–112; fear campaigns 49, 71, 76; gimmicks 56; Kolynos strategies 35; percentage of sales 173; placement of dentifrices 106; professional images 184; quality of dentifrices 195; radio 52, 59; standards for magazines 82; strategies (1800s) 11–13; tie-ins 62; trade-in strategies 24–25
Advertising Age 86, 148

advertising expenditures: (1920s) 24; (1940s) 81; (1953) 105; (1959) 146; (1964) 158; (1965) 174; (1970s) 194; brushes (1960s) 119; brushes (1981) 124; brushes (1990s) 128; dentifrices (1964) 185; Dr. Lyon's 35; Dr. Lyon's (1930s) 56
Aim 194
Albright, Andrew 20
Albright Tooth Brush 19–20
Alexander the Great 9–10
Alstadt, W. R. 152
Alter, Jennifer 124
American Dental Association (ADA) 13, 95, 107–108, 109–113; accepted dentifrices 45; and ads 103–104; and approvals 107–108; and brushes 117–118, 124–125, 130; and fluoride, after Crest 157–161; and marketing battles 161; and plaque fighters 167–171; and power brushes 139–142; reaction against recognition of Crest 147–153; recognition of Crest 145–153; and whiteners 164–166; *see also* ADA entries
American Medical Association 23, 147
Amm-I-Dent 80–83
ammoniated dentifrices 80–88; evaluated 84–86; launch 82; market share 81; new entrants 83–84
Amos 'n' Andy 52
ancient times 1–10
anti-enzyme dentifrices 93–95
antiseptics 43, 52, 66
Aqua-Fresh 194
Aristotle 9–10
Arm & Hammer 161
aromatherapeutic paste 171

bacteria 43, 65
Bah, Habib 201
baking soda pastes 161–162, 166
Belden, August 20
Berry, Halle 171
Blatnik, John A. 110
bleaching, of bristles 24
Bliven, Bruce 99–100, 153
Block Drug 81

Blumenthal, Deborah 8
Bobrinskoy, George 6
body weight and brushing habits 129
Born, David 125–126
Bost 55–56
Bost, William Dale 55
bottle, squeeze 107
brand loyalty 102
brands, number of (1949) 88
breath, bad 44, 77–78, 110, 192
bristles 19, 23–24; attachment of 20; hog 9, 27; natural 27–29, 125; nylon 27–30; origin of hog 23–24; slanted 125; synthetic 125; treatment of 24; tufts of 19
Bristol-Myers 36, 106, 157, 186
British Dental Association 154
Brody, Jane 141–142, 168–169
Broxodent 140
brushes: advice on 121–122; after use treatment 18; as agents of infection 125–126, 130–131; boiling of 23; borrowing of 126; buying advice 126, 128; chemicals, impregnated 122–123; children's 119; condition of 25, 117–118, 123; development of 18–20; efficiency of 16; evaluation of 31–32, 118; favorite colors 126; free from schools 15–16; handles 119–120, 128; hanging of 18; hole in handle 18; ideal type 1943, 32; imported 19, 20; innovations 120, 133; invention of 10; musical 131–132; not hygienic 16–18; number of brands 125–126; ownership statistics 19; power 134–144; prices of 29, 32–33, 118, 123; profits from 20; purchase advice 23; replacement time 29, 123; retail display 19–20; shape of 120; sterilization 16; sterilizers 130–131; surveys of 117–118; trade-in plan 24–25; treatment of 23; unhygienic 21–23; v. dentifrices 68; where bought 123
brushing: drills for children 18; how to 16, 17, 21; and income 121; number of times 121; recommended time of 129; time spent on 25; usage statistics 21; with water only 122
Bryan, Arthur 43
Buckleitner, Warren 132
Bunzell, H. H. 66
Burrell, Kenneth 165–166
Business Week 95

Calox Tooth Powder 76
Campbell, Jean 168
candy industry 185–186
Captain Kangaroo 160
Carmichael, Mary 143
Carter, Theora 16

Castle, Bob 187
Cattrall, Kim 171
Catullus 7
cavity prevention 81, 82, 190
cavity reduction 160; campaigns 158–161
Cazenne, Pierre 8
cease and desist orders 109–110
celluloid 18–20
Center for Corporate Responsibility 191
chalk, precipitated 39–40
Changing Times 121–122
Chappell, Thomas 199
charcoal 11
Chase Manufacturing 135
checks, delayed cashing 56
children 160
China/Japan war (1937) 27
Chinese, ancient 8
chlorophyll dentifrices 90–92
Chunky Corporation 186
Clarey, J. J. 84
Clark, Blake 75
Close-Up 164, 165, 194
cloth, linen 9
Colgate 49, 128, 133, 157, 159–160; Dentagard launch costs 168; fights Crest recognition 152–153; origins 36
Colgate Baking Soda & Peroxide with Tartar Control Toothpaste 200
Colgate Dental Cream 77–78
Colgate Gardol 97, 114–115
Colgate-Palmolive, and Darkie brand 196–198
Colgate Platinum Whitening Toothpaste with Fluoride 200
Colgate Ribbon Dental Cream 43
Colgate Total 182, 200
Colgate v. Crest 187–188
companies, parent 95–96
Connecticut State Dental Association 150
consent orders 75
Consumer Bulletin 118
consumer buying habits 102, 120–121; for dentifrices 93
Consumer Reports 42, 84–86, 88–89, 97–98, 126, 136–137, 148, 150, 177–179, 180–182
consumer usage, power brushes 142
Consumers' Research Bulletin 31–32, 45
containers, dentifrices 107
contests 25–27, 57–59
copywriter, Pulitzer winner 106–107
cork, burnt 9
cost of powders (1944) 45
counterfeiting, of Colgate paste 201
coupons 20–21, 52
Creig, Ralph 110–111

Crest 99, 106–107, 145–155; conversion to after acceptance 153–154; number of varieties (2006) 155
Crest Tartar Control Formula 167
Cue 158; cost of failure 188
Cunningham, R. M. 77–78

Danzig, Fred 52, 193
Darkie (brand) 196–198
Davis, Robert 130, 200
decay 77; 92–93
deception in ads 63–78
Demmings, Dara 197
De Niro, Robert 171
Dentagard 168
dentifrices: advice on worth of 42–43; ancient formulas 5, 7, 8, 10; bleachers 42; children's 180; confusion from tube sizes 188, 190; effectiveness of home-made 39–40; evaluated 177–179, 180–182; evaluated (1936) 41–42; evaluated (1949) 88–89; evaluated (1954) 97–98; evaluated by FDA 190–191; evaluated by U.S. Army 191–192; for children 199; formulas 11; home-made 10, 39–40; home-made formulas 39–40, 45, 74; international cost of 179; liquid 43–44, 76; market static 60; number of brands (2004) 200; percentage that use 199; powders evaluated (1944) 45; prices of (1949) 89; public expectations 68–69; pump dispensers 196; rate of new products 199–200; safety of (1940) 44; safety of (1930s) 42; sizes of tubes 176–177; v. dentists 40, 51, 68–69; varieties of (1990s) 181
dentists 51, 60, 120; and brush choice 130; buying recommendations 120; and power brushes 140–141; recommendations of paste 172; soliciting of 161, 173
detail men 51
Diallo, Saifoulaye 201
Dickson, Charles H. 40–41
diseases: contagious 21; made-up 74; mouth 68
Dr. Cornish's Tooth Powder 87
Dr. Lyon's Tooth Powder 34–35, 56–57, 71, 75–76, 176
Dr. West's Germ Fighter brush 122–123
Dr. West's Miracle-Tuft Brush 27–28
Dr. West's Toothbrush 19
Doty, Roy J. 91–92, 148
Dowd, Timothy 133
drugstores 174
Dudding, N. J. 122

electric brushes 134–144
Electric Motor Corporation (EMC) 134

endorsements 106
Ephraim, Jerome W. 68–69
EpiSmile 165
expenditures, dentifrices (1930s) 43
exporting, Kolynos 35
exton 27–28

Fact paste 185
Fact v. candy industry 185–186
false advertising, cases 75–78
Federal Trade Commission (FTC) 36, 71, 75–79, 109–116; and dentifrice ads 192–193; *see also* FTC entries
Feldman, Bernard 16–17
film (on teeth) 38, 64
finger, as brush 17
First District Dental Society (NY) 66
Fitch, Samuel 5
Flemming, Arthur S. 112
Flodent 43
Flood, Robert 105–106
fluoride 80, 99–100; pre-1960 dentifrices 145–146
fluoride paste 98–100, 145–155, 192; after Crest 157–161; intensified marketing 160–161; percentage of market 195
Food and Drug Administration (FDA) 66–68; evaluation of paste 190–191; and plaque fighters 169
Forhan, Richard J. 36
Forhan's 36, 42, 54, 78–79
Fortune, Mark 197
Fosdick, Leonard 104
Fosdick, Leonard S. 93–94
Fouchard, Pierre 6
FTC complaint, Gardol 114–115
FTC consent order, Dr. West 122–123

Gardner, William 23
gel toothpastes 194
General Electric 135–140
Gillette 144
gingivitis 78
Glass, Richard T. 125
Glasser, Ren 8
Gleem 96
Godfrey, Arthur 159
Goldstein, Alan J. 166–167
Goodman, Walter 97
Gordon, Samuel M. 69, 73
Goulding, Peter 48–49, 100, 174
Greeks, ancient 7
Grimm, John E. 188
Gross, Leon R. 114–115
Grove, Carl 80
Gruebbel, Allen O. 117
gum inflammation 191

gunpowder 8
Gwynne, John W. 110

Hackett, Catherine 63–64
hair, animal 5–6
Hall, Trish 128
Hall, William Henry 11
Hart, Malcolm 59
Hasbro 131–132
Hawley & Hazel Chemical Company 197
Hein, John W. 103
Hellenbrand, Harold 100
Higgins, Marguerite 106–107
Hinkes, Harry 116
Hippocrates 5
Hittner, Patricia 181
Hommel, Martha 6
Hope, Bob 52, 62
Hopkins, Claude 49
Howe, John 187
Humphrey, William V. 186
Hygeia 23, 39–30, 73
Hyman, Richard 123–124

industrial espionage 173
Ingallis, Albert 44–45
ingredients, special 78
Interfaith Center on Corporate Responsibility 197
Interplak 142
inventions, public rating of 129
Ipana 36, 42–43, 52, 75, 97, 106; death of 186–187
Ipana Troubadors 36
irium 38, 78

Jenkins, G. Neil 88
Jenkins, N. S. 35
Jeserich, Paul H. 111, 150
Journal of the American Dental Association 48, 103

Kanner, Bernice 166–167, 170–171, 179, 194
Katz, Susan 168
Kelly, Maurice 170
Kesel, Robert G. 117–118
Kinter, Earl 112
Klein, Howard J. 186
Kneiser, Albert H. 88
Kolynos 35–36, 71, 107–108

Laird, Kenneth 25
Lane, Annie 15
Larrabbee, C. B. 69–70
Lasater, R. L. 134
Lasker, Albert 36–38
Lasker, Edward 52

lawsuits, frivolous 129
Lehn & Fink 56
Leonard, Veader 66
Lesch, George H. 188
Lever Brothers 49, 107, 157
Levine, Jonathan 171
Link, Henry 89
Listerine 97
Listgarden, Max 200
Literary Digest 16–17
Luckman, Charles 59–60
Lyon, Israel Whitney 13–14
Lyons, Harry 103, 111
Lyons Tooth Paste 101
Lyon's Tooth Powder 13–14
Lysol 17

Macleans 162
Macmillan, Hugh W. 18
Macuithey, James C. 190
mailouts 57, 155
Maisel, Albert 93
Mark, Reuben 161
market share of brushes: (1937) 28; (1939) 30; (1960s) 120; (1981) 124; (1990s) 126, 128–129; (2000s) 133; power 138; power (2000s) 144
market share of dentifrices: (1930s) 43–44; (1940s) 36; (1949) 82; (1952) 91; (1954) 95–96; (1950s) 146; (1960) 172–173; (1961) 157–158; (1965) 174; (1960s–1970s) 154; (1970s) 194; (1975) 193; (1982) 196; (1980s–1990s) 154–155; (1990) 179–180; (2007) 201; world (2000s) 183
marketing philosophy, Pepsodent 60
marketing strategies, giveaways 43
marketing, test 55
mass marketing strategies 193
Massachusetts Institute of Technology 129
Mayfield, Eugene Andrew 173
McCall, John Oppie 21
McCormack, O. J. 106
McGhee, Robert 159
McGill, Douglas 198
McGillan, Frank 143–144
McLean, David 5, 27
medicines, patent 13
men-in-white ads 76–77, 184
milk of magnesia 73
Miller, T. K. 88
Miner, Leroy S. M. 151
Mitchell, Edgar 195
Mitchell, Edgar W. 167
Morrey, Lon 7
Motodent Inc. 134

Nader, Ralph 191
Nagle, James 104–105
National Association of Broadcasters 184
National Confectioners Association 186
National Council of Churches 196–197
natural toothpaste 199–200
Neff, Jack 144
New York City Department of Consumer
  Affairs 188, 190
New York City Health Department 18
New York City Police Department 18
New York Journal of Dentistry 102–103
Newsweek 153
nineteenth century 10–14

Oklahoma State Board of Health 40
Oral-B 133
oral hygiene: government promotion 18;
  lectures to children 16; professionaliza-
  tion of 7; state of 15–16
Osborne, Oliver T. 21
Osher, John 143

Pader, Morton 7, 165, 175–176
Palmer, Bissell 69
Parker, Sarah Jessica 171
Patton, Charles 153
Pearlman, Sholom 110
Pebeco 49, 52, 54, 88
Pell, Claiborne 191–192
Penicillin dentifrices 92–93
Pepsodent 36–38, 42, 49, 57–59, 62, 78,
  115–116; ads 51
Pepsodent Chlorodent 90
Pepsodent Liquid Dentifrice 43
peroxide 165–166
Philipps Dental Magnesia 41
pills, chewing 8
pink toothbrush 74, 109
Place, Geoffrey 160
plaque and tartar, defined 168–169
plaque, dental 38, 49
plaque fighter pastes 167–171
Plaut, Edward 56
Plus White 164
police officers 18
Popovich, Bette 199–200
powders 34–41; ads 49; v. paste 34–45, 56,
  82–83, 89, 93, 101
power brushes 134–144; buying advice
  136–137, 139, 141, 142–143; cheaper models 143–144; computerized 144; consumer
  reluctance 136–137; and dentists 139–141;
  early efforts 134–135; evaluation of 138,
  139, 141–142; more expensive models 142;
  new entrants 137–140; prices of 141–143;

sales of 137; shock hazard 135–137; status
  of 142–143
Proctor & Gamble 96, 99, 128, 145–146,
  151; fluoride campaign in UK 154
product pricing 39
Professional Dental Products 81
profits 102
Pro-phy-lac-tic 24–25
pump dispensers 196
Py-Co-Pay 120
pyorrhea 36

Ramirez, Anthony 9–10, 179–180
Ramirez, Eddy 131
Rapoport, Sheva 192
Reach brush 125
Rembrandt 182
retailers 21, 101–102
Rettig, Richard G. 36
Revett, John 186
Riesz, Peter 153–154
Romans, ancient 7–8, 10
Royce, Elliott 187
rubber, hard 20
Rubberset Company 19–20
Rubifoam 49
Rusk, Howard 104
Rystan Company 90

sales of brushes: (1940s) 32–33; (1961) 118;
  (1964) 120; (1960s–1970s) 123; (1990s)
  126; (2000s) 129, 133; (2005) 201; power
  (1960s) 139; power (2000s) 144
sales of dentifrices: (1930s) 41; (1940s) 81;
  (1952) 91; (1950s–1960s) 174, 175; (1960)
  146; (1964) 158; (1960s–1970s) 154;
  (1970s) 177, 194; (1981) 194; (1982) 195;
  (1990s) 199; (2000s) 201
sales of oral care products (2000s): U.S.
  182–183; world 183
sales outlets 174
salesmen 51; traveling 21
Salmans, Sandra 160
salt 6, 40–41
Salzman, Jack 194–195
samples 51, 155, 188
sampling: to dentists 34–35; of professionals 54–55, 57
Sarazin, Jules J. 17
Schaper, Armin 186
Schiller, Zachary 167, 200
scratch test 71
Segalas, Hercules A. 154–155, 195
seizure, paste 109
Sensodyne 180
Sfikas, Peter M. 129

Shaffer, Michael 199
Shaye, Katja 181
Sheffield, Washington Wentworth 10
Sherman, Stuart 59
Shuchman, Abe 153–154
silica 161
Sloan, Pat 128
slogans 34, 35, 36, 49, 52, 146, 163; Colgate 49; Crest 107, 162; Ipana 107; Pepsodent 52
Smigel, Irwin 165
Smith, Douglas 36–38
smokers 49, 55, 180
Snyder, John Avery 140
solicitation, of dentists 51
Solomon, Goody 10, 137–138, 173
Sozodont 11–13
Spieler, Eric 181
SpinBrush 143
Squibb 135
Squibb's Dental Cream 77
stain removal 55–56
stains, smoking 115–116
sterilization 23
sterilizers for brushes 130
Sterling Drug 101–102
Stevenson, Richard 199
Stewart, David C. 185
Stookey, George 159
Stores 142
Stripe 107, 159
sugar 86
Sulloway, Cyrus 15–16
super protection pastes 171
supermarkets 174
Susman, Truman 170
Sykes, McCready 68

tartar 168
tartar pastes 170–171
Tartaroff 65
Teel 43–44, 76
Tek brush 28
television ads, FTC charge 115–116
Thacher, W. 18–19
Thain, Gerald J. 192
Theberge, Leonard J. 173
Theophrastus 5
Thumser, Maryanne 128
Tom's of Maine 181–182, 199–200
Tooth Tunes 132
Toothmaster 134

toothpicks 5
Tracy, Eleanor Johnson 167–168
trade practice conference 111
triclosan 171
Trimarco, Mark 129
tube, paste, invention of 10, 11
Twain, Mark 11
two for one offers 20–21
Tyler, Ralph 174

Ultra-Brite 162; launch 188
United States Army, evaluation of dentifrices 191–192
United States Congress, House subcommittee hearing 109–110
unsanitary practices 10–11
urea, synthetic 80–81
urine 7

Vibra-Dent 135–136
Violight 130
Volker, Joseph F. 84

wafers, in lieu of brushing 86–87
Wallace, Donald A. 78
Wallace, J. Sim 32
Wallack, Lydia 139
Washington, George 10
Weissman, H. A. 34, 56
West, George N. 19
Western Company (Weco) 19
Whall, Clifford 161–162
Wharton, Don 10, 49, 102
Wharton, W. R. 66–67
whitener pastes, prices 166
whiteners 14, 48, 74, 192; efficacy of 166–167
whiteness 5, 7, 35, 64–65
whitening campaigns 164–165
whitening dentifrices 162–167
Whitney, Craig 188, 190
Williams, D. H. 101
Wisan, J. M. 117
Wood, Grant 196
wood sticks 5, 7–8
Woodside, J. T. 19
Worcester, Salt Company 40–41
words, made-up 38
Wright, Donald E. 88

zircate 159